NO JOB FOR A MAN

NO JOB FOR A MAN

A MEMOIR

JOHN ROSS BOWIE

PEGASUS BOOKS
NEW YORK LONDON

NO JOB FOR A MAN

Pegasus Books, Ltd.
148 West 37th Street, 13th Floor
New York, NY 10018

First Pegasus Books cloth edition November 2022

Interior design by Maria Fernandez

ISBN: 978-1-63936-246-2

10 9 8 7 6 5 4 3 2 1

Printed in the United States of America
Distributed by Simon & Schuster
www.pegasusbooks.com

CHAPTER ONE

MUGGINGS AND THE METROPOLITAN OPERA: AN OVERTURE

W hat was it like growing up in New York City?

No one who grew up in New York City actually knows how to answer this question until they meet people who *didn't* grow up in New York City and realize what a weird, incredible, terrifying experience a New York City childhood was. It's disingenuous to say our childhoods were normal, because they weren't, not even remotely, and we may be justifiably accused of living in a bubble if we suggest otherwise. Our parents did something very strange by raising us in New York City in the 1970s and '80s—particularly in Hell's Kitchen, where I grew up, steps from Times Square, long before it was Disney-branded. We were gifted and cursed. Our metropolis offered us everything without caring whether we survived or, if we did, what was left of us.

Growing up in New York City meant that when you were a really little kid, you knocked over another really little kid at a public playground in Central Park near the West 70s, felt bad immediately, picked the kid up, and dusted him off, and his grandmother saw the whole thing. The grandmother came over to your dad and said, "That was nice of your son." And your dad almost started crying because the grandmother was Ingrid Bergman, the star of *Casablanca*, his favorite film.

Growing up in New York City meant you got mugged when you were nine by two kids who were about eleven. They shoved you against a wall in Riverside Park and threatened to kill you, so you gave them everything you had—a dollar and your library card.

It meant that in elementary school you went over to a friend's house and met her eccentric dad (long hair, huge moustache, nasal voice) and years later realized you had been in the Manhattan Plaza apartment of the real-life inspiration for Kramer.

It meant your mom's friends were gay and witty and hilarious and opinionated, and you watched at least three of them waste away, walking with a cane and stricken with a damp death rattle before they were forty, victims of an illness that had only recently been named. You placed a small pebble on Andy's gravestone a year after he passed. You were seventeen.

Growing up in New York City meant your dad would let you use his Metropolitan Opera tickets so you could take your senior-year girlfriend to see *Rigoletto*, which was both precocious and romantic and is remembered with a glow so golden and gauzy you sometimes wonder if it actually happened, but it did; you have the ticket stub in a box in the garage.

It meant the local news always kept you nice and up to date on the Son of Sam, the suddenly-vanished-into-thin-air Etan Patz, the hogtied-and-killed-by-the-police-for-the-crime-of-graffiti Michael Stewart, and other stories that made you carry your keys like Wolverine's claws—sticking out from between your fingers—so you could defend yourself against the criminals and maybe even the cops.

It meant your cultural education came every Wednesday morning when you picked up the *Village Voice* on the way to school, learning about a performance artist who stuffed yams up her ass, De La Soul, John Woo and his generation of Hong Kong filmmakers, the art-rock collective known as Missing Foundation, and the complex and fascinating saga of a dangerous BDSM predator who was revealed to be a trader at Bear Stearns (the so-called Dangerous Top). You kept the paper tucked in your desk, so you could peek at it during first period algebra.

Growing up in New York City meant every talent show at your high school featured someone singing "Always & Forever" by Heatwave, followed by pasty kids whining their way through the Cure's "Just Like Heaven" on cheap guitars.

It meant you watched the sunrise sitting on a bench in the dead center of the then pretty dicey Tompkins Square Park (you went to Washington Square Park to buy street herb; you went to Tompkins to cop the heavier stuff . . . I mean, *you* didn't, but you knew some people who had already graduated). It was five A.M. and you were surrounded by the elaborately huge tents of the homeless with a girl you really should have kissed but didn't, and you lived to tell the tale.

It meant you went to the Halloween parade in the West Village and heard a familiar chorus around the corner. You stood on your tiptoes to watch the Village People cruise by singing "In the Navy" on the back of a flatbed truck.

It meant your camp counselors had a dance routine for the Ramones' "Rockaway Beach" (your introduction to such history-shifting music).

It meant you tanked the entrance exam for Hunter College Elementary School at age five. Confused by the interview and dazzled by the paneled office's gray lighting, you didn't know the answers to questions or even why you were being asked them. When you didn't get in, your dad blamed "racial quotas," which, God help you, you used as an excuse to dabble in your father's quiet racism.

Growing up in New York City meant you went to high school with a Wayans brother who made fun of your big feet (you were/are a size twelve and only five foot eight.) "Damn, son," said Shawn Wayans. "You got some big-ass feet."

It meant you briefly dated a girl who babysat the daughter of Jerry Harrison of Talking Heads.

It meant burly white guys in an IROC swerved at you in Maspeth once while you were walking home with two really hot goth girls from your high school. In an attempt to impress the goth girls, you flipped off the burly white guys. They did a U-turn, pulled up on the curb, shoved you up against the wall, and punched you in the Adam's apple until you apologized. This did not impress the two goth girls, so instead of . . . whatever you had in mind . . . you went back to one of their places and glumly listened to Depeche Mode's *Black Celebration* on a stereo that had virtually no low end.

It meant you made out with a girl on the Governors Island ferry as the sun set behind the Statue of Liberty, and you saw New York City as your Scottish immigrant grandparents must have seen it: beautiful and stuffed with so much opportunity that glass and steel buildings could hardly have contained it, and so it poured out invitingly onto the streets.

It meant you and your friend Sybil went to see saw Jim Carroll and Richard Hell read at the St. Mark's Poetry Project. Richard Hell read a poem about fucking a deer and compared the animal's labia to bubblegum. You were so inspired you started writing your own poetry, and thank God in heaven it's all gone, lost in one of several apartment moves in the nineties.

Growing up in New York City meant you were engaged and terrified and in love. It was raucous and dangerous and sexy and funny. Every band came to your town; every book was available; every record was on sale, even if you had to go through the import bins. The winters were merciless; the summers, too, but at least in the summer there was free stuff, and hey, Toots and the Maytals played at the bandshell in Central Park! Bill Beutel on *Eyewitness News* tracked the city's climbing murder rate, and President Ford tried to kill us, but we were all there together. Constantly inspired, constantly terrified. It was too much, always too much, but goddammit, it was *ours*.

CHAPTER TWO

I WOULD LIKE TO MEET RHODA

We sat on my parents' bed in their small bedroom, one of two in our teensy West 40s apartment, to watch the only TV in the house (the living room had the stereo and Dad's vinyl: show-tunes, folk, Scottish folk, Gilbert and Sullivan, early Beatles—nothing past *Help!*, and not even the actual Beatles album *Help!*, the cash-in soundtrack with a couple of shoehorned score moments—and most of the Bill Cosby comedy albums). In the evening, the streets were quiet, but in the morning massive *New York Times* trucks went rumbling along, shaking our buildings, urban roosters that crowed and woke the household daily. The bed took up most of the room. Between it and the TV cabinet, there was only an alley of about eight inches you could walk through. The TV was a black-and-white set, no cable (still exclusively a bauble of the wealthy), with aluminum foil on the rabbit ears and scuff marks on the side where my dad hit it in a vain attempt to tame the oft-flipping picture. I'm pretty sure it's about 1977 because:

1. My parents are still together.
2. They're smoking.
3. We're watching *Rhoda*.

Rhoda was a spinoff of *The Mary Tyler Moore Show* about Rhoda Morgenstern, Mary's native New Yorker neighbor, and her return home from her sojourn in Minneapolis. I never missed an episode. It took place in Manhattan! Where I lived! (Upper East Side, two subway rides from Hell's Kitchen, but still!) And everyone was so funny, and they said what they thought, and when they yelled they were hilarious. Was such a life possible? My parents yelled at each other about . . . well, I couldn't really tell. Money? Dad's drinking? Mom being, in Dad's words, a "dizzy bitch"? That was the yelling I was familiar with. But funny yelling? A new frontier. And they thought of these witty ripostes so quickly—it was astonishing. Rhoda would say things like, "I have to lose ten pounds by eight thirty." Obviously, I didn't know she had writers. Obviously, I didn't know she'd spent all week rehearsing this tight joke.

Obviously, I asked to visit Rhoda.

"What do you mean?" asked my mom.

"Where does she live?" I countered.

"Upper East Side."

"Right, that's what I thought." I nodded, already very psyched about meeting this funny lady in her headscarf. "We should go visit her."

My parents exchanged a glance—extra poignant to think of them bonding over anything at this point in their marriage, in the grand scheme of things, just minutes from its end—and my mom, as delicately as she could, tore my heart out through my ears. "She's not real, hon. She's just a character."

"Yeah, Tiger," said Dad, drawing on his Vantage, his eyes a little aglow at getting to explain something to someone. "These are just actors."

I started to cry. It wasn't the blue Vantage smoke blocking the TV that made me tear up. An illusion was gone—these people were not actually that funny, that honest, and things did not end that tidily *anywhere*. I went to bed early that night. The following morning—amid the bustle of three people vying for one bathroom, my dad on his way to the paper company, my mom waiting to have the small apartment to herself, me getting ready for school—I had my earliest, clearest idea of what I wanted to do: I wanted to get into that alternate world inside the TV, where people said smart and funny things, where when they fought, they made up twenty minutes later. It was a vastly better world, I decided, than the one we actually lived in. I wanted to be an actor.

Hell's Kitchen is the theater district, encompassing both Broadway's great theaters and a dozen or so smaller playhouses that lay tucked away on residential blocks, before tunnel entrances, and on the darkest corners of seedy streets quickly populated by sex workers and junkies the second the sun slips behind New Jersey. That's where I grew up. We moved from Rego Park in deep Queens (near a Woolworth's I called "Werewolfs") and into a third-floor Hell's Kitchen apartment in a six-story walkup, each stack of apartments connected by a long-dormant dumbwaiter. There was a window-sized opening to the dumbwaiter in every apartment, painted shut for years. The building was from 1913-ish, and while the dumbwaiter may have been a handy way to transport groceries in that era, to me it was only ever a reminder of how old the apartment and building were. Add to that a gas stove that had to be lit with a match, exposed heating pipes that stayed extremely hot in a vain effort to counter the icy winds off the Hudson, and, obviously, no air conditioning to help you weather heat waves and fetid garbage strikes. The city was bleak and weird and was going through such a dire economic period that we were denied federal relief, leading to the famously inflammatory—but not false—*Daily News* headline FORD TO NYC: DROP DEAD.

Asleep one night in the summer of 1978, a rare and abrupt silence woke me up like an M-80—the firework that bad kids insisted was "a quarter stick of dynamite." There was always an ambient hum of electricity and anxiety and sirens, so its sudden absence was a jolt. I lay in my bedroom for a while, unable to figure out what was wrong. At age seven you're forced to take so much for granted, as every other question is answered with, "Ugh, I'll tell you when you're older." Finally the silence grew too intense. A soft orange flicker emerged from the living room, and I padded out in my pajamas.

My mom sat on the couch, having just lit two candles. "It's a blackout," she said, smiling, maybe genuinely excited at the "business as unusual" of it all, maybe just putting on a brave face for her son, who looked confused. "All the electricity went out. Lights, TV, refrigerator, everything."

"Where's Dad?"

"Asleep," she said with tight lips—probably implying that he'd been drunk before he was asleep. I curled into my mom's armpit. She had long, straight hair like Crystal Gayle's and enormous glasses with brown frames, and she wore a maroon turtleneck sweater over her pajamas. She smelled like cigarettes and soap.

"Is everything OK?" I murmured.

"Yes, pumpkin. Everything is OK." I fell asleep next to her in the dark living room.

The next morning, the three of us walked around the neighborhood. Dad tucked a polo into his khaki shorts. He was still a relatively spry forty, and if he was hungover, it didn't show. There had been looting uptown, but Hell's Kitchen had been spared any major incidents. There were cars on the road, and maybe a couple of buses, but all the stores were locked and dark, and the bright summer sunlight did nothing to stop the eerie dimness that overtook the city that morning. In a doorway, I saw a middle-aged couple kissing passionately, like they were cheating or dying. The affection was striking and so open. Is this what happened in a blackout? Is this what people did when stores closed? Is this what abandon looked like? I walked between my parents, holding both their hands, a conductor of whatever depleted affection still passed between them. This was the only way they ever held hands. I had never seen them kiss. It wouldn't be long now before holding both their hands at the same time felt like a grim denial.

If all of this sounds a bit too *Angela's Ashes*, let me add that we didn't starve, and my dad, while a drunk by his own admission, was not a blackout drunk. No bankruptcies. It's Manhattan; nobody drives except cabdrivers and visitors from New Jersey, so he had no DUIs. He held on to his job throughout ninety percent of my childhood. I attended a mediocre public school and then transferred to a slightly better one to join their "gifted program," despite my choking hard during my Hunter interview. Both were in decent buildings, with none of the truly awful decay present in some NYC schools. Truth be told, our apartment's crude amenities and the random violence that spread like seafoam in our neighborhood were balanced out by one consoling fact: the magnificent *theaters*. Inside them were not just different worlds but something even more dizzying: alternate timelines, threads of existence where action led to action and then to a climax, and people who occasionally sang their thoughts. We didn't have a lot of money and didn't spend a lot of money (God, we ate a lot of Wheatena and Swanson TV dinners, and I sometimes washed my hair with dishwashing liquid),* but my parents prioritized the theater. We saved up or went to TKTS, the half-price ticket booth in Times Square, or just waited until a show was deep into its run and prices had dropped.

The first Broadway show I saw was *Annie*, that 1970s take on the Great Depression filled with melodies friendly but rarely cloying.

---

* Which led to me writing what I think was my first joke—based on the popular Joy commercial that proclaimed the detergent would make it so you could "see yourself in the plate!" I wondered if my mom could "see (herself) in my hair." It *killed*.

People knock *Annie* all the time, and I see their point. Sure, the sun might not come out tomorrow, that's tough yet fair, but Annie is an old friend about whom I will not speak ill. Plus, it was filled with actual children! On stage! They were playing pretend, and people were paying to see it; I was still playing pretend on spec. I saw *Sweeney Todd* a couple short years later with its second-string cast (George Hearn and Dorothy Loudon who, that's right, I had seen as Miss Hannigan in *Annie*) putting on a performance that was riveting, terrifying, and starkly postmodern before I had a word for such a thing. ("What happens then? Well, that's the play," Sweeney sang about his show in the opening, adding, "And he wouldn't want us to give it away." Imagine being eight and having art's artifice called out in front of you so boldly and being unable to give it a name.)

But we also saw performances so esoteric and just . . . *off* that ticket prices were charitably low. The *Village Voice* used to have a "Free or Under $2.50" section in the arts listings that my mother would cut out, post on the fridge, and pore over for family-friendly outings.* This quest for low-cost entertainment led us to a strange, hippie children's theater, an avant-garde production of *Frankenstein* played in front of a drop cloth at the Society for Ethical Culture on West 64th Street, a disco version of *A Midsummer Night's Dream* in Tribeca starring my Sunday school teacher with—according to the mimeographed program that I recently located—a young John Goodman as Oberon and a still younger Nathan Lane as a Rude Mechanical. I had a mild crush on my Sunday school teacher, and she was a phenomenal Helena. Church was an unquestioned thing that we did every Sunday without fail, and disco Shakespeare was the best thing to come out of it.

---

* Abe Simpson voice: "And I wore an onion on my belt, which was the fashion at the time . . ."

But the show that burned into my memory like a white-hot brand—a strange glow I still feel in my heart whenever I perform—was *The Snow White Show*, performed at the 13th Street Repertory Theatre. It was a musty old place that, like a lot of old buildings in New York, always smelled like it had just been quite wet but was now dry. *The Snow White Show* required young audience members to get on stage and play the seven dwarves. The actual cast had only three parts: a beautiful young actress to play Snow White, a beautiful older actress to play the Wicked Queen, and a lanky stoner with a perm to play Prince Charming. The dwarves? We waited for our cue in the audience. In the meantime, there were plenty of in-jokes for the parents to enjoy. While explaining how mean she is in song, the Wicked Queen trills that she gives away the ends of movies, leaning in to confide, "Rosebud is the name of the sled," which cracked up my dad, who explained the gag to me later that day—thus spoiling *Citizen Kane*. It didn't matter. The mood in the dingy sixty-five-seat theater was effervescent, even though the place wasn't full. The show was just so silly, so committed to being silly, and so literally inclusive: You're so in on the joke that we need you on stage to hit the punchline. I couldn't wait. This was my chance to be . . . Annie, maybe? To be a performer, to get up and have the ability to make people enjoy me the way I enjoyed Rhoda? A bigger, shinier version of myself? I wasn't entirely sure what the endgame was, but I was going to get up and make it happen.

And so they asked if the kids in the audience would come up and play the dwarves. It was time—maybe not time to join the pretending pro circuit but time to at least become a pretending amateur, a "person who pretends in front of other people." I was ready, or so I thought.

When I looked at the skeletal, well-toasted Prince Charming beckoning me onto the stage, my world flipped over, the earth gave out, and a deep, burning panic crawled across my back. I started to sweat. There were no surprises here; I'd known this was the deal going in. I knew this was what was required, postmodernism grabbing me by the hood of my OshKosh and demanding that I be part of the show. Yet I sank down in my seat, murmured something like "no thanks," and the Feeling-No-Pain Prince Charming backed off. "That's okay, man, we can make do with . . . let's see . . . five dwarves. Sure, yeah, it's cool."

I sat quietly seething at myself for the rest of the show. The kids on stage were given Warriors-style denim vests that said DWARVES on the back in metal studs, and they were led about the stage and told to hover over the sleeping Snow White. One of the kids—really little, younger than me, let's say four—brought the house down with a simple question. He had been picking his nose and reaching into his pants to adjust himself in the way that unself-conscious four-year-olds do, when he suddenly stopped the show by asking, "Hey! Do you know what the doctor did to my mommy's tooth?"

This *destroyed*. The laugh the audience gave him was not from the belly, it seemed to start beneath the earth from some primal place before language. The walls shook. The laugh was real, it was spontaneous, it was pure and unaffected. I've since seen Mike Myers improvise in person, I've improvised *with* Robin Williams, I've watched Sarah Silverman polish new material at the old Largo on Fairfax in L.A., and any one of them would have sold their soul to get the laugh that kid received for his dentist line.

I went to bed that night disappointed in myself and deeply jealous of that brave little dwarf whose mom had been to the dentist. My father seemed disappointed that I didn't get up to play a dwarf—not because he wanted his son to be an actor, no, but because it showed a flippant disregard for the whole venture. It was participatory children's theater: Get off your ass and participate! The afternoon had gotten off to a bright start, but his son's cowardice had irked him. A few beers were the only possible cure to this annoyance. He settled into a buzz that evening and commented: "Probably just as well. Remember what Spencer Tracy said: 'Acting is no job for a man.'"

"Spencer Tracy?"

"He's the judge in *Judgment at Nuremberg*. You should see that, Tiger. Maybe Judy Garland's best work."

"Dorothy?"

"Yeah. In a movie about bringing Nazis to justice."

It was an inauspicious non-start to my acting career. Aside from my newly discovered deep fear of getting up in front of people—no small roadblock for an aspiring performer—there were other concerns about acting: feeding one's family while doing it being chief among them. The bulk of my current actor friends grew up in the suburbs, and the actors they saw were best-case scenarios: Actors who had gotten jobs on TV or been cast in movies. Actors who won trophies or at the very least presented trophies to other actors at awards shows. Actors who knocked over appreciative audiences with one-liners. My friends saw no struggle, no staggering gaps in employment, no existential crises brought on by an audition that "went another way," just these glorious, finished products, and it fueled them with an optimism that had not a single foot in reality. While they were watching the Oscars and the Tonys and *Welcome Back, Kotter*, I was watching Anthony's mom worry about making rent in Manhattan Plaza, even though Manhattan Plaza was subsidized housing designated for artists who struggled with rent in more traditional settings. She'd done a couple plays in smaller theaters and tried to supplement that with wardrobe work in the bigger theaters, but it didn't add up to much. Years later, when I was in my late twenties (she had to have been in her late fifties), I saw her applying for a hostess job at a cheesy Yuppie bar on Tenth Avenue. I averted my eyes, finished my drink, and slunk out the side entrance.

My friends' parents who were actors—living in the theater district, there were about a half dozen—seemed to lead a life of constant uncertainty. They seemed stuck on a small propeller plane with a dead pilot, spinning wildly over the Andes. Later on, in my teen years, I remember being on the phone with my friend Patty and hearing her dad crying in front of her because he didn't get an arc on *Kate & Allie*. Before that, I can recall Jeremy's dad stopping my mom and me after school, begging us to take Jeremy home with us because Jeremy's dad had a big audition and didn't want to "bring the kid." The wild-eyed thirst in Jeremy's dad's eyes haunts me to this day. It was a compulsive gambler's desperation, facing awful odds yet needing to play another hand.

Acting looked like a well-oiled tightrope, from which you fell constantly and snapped your tibia because there was absolutely no net. My father hated his job, but at least he had a job, steady work as a customer service manager in the paper industry. (If that sounds familiar, it's very close to what Michael Scott did on the American version of *The Office*.) On his good days, my dad *was* Michael Scott—the self-proclaimed funniest guy in his office with an eye always on the door. On his bad ones, he was also Michael Scott: the guy telling jokes that necessitated a "Black voice" for the punchline and would get you pepper sprayed and reported to HR today. But in my eyes, my father's life represented a grim template of adulthood: You hated what you did. You did it to feed your kid. You drank to cope.

◆

When I was seven years old, just as I was beginning to wrestle with how to put food on my future family's table, my parents split up. Their divorce had felt inevitable. They fought constantly, and my mom had recently bought a trundle bed so they wouldn't have to touch, even while asleep. The palpable, almost chewy tension in the house had gotten so bad that my father, in a fit of drunken resentment, had recently taken an antique samurai sword from his big red trunk of edged weapons (a collection he insisted I not call "the swords," as it included rapiers, daggers, a couple Bowie knives—no relation and we pronounce our name like *Maui*) and thrown it at my mom. There's still a nick in the wall where the sword (or *katana*, as my father would say) cut through the paint and chipped the plaster. I didn't hear this story until years later, but when I was growing up, there was always a sense of danger around my dad—a weird unpredictability, which is odd, because you could set your watch to him coming home drunk every Friday night. It was such a reliable occurrence that I started to refer to my father's "Friday night face" with a sense of rue that did not fit my young years. But the unpredictability lay in which version of drunk dad returned home: Maudlin drunk Dad? Cheerful drunk Dad? Angry drunk Dad? An ill-flavored cocktail containing some or all of the above?

My parents' separation, while expected, wasn't as ugly as some. There was no long, drawn-out custody battle, and I never had to take the stand and pick my favorite parent, but it was ugly in the sense that there was no "we're still a family" speech; my dad just came in one night, by himself, my mom sitting silently in the other room as I was on my way to sleep, and told me he was moving out. When I started crying and asked him, "You're getting a divorce?" he softly corrected me. "No, we're separating. No one is talking about divorce yet." My mom coldly confirmed this the next morning, adding, "It's his idea. He wants to move out."

This brought the family to a détente of sorts. Yelling was replaced with a kind of seething mutual hostility. Hot on the heels of my parents' separation was another seismic incident: A young girl I'd grown up with, "a latchkey kid" (a phrase recounted with a clicking tongue by many a judgmental parent), was making the four-block walk home from school one day while her single mom was at work. She was pushed into her apartment by a stranger and raped. She was nine years old.

My parents tried to keep this from me, but one day at the playground she told me all about it herself. There was a dead-eyed detachment, but still an "I've got you on the edge of your seat" tone to her retelling; she recounted it breathlessly as if she'd seen it in a movie. When she was finished, she climbed a ladder and went down a slide, Central Park West's beautiful old buildings staring down at her. The effect of the rape pulled the earth out from under me—no one was safe. Children were vulnerable. My mom became very protective, insisting I come to her office after school (she was working at a small book design firm on the Upper East Side) and then go home with her. When her boss was at work (her boss who did not like kids and who would not have tolerated a kid doing his homework in her workspace), I was to sit across the street at Burger King, do my homework, and wait for her. Two hours at a Burger King in 1981 doesn't make you feel "safe" per se, but the choice was presented as pretty binary: Burger King for homework or sexual assault.

I never blamed myself for the divorce (or if I did, it's buried so deep that literal decades of therapy have not unearthed it), but I was definitely mad at my parents and, by extension, the world, which felt very much like it was closing in on me—the aftermath of the Jonestown massacre was all over the news too, and I felt weirdly, personally bruised by the reports of those parents squirting cyanide-laced punch into their children's mouths. This all added up to my understanding that the world is out to get you. No place is safe. Be afraid.

I started losing my temper at school and spending time in the principal's office, brazenly telling my second grade teacher that I had had "enough of [her] crap." I had a massive overbite—you could stick your thumb into the space between my top and bottom teeth—and had been prescribed a massive full-mouth orthodontic contraption called the Frankel device. It was an unsightly apparatus made of enamel and wire. It has since been discontinued, but I strongly encourage an image search for it. You couldn't eat while wearing a Frankel device, and talking was a chore except in this clenched-teeth Bogartian fashion that made me sound even angrier than I was. I took it out during a principal meeting, and the principal—gaunt, tired, and smelling of public school, perfume, and wine—asked me if I resented the device. I answered, "No, but it hates me." A solid enough joke for a grade-schooler, and my mom laughed, a WASPY cough of denial—"Can you imagine resenting orthodontia?"—but it was also a lie. Of course I resented that thing. It made it hard to talk and eat, it annoyed my teachers, and it may as well have been a large BULLY ME sign on my back. The kids—a melting pot of douchebags—called me Jaws, not for Spielberg's shark but for the metal-toothed Bond villain played by Richard Kiel in two of the Roger Moore movies. It was, quite simply, one more fucking thing to deal with in late seventies New York. Divorce and crime and air pollution and orthodontia. Everything scared me. Everything made me angry.

Don't think me purely the victim—I was just as capable of lashing out at people in a lower caste. I farted horrifically in music class one time—a stereophonic burner on a wooden chair that made a head-turning sound. Everybody, even the teacher, stared at me, so I looked accusingly over at Ned Simmons, a kid with horn-rims and preternaturally greasy hair who was by any estimation even lower on the social ladder than I was.

"No, John Bowie," he barked, slamming his desk at the sheer injustice of my charge. *"No."*

Nobody believed me anyway, and neither Ned nor I got invited to many birthday parties that year, so my punching down yielded no dividends. I recently felt a great calming warmth when I googled Ned and learned he's an inventor who once won quite a bit of money on *Jeopardy!*

Once, while sitting around at my grandmother's house on Long Island, I got bored watching my dad get drunker and drunker in front of the TV (watching Tyrone Power? Errol Flynn? Humphrey Bogart?), so I sulked outside and watched a neighbor girl (upon whom I had a

chaste crush) talk to her boyfriend. They seemed really happy. I have
no idea if they actually were, but her parents were still together. He
was tall, handsome in a late-seventies way (feathered hair and a thin
moustache). Their vitality, their joy, the breezy way they talked to each
other, the gentle way he moved her hair over her ear—all of this filled
me with outrage. Out of nowhere, eleven-year-old John thought it a
good idea to throw a pebble at the guy's car. It hit the passenger side
window, chipping it slightly. I rushed into the house, choking with
tears and shame, and ran to the room where I slept. The boyfriend came
in and—in what was a pretty measured tone, considering—told my dad
what had happened. I shook in my grandmother's room, waiting for
my dad to come in and spank me. He did not disappoint. In hindsight,
this all makes sense: Alcoholic dad (raised by an alcoholic dad) fills
son with weird rage, years later son finds that alcohol quells said rage,
then alcohol starts to not quell rage, and, God bless him, son keeps
trying, but I think the cycle might have stopped with this generation.

◆

One early Friday evening in 1980, Dad arrived at my mom's apartment to pick me up, having already had a couple of drinks. He was
a little sweaty, his normally slick Alberto VO5'd hair disheveled—a
couple strands out of place and dangling over his forehead, which
was marked by two scars, both of which were sustained when he put
his head through a window at a tavern in Hamilton with his Colgate
fraternity brothers. He was not able to hold eye contact for very long,
and his modest silk tie was loose.

The arrangement was thus: dinner with him every Thursday, and
spend the weekend at his place in Queens every other weekend. My
mom had gone back to work as a temp secretary by this point and
probably relished the occasional quiet time at home.

Friday night, early 1980s. The jazz years, let's call them—my father in his post-divorce malaise had been going to a club called Eddie Condon's after work, listening to some regulars play standards and bringing dates he'd met at church where he was, to hear him tell it, "getting more ass than a toilet seat." He took me to the club occasionally. The staff looked the other way from the little overwhelmed boy sitting in the dark, smoky nightclub, amber lights shining on paunchy older guys blowing clarinets. My dad would drink beer and order me a Jackie Cooper, which would cause a waiter to scrunch up his forehead, go to the bar, get into an increasingly exasperated conversation with a bartender (imagine someone more exasperated than a bartender at a jazz club), and then slink back to our table. "I'm so sorry," the waiter would say. "Neither Gary nor I have *ever* heard of a Jackie Cooper."

"Ah," my father would smile with a level of smug you could see from space. "It's a Shirley Temple for boys."

It was here one night where ten-year-old me was introduced to a very old man named Johnny Marks.

"John! This is Johnny Marks!" Suddenly every man in the club was standing over me, each smelling drunker than his peers. Mr. Marks loomed over me, an enormous grin spreading over his face. Skeletal but friendly.

"Johnny Marks wrote 'Rudolph the Red Nosed Reindeer'!"

Ten is a weird age for this kind of thing—you're just turning the corner from being impressed by Rudolph, but you're still too young and snotnosed to be gracious about it. Correct response here should be "It's an honor sir," along with a handshake. I managed a feeble "Oh . . . Cool!" He extended his hand, and my father whispered, "Shake, Tiger," and I did, with the kind of weak non-grip that little kids have. This disappointed everyone, including Mr. Marks, who only had a few years left on this earth. All these tall, drunk men turned away with a collective shrug.

But this was not one of those nights. Dad had gone to Condon's alone and had come over to our apartment to pick me up. Even drunk, he was a good-looking guy—maybe not a head-turner, but he had a strong jaw and slate blue eyes under neatly cropped coal-black hair that was only now in his late forties beginning to be tempered with silver. A winning smile you could hear over the phone no doubt helped his work. His Brooks Brothers blazer was open. He was ready to take me out to the new apartment! In Jackson Heights! But first! An ethnic joke! "Do you know what a Polish cheer looks like?"

My mother, after a deep but unregistered sigh: "What, Bruce?"

"Clap your hands!" he yelled, while stomping his feet.

"Stomp your feet!" he yelled, while clapping his hands.

"We're number one!" he yelled, extending two fingers in the air.

He laughed a little too hard at this joke, which he *had* to know was subpar—my father was funnier than this. But drink impairs judgment, and my mom mumbling "Good one" did not notify my father that he had just bombed, hard, in front of his son and soon-to-be-ex-wife.* I grabbed my bag and headed off for the weekend.

My father was not the sort of racist who self-consciously and vehemently denied being a racist—he acknowledged his prejudices. He made it very clear that he had no problem with Black people, but there was a difference between Black people and N-words (and this being the seventies, I need not explain that he used no such code). My father would literally scowl when he saw Black youths wearing anything other than suits on the subway. He scorned affirmative action, as it was *allegedly* the institution that kept his son out of the prestigious Hunter school. With all the television we watched, I did not see an episode of *The Jeffersons*, *Sanford and Son*, or *Good Times* until I was in college

---

* They were on their way to getting divorced, but he was dragging his wingtips on the final signing.

(there was a strange dispensation made for *Diff'rent Strokes*, at its core a twenty-five-minute white savior story). His racism disguised itself as a certain cold practicality: divesting in South Africa would only hurt the poor Black people who would be fired if the money dried up, plus "Mandela killed a cop, you know—people never talk about why he's in jail." Everyone has a chance to better themselves, some just choose not to. He had Black friends through church but claimed he had been very scarred by being mugged by a Black guy while in the service.

I wore his scars and a couple of my own for a while, having gotten mugged at nine and then again at fourteen by Black kids. It's a horrible thing to admit, but racism seemed an easy and lazy way to organize my anger: These kids apparently don't like me because I'm white, therefore, I don't get to like them because they're Black. And I can make snide comments and rude jokes to back that up. But the strangely glorious thing about being a New Yorker is that if you stick around and pay attention, you will eventually be mugged by every color of the rainbow. The junkie who tried to steal my saxophone from band class? Bright white. The bully who hit me harder than I've ever been hit while I was at summer camp? Asian. It should have been clear that it was not about race but about me being eminently muggable, but kids are simple and often not too bright.

Among the scariest things to happen in my childhood happened at the hands of my fellow Irishmen. After church one Sunday when I was about ten, I talked my parents into taking me to lunch at one of those sawdusty Irish pubs near Herald Square. I thought it would be nice to celebrate Mom's Irish heritage and by extension my own and to pretend we were a cohesive family unit together. Terrible idea, that. It was nearly St. Patrick's Day, and Dad enjoyed the seasonal drink specials while Mom got quieter and steelier. I excused myself to go downstairs to the bathroom.

Sitting on the toilet, too tense to poop and too anxious to leave, I heard several young men come in. Ruddy, rowdy, and shitfaced, they grew tired of me occupying the stall and started pounding on the door. I froze. I definitely didn't want to come out now; I had no idea what awaited me. I just . . . sat there, staring at the black and white tile on the floor while the stall's wooden door hung on for dear life.

"Leave him alone, he's fucking shitting," quoth one of the youths.

"I don't care if he's fucking shitting," retorted another. "I need to get in there."

I guess I had been away from the table for a while. After several minutes of pounding on the door, I heard my dad's slurring voice. "Tiger?"

"Hi!" I managed.

"Come on out."

I pulled up my pants and stepped out to see my dad standing amid all of these other drunks. The only sober person in the room was ten-year-old me. My dad gruffly grabbed me by the arm and said, "Let's go." That should have been it, but allegedly somebody shoved him. Not too much, but just enough for my dad's beer muscles to activate. What happened next walked the delicate line between scarring and hysterical. My dad turned and tried to kick the person who shoved him. It was not the balanced, from-the-side type of roundhouse kick you see in kung-fu films (and my father and I had seen dozens). No, my father kicked straight out like a Rockette. Leg up and forward at a loose ninety degree angle. The problem with that combat approach is that it can leave you off kilter, especially on the damp tile of your average Irish pub around St. Paddy's. He went down, straight down, his grounded leg slipping out from under him, most of the fall being absorbed by his left elbow.

"*Uck*" was the sound he made.

Now, finally, everybody in the room was frozen. No one knew what to say or do. A drunk in his early forties had just basically disintegrated in front of all of us. Finally one of the young redheaded door pounders remembered that we were near a cherished saint's day, and he extended his hand to help my dad up.

My dad took the stranger's hand. He murmured thank you and, chastened, we went back upstairs. I promptly told my mom everything that had happened.

Enough incidents like this happen and you realize that there are just some unpleasant people of all colors in the gorgeous mosaic that is New York City. I'd love to tell you that I'm free of all racism—picture me wiping my hands with a satisfied "Well, that's sorted"—but I've tried to come to terms with my own prejudices and correct it in my kids.

I'm not sure if my father ever got there, but he gave regularly and quietly to the United Negro College Fund. I was surprised to find a check on his dresser once. I held it up with a quizzical look on my face as if to scream, *You say awful things and yet you give to the UNCF?* He shrugged off my surprise. "It's a good cause," he said, and that was that. Maybe he thought the donations canceled out his votes for people who used terms like "welfare queen" and his ethnic jokes that were far more upsetting than the Polish cheer.

On his custody weekends, we took the subway to Jackson Heights, sometimes two trains if there was a track problem, which meant waiting on the elevated platform at Queens Plaza in all sorts of weather. The cold would usually sharpen my dad up a bit; he'd ask how school was going, and his sullen son would respond, "Fine."

He'd mimic me. *"Fine."*

"It's fine. What? Math is hard. I have a crush on a girl named Cathy. She thinks I'm dumb. I told her I liked her scarf, and she said, 'It's a bandanna,' and then she flat out said, 'You're very uneducated.' In front of her friends, who laughed at me. I like English, and I like history."

"Well, you need math, too."

"Do I? I don't think I'm going to do anything that needs math."

"Even actors have to do their taxes."

"Don't even know if I wanna be an actor anymore . . ."

He tousled my hair, probably because he'd seen dads do that sort of thing on TV, but it felt rough, clumsy. "Well, what do you wanna do?"

"I don't know," I shrugged, looking into people's apartments. From the platform you could see an advent calendar of tenement windows. People going about their nights only steps from the subway tracks. Sometimes I look back and marvel at how densely packed the city was. How did any of us ever sleep? "Maybe be a writer? I'm young, still. Right?"

"Yes. But it's nice to have goals."

What were your goals? I didn't say. *Did they involve working in customer service for the paper industry?*

Dad drank a little more that night.

"What's your mom up to this weekend?" he asked once we were back at his apartment—a very tidy studio decorated with his weird collection of old bottles, his fantastic books about movies, that Picasso drawing of Don Quixote that so many dads had, the edged weapons, and in an out-of-character, decidedly whimsical touch, a series of small watercolors of vegetables that my father had bought from a local artist. Tiny little broccoli. Tiny little cauliflower. They framed the entryway to the dinette.

"Don't know." I pretended to be lost in a book.

"Ah. I see. It's a 'don't tell Daddy' situation."

It was, absolutely. My mom only had two long-term-ish relationships after the separation, and both were awkward for me. This first one was with a priest from our church, a divorced Episcopal clergyman who smoked more than my dad and always looked kind of sad. Her next one would be with a friend's dad—in fact, the dad who cried over not getting a role on *Kate & Allie*. Both made me very uncomfortable; the guys came over, and in the small apartment, I could hear my mother panting, which I do not wish on anyone. You never realize how small an apartment is until you've heard your mom in congress with your friend's dad. She had expressly asked that I not tell my dad that she was seeing Father Conrad. Her secret was safe with me, although I was clearly not a very good liar. It was in my best interest to keep my head down about this stuff and just get to sleep before my dad started snoring. His snoring was legendary. Decades of smoking had given him untold bronchial problems, and the sounds he made while sleeping ensured that he would be the only one sleeping within a mile.

The next day over a dinner, my dad made of delicious toasted cheese and grilled Spam sandwiches, we watched *WKRP in Cincinnati* on TV. I got about half of the jokes, but those jokes made me laugh really hard. The quiet deadpan of Howard Hesseman and the active exasperation of Gordon Jump seemed like sorcery to me. *How could they do that without laughing themselves?*

Maybe there'd be a good movie on the late show on channel 5—I could ask my dad to let me stay up late for an old film. *Angels with Dirty Faces*, an underrated gangster tragedy with both Bogart *and* James Cagney. *Double Indemnity*, which was too slow for me when I was little but is as perfect a noir as has ever been committed to film. *Casablanca*, of course, starring our old playground buddy Ingrid Bergman (my father told the story of meeting her through me time and time again) and Bogart again, this time as the bar owner Rick, who is terribly selfish until he is gorgeously selfless ("They didn't know the ending when they started shooting!" my father would gasp.)

"*The Grapes of Wrath!*" he chuckled appreciatively, leafing through the *TV Guide*. "Have you ever seen a John Ford movie, Tiger?"

"I don't think so. Westerns, mostly, right?" I knew enough to say that. My dad had those movie books all over his apartment—enormous coffee table tomes about war movies, the great Westerns, extensive works on the filmographies of both Humphrey Bogart and the largely forgotten matinee idol Tyrone Power.

"Mostly, but not exclusively. The thing about John Ford—every frame is a picture. You could take any frame from any second of any

John Ford film and it would be the most perfectly composed shot you'd ever seen."

"OK. Let's watch."

The movie was not a Western, and it was slow, but he was right—every frame was beautiful. Everything made visual sense. You could see where everything was in relation to everything else; it had a sort of rhythm and balance to it. There was, however, one frame, early in the film, where the screen was black before Henry Fonda lit a candle.

"Well, that's not a picture," I said.

"OK, not *every* single frame," he rolled his eyes. "Don't be pedantic."

"What does 'pedantic' mean?"

"Overly concerned with details, in a sort of precocious way."

"Pedantic," I repeated, savoring the sharp consonants of a new word.

"He's good," I said, marveling at Fonda's wholesome naturalness. The unblinking eyes that stared down his scene partner while his voice hardly ever raised above conversational volume. "It's like he's not even acting."

"Ahead of his time. Really understated. Really screwed up guy, though."

"Hmm?"

"Five wives. *Five.* One killed herself. And his daughter is a fucking disaster area." He sipped his beer and farted. "Actors are a mess."

I watched Henry Fonda as he walked through frame after perfect frame. He seemed so focused, so righteous in his Tom Joadiness. Did you *have* to be a mess to be this good?

The night wore on and my dad drank until he was maudlin. And then suddenly energized. And then, just as abruptly . . . both. He did push-ups or forward rolls in the hallway of his large studio apartment and then sat on the side of the couch where I was lying and weepily told me, "I love your fucking mother" until I fell asleep.

We got up early as we always did on Sunday mornings. Jackson Heights could be quite drab, but beautiful sunlight filled the apartment, and my dad would serve me a bowl of Total with very cold milk, and I'd eat it quickly before it got mushy.

"You were snoring a lot last night," I complained. He had woken me up with his cavernous, percussive breathing.

He smiled at me, and his vengeance was swift: "You were talking in your sleep. Bouncing up and down on your belly and murmuring something about 'Cathy.'"

I sank in my chair a little. The room darkened. Mortification hung over me like one of those lead blankets you get at the dentist's office. I felt my face redden. For a moment I thought it might even be true.

Again with the slightly-too-rough hair tousling, followed by a smirk. "I'm just joking," he said. "It's OK, Tiger. My dad used to tease me, too."

It felt very far from OK. It felt like this reference to my really nascent sexuality was dragging me into something—Adulthood? Masturbation?—for which I was not ready. I just got very quiet on the long subway ride to church. Dad was an usher at Mass, and he was charming, effortlessly charming as he welcomed people into the place. Sometimes the effort showed, and you could watch the smile vanish from his face as soon as someone turned their back. My mom met us at Mass, and I said my goodbyes to my dad and went home with her.

"How was your weekend?" she asked, as we walked up Madison Avenue.

"Fine," I said.

◆

I found church incredibly boring as a child (I wish someone had explained the structure to me—how we read an old story, and then someone put it into modern terms, analyzing a text like in English class, because that I *might* have been into), but my parents insisted on going, and it seemed especially important to them after the separation—a sad grasp at constancy. My post-separation personality was just getting worse, angrier; I was more cutting in my language, needlessly bitchy and mean to my peers, by whom I desperately wanted to be loved and admired. I was funny, sure, great, but had no idea how to deploy it, so I figured why not just be sarcastic to people I cared about—that way they would *know* I was funny and would like me, even though I had just called them "Baryshnikov" for tripping over a desk leg. When this was not appealing to others, when people avoided me or, worse, scolded me, my response was often to flip over a desk in an absurd rage.

These violent outbursts were coupled with creeping, persistent dizzy spells—vicious episodes that made the ground suddenly lurch out from under me, sending me into the wall, shaking. And chronic insomnia. I'd lie awake in my room where I had one of those old eighties-era digital clocks with the numbers on tabs that flip down. A little click meant a minute had passed, and a bigger click meant a whole hour had passed. I would worry about worrying, worry about losing sleep, worry that lost sleep would send me into dizzy spells, worry that dizzy spells would make me miss school, worry that that would mean I'd get held back, worry that that would make me lose sleep. My folks sent me to a neurologist; then to an ear, nose, and throat specialist; and then finally to a GP, who talked to me and found that the dizziness was just a physical manifestation of this steady anxiety that had been following me for as long as I could remember and has kept pace with me until today. I probably should have gone to therapy. As I would've been very resistant, I probably should have been *forced* to go to therapy. But therapy for kids was super rare at the time, even in Manhattan, and if you did go, it meant you had money to spend on something as wildly self-indulgent as talking about your feelings. My mom sent me to self-defense classes—very chic in the New York of the eighties—and the exercise did me good; the dizzy spells dissipated. But there was still this extra, fidgeting energy and weird, misplaced anger that colored everything around me and made sitting still in church nigh impossible.

To counteract this boredom, I joined the choir. And from there, obviously, it was short trip to lower Manhattan's vibrant performance art scene.

I am by no means a singer, but I can carry a tune and I have a decent ear, and for some reason my fear of getting up in front of people didn't extend to the choir: There was an anonymity in being just another kid in a black cassock singing with nine other boys. I wouldn't be up there alone. I'd be clumped together with others. The choir mother—think slightly less religious den mother, in charge of making sure the boys got to where they were going—was a very friendly midwestern woman with a phenomenal perm named Carol. Just about six years later, she would become my stepmother; my joining the boys choir was how she and my dad first met.

The choirmaster was this very stern, very blue-blooded guy named John Morris, an effete "confirmed bachelor" who lived downtown. I mention this only because aside from his abiding faith and his deep love of liturgical music, he also had one foot in the lower Manhattan arts scene of the 1980s. As such, the boys choir of the Church of the Transfiguration was hired circa 1983 for a performance art piece called *The Piano above Heaven*, written by a friend of his.

God, I was nervous. Sweaty. My teeth were clenched and I was in a state of intestinal distress. We hadn't seen the whole script—we had just seen our parts—and from what I'd seen, I had no idea who this was for or why anyone was doing it. We were to chant non sequiturs while standing stock-still behind the writer, a tall, blond, handsome man who looked to be in his thirties (but kids are terrible judges of such things, so he was probably in his twenties) named Eric Schmidt, who stood at a music stand and recited this odd . . . poem? Spoken word piece? Yes, I was in Manhattan, and yes, it was the early eighties, but I was about eleven years old, and you'll forgive me for not being aware of Laurie Anderson or Klaus Nomi or any of the performance art icons of that era. *The Piano above Heaven* was, as we say now but unfortunately did not say then, a lot to process.

In a Tribeca gallery on a very dark, very cold November night, the small audience (let's say about twenty-five people) giggled nervously upon seeing an Episcopal boys choir step timidly into the art space. Under a strobe light, we threw costume jewelry into the crowd, the effect being a slow, shiny rainfall that sparked an amused *"Ahhhhh"* from the small audience. Weird chunks of text stay with me: "Mendelsohn, goodbye!" and "Your doll's bottle's nipple where it fits into your mouth!" and Schmidt himself saying, "Fuck artifice!" which shocked me so much I looked around at my fellow choirboys in a fit of uncharacteristic pearl-clutching.

While walking back to the subway that night, my separated parents and I tried to figure out what they had just seen and what I had just participated in.* My mom still thought it was really impressive, and said she was proud of me. My dad, however, admonished me: "When he said 'fuck,' you looked around at your buddies. That was unprofessional."

Fair point. We were being modestly compensated, and I had broken from my role of innocent-looking cherub, there to balance the profanity. We had not been warned about the cursing, and I was taken aback, but performing is about commitment, and although it would be years before it was codified as such, *The Piano above Heaven* is where I learned that. What Rhoda does? It's hard. It's work. It's a job.

The other lesson I took to heart that night?

Everything will impress Mom. Nothing will impress Dad.

---

* We got nowhere, and hindsight doesn't give us much to go on: *The Piano above Heaven* leaves little internet trail, save for a shot of Schmidt performing it in Chicago, sans boy choir, sometime in 1983.

CHAPTER THREE

THE OTHER STAN LEE
AND HIS NOVELTY GLASSES

T hey outnumbered me. There were four of them, and though they were each the size of my thumb, there was something about them that said that while they weren't necessarily going to start a fight, they could finish one very quickly and I would be much the worse for wear. Yet there was also a pronounced dorkiness to their aesthetic. They were not in great shape, they were not dazzlingly handsome, and they looked like they held strong opinions about comic books and actors who had played Dracula. There were many iterations of the group spread across the shelf, but it was this particular dead-on black-and-white image that really stuck with me, following me as I walked up and down the crowded cassette aisle at the Tower Records, past the cash registers, in the back of their flagship store near Lincoln Center. I'd heard of them before, of course—this was New York City, and my camp counselors had once danced to one of their singles at a talent show—but I didn't own anything by them. Still vaguely scared of the cover photo, I turned the cassette over and read the song titles, which were hilarious. "Beat on the Brat." "Today Your Love, Tomorrow the World." The one that struck me as the funniest was "Now I Wanna Sniff Some Glue." That imperative "now" takes a weird idea and gives it an immediacy that gets more darkly hilarious the more you think about it.

"Well, Joey, did you get the groceries?"

"Yeah. And I stopped by the newsstand and picked up the paper."

"What do you want to do now?"

"Now? Now I wanna sniff some glue."

I bought the Ramones' self-titled debut album on cassette sometime in the spring of 1985, just around my fourteenth birthday. It had been a tough year. The summer before, at a lush, pastoral Episcopal camp in Connecticut, I had done the thing you were supposed to do—stood up to a bully—and been punched so hard I seemed to evaporate before reassembling on the ground. Shortly thereafter, a cadre of beautiful girls were giggling uncontrollably right across the campfire from me. It was nothing I said, and I took a tragically long time to discover that they were laughing at the testicle that had found its way out of my too-short trunks to take to the air.

The following school year had not been an improvement. I'd spent the whole year pining à la Charlie Brown for a Little Red-Haired Girl, and when another boy asked her out in front of me, I managed a less-than-impressive "Wait—me, too?" She kindly took a couple of hours before calling me to let me know, gently, that she had decided to go with the guy who had *actually* asked her out and not the guy who had asked to be included after the fact.

This sort of nerdery might have been reflected in exemplary school-work, but no, my grades were only okay—a mean in the low 80s, NYC still using numbered grades—and my visits with Dad were getting quieter and more separated from normalcy, bizarre little pauses in my day-to-day life that occurred every other weekend. All of my answers to his very reasonable questions about school and life were being shortened to "fine," and he hardly ever asked follow-up questions. I was starting to form my own cinematic opinions and push back lightly on his. Maybe *Platoon* wasn't a masterpiece, per se, and maybe *Ladyhawke*'s synthesizer score was wildly out of place ("Anachronistic?" he said, reminding me who was boss.) Maybe Ronald Reagan was a doddering old fool who was pushing us perilously close to an unwinnable war, and maybe his work in the 1940 Western *The Santa Fe Trail* was ghastly not just in his wooden performance, but in the fact that the film's bad guy was the abolitionist John Brown, as clear-cut a hero as American history has provided us. "Why the fuck are we watching this? Is there nothing else on?" As I got deeper into high school, my politics moved to the left and therefore further from my dad's (and I'm even further left now, tossing that adage about everyone growing conservative with age to the wind).

My mom and I were getting snippy with each other, too. I needed a little more privacy right as I was suddenly taking up more space. She was lonely, I now realize, and I don't think she had any long-term relationships after I entered high school. She lost her temper only once, and she really had the right to do so. One night, she had made me go finish my homework when I had begged to watch more TV. I stewed in my room and scribbled something awful on my worksheet. I'm pretty sure it was something akin to "priest-loving whore." She wasn't even dating the priest anymore. More to the point, she was absolutely right: I did have homework to finish. My mom didn't deserve this outburst of misdirected rage, and I knew it immediately after I wrote down the epithet. What a callous, stupid thing to say. A wise man would have just torn it up and thrown it out, but I was so filled with guilt . . . that I decided to show it to her and beg her forgiveness.

This was a massive error in judgement. I called her meekly into my bedroom and said, "Mom, I'm really sorry," showing her the worksheet. She looked at the paper, iced over, and retreated to the living room.

After a brief, horrible silence, there was a crash—mom had pulled over the small two-shelf bookcase, sending her mystery novels all over the floor. She screamed a bunch of things through tears, but the one that stuck was "Did you ever understand that I might have wanted to get remarried?" When pent-up Irish rage explodes, you better duck. So I did. I retreated to my room for the rest of the night wrapped in self-disgust. In the morning we didn't discuss it. It was as if nothing had happened. The books were already back on the shelf.

◆

I took the Ramones cassette home and put it in the shitty Coby stereo we'd bought in Port Authority.* The cheap speakers distorted everything, so what came out was a buzzing aggression the likes of which I'd never heard; the album sounds pretty raw through great speakers, but the level of distortion coming at me was cacophonic. It was brand new (loud, obnoxious) and yet totally familiar, being based in the pop foundations of sixties AM radio. It sounded how I felt, in a way that showtunes and Top 40 and mild folk could never approximate. This was music that was scared, and angry, and snotty, and funny. This was music *for me.* I was heading into a high school with a superpower: punk rock.

Shortly thereafter I stepped into Postermat on 8th Street, a vast, deep store lined on its western wall with punk T-shirts brandishing intimidating, confrontational logos (the Misfits skull, the Circle Jerks slam dancer), all daring you to buy them. And there it was: the Ramones T-shirt, in black, with what I later learned was Arturo Vega's logo at its center: the eagle from the Great Seal of the United States carrying not an olive branch but a baseball bat. Across the top, the

---

* An off-brand Sony knockoff that was reasonably priced at the sort of appliance store that you would find in a bus depot.

word RAMONES. Direct. No article. The band referred to themselves as *the* Ramones in every live recording I'd heard, but according to the shirts and album cover, they were just Ramones. This shirt told people what they needed to know—that this music spoke, to a certain extent, to me and for me.

This music had everything I needed. It was loud, silly, juvenile, and so dumb it was smart. There was this appealing, accessible amateurishness about it. I took alto saxophone at Wagner Junior High and could read just a little music, and even I knew there were only a few chords being played on the record.* It wasn't about craft. This was direct. This was about doing *something*—starting a band, playing shows, releasing records—before you really knew *what* you were doing. There was no college that could or would teach you to play like that. By 1985 there were eight Ramones albums to listen to, and I had a lot of catching up to do.

And I didn't stop there. I had been on a diet of the era's technopop (Howard Jones, Depeche Mode, Thomas Dolby) and more guitar-based stuff like the Cure or my Scottish brethren Big Country, but all those guys could really play. They were occasionally virtuosic, even. But with the Ramones—and punk rock in general—there was something different going on. "We are at a fairly low skill level, but we're doing this and you can, too," it seemed to say. And then eventually, years later, "We're doing this, so why *aren't* you?"

The Ramones opened a door, and through that door came a bunch of bands with this aggressively goofy aesthetic. Sometimes a song title would catch the eye. "She's a Hunchback" led me to the hooky and tasteless pop-punk of the Dickies, just as "Pervert Nurse" led me to Orange County's surfy D.I. Sometimes it would just be the name of

---

* I was perpetually second chair and a thorn in the side of the long-suffering woodwind teacher, Mr. Modrow, bless his heart. If you can hear me, sir, I'm sorry for wasting your time.

the band—the boomer-scaring Dead Kennedys being a band whose controversial name led to interesting music, Canada's Nunfuckers less so—that would get me to buy a record. The import bins at Tower Records became the small hallway of Second Chance records and the spooky speakeasy-ish basement that was Some Records, tucked off the Bowery, and yeah, a lot of the bands sounded the same, but there was great joy to be found in noticing the little differences. The drums on D.O.A. records were mixed higher than Hüsker Dü drums, but "The Enemy" and "These Important Years" seemed to use the same chord progressions. Some of the music was performed by people—say, Bad Brains or Descendents—who could really play. But even with the virtuoso bands, the bands who could *really* shred, there was a sense of gleeful amateurishness—no stage sets, no makeup, sometimes you wouldn't even get an encore. Bands like Duran Duran were glamorous rock stars, bestowing music upon us from the great heights of their rarified British air, abetted by stylists and the best gear money could buy. But these punk rock guys were my classmates. My dungeon masters. They actually worked at the record stores into which I ventured.

Which is not to say that I felt totally welcome. Punk rock was scary. These were people who were brought together by sarcasm and generalized anger—there was no trace of hippie, love-bombing inclusion. And God, how terrifying to be called a poseur, a fake punk who just liked the music and couldn't embrace the lifestyle or didn't put Elmer's glue in his hair to make it stand up. Punk rock was made by amateurs, but you had to be the right kind of amateur.

"What's this?" Dad asked when he heard the opening drums, chords, and snarling vocals of "Holidays in the Sun."

"The Sex Pistols," I said. I had put a cassette in his stereo, a complicated component system whose installation had made my dad curse a lot. (A *lot*. Screaming at *the motherfucking back of the motherfucking stereo that doesn't make any motherfucking sense.* If he was drinking to take the edge off, it just made him more pissed at this stubborn appliance. I almost called my mom and asked her to come get me because I was scared, but I was too scared to even do that.)

"Oh, this is the Sex Pistols?" He'd heard of them, of course. They were the face of the "punk rock scourge" that local news had used to scare people his age just a few years prior. He listened. "Can't understand the words."

"Yeah. You kind of have to train your ear."

"It's just yelling," he said, with a voice that said *You know I'm right*, even though I didn't.

"It's not always about melody," I persisted with the breathy tone that indignant teenagers are known to present.

"Music's not about melody?"

"No, it's about emotion. Or individuality. It's about rebellion."

"Ah," he said, and went back to his cooking. He was an excellent bachelor cook, and tonight's main course was burgers with thinly sliced onions mixed into the meat. "So you can be a society of individuals. Together."

Again—the smug grin that said *You know I'm right*, which again, I didn't.

"How's work?" I asked.

He chuckled ruefully. "It's a paycheck."

Mom was more receptive. She was either genuinely interested or just trying to distinguish herself from Dad. She didn't get punk rock per se. Born in 1942, she was even older than a lot of my friends' boomer parents. But she didn't stigmatize it, and she listened with me and laughed at the boldness of titles like "California Über Alles"—after making sure Dead Kennedys were not actually endorsing Nazism, just using the iconography to make fun of Jerry Brown. The upside of my mom's pro-John enthusiasm was her listening to what interested me, checking in on my tastes. Partly to just monitor me, sure, but also out of a genuine curiosity. It was a very big step for a woman who had gone to Catholic school in Ohio to approach an album called *In God We Trust, Inc.* with an open mind, but she often surprised me.

◆

I started going to shows before I was supposed to. The clubs in New York in the mid-eighties had an arbitrary sixteen and over rule at the door, but sometimes they didn't check ID. So I pushed my luck and started going to shows at fourteen. Not knowing any authentic punk rockers—or, rather, being too intimidated to talk to them at school—I took my friend Abe to see the Dickies at the Ritz, an old ballroom converted into a concert venue in the early eighties. If I couldn't make friends with the punks, I would try to make my friends into punks. Abe was tall and lanky with a thick head of hair that added inches to his height. He was not necessarily into punk rock but was curious to look inside a subculture and generally pretty game for an adventure. Abe was also ridiculously funny, and I thought he might enjoy a ridiculously funny band on that level. He was prone to absurdist sight gags like taping a picture of Miles Davis hanging with Dennis Hopper on his wall only so he could sing in his best Roger Daltrey, "I can see for Miles and . . . Dennis." Or doing a credible John Cougar Mellencamp while he sang, "Little ditty . . . 'bout Moshe Dayan" (which is the most eighties joke in the world, included here to give a greater sense of time and place). I hoped Abe would be drawn to the loud silliness of the Dickies the way I was, and then, poof, I would have a friend, a partner to take with me into the untamed frontier of punk rock. The deal was simple: Abe's dad would drop us off in front of the club at eight P.M. My mom would pick us up at midnight, same spot. The doorman let us in, and two smells ruled the old ballroom: clove cigarettes and Aqua Net, a now extinct aromatic mélange I can still summon if I close my eyes. Abe and I got there right after the doors opened, naïvely thinking the show might start around then.

It didn't. We positioned ourselves above the fray, at the edge of a balcony that looked out over the hall. Kids wandered in and a big screen in front of the stage played kitschy, random content like old Russ Meyer clips, Nancy Sinatra's "These Boots Are Made for Walkin'" video, or the scene from the 1966 *Batman* movie in which Adam West is forced to use his bat shark repellent. The atmosphere of fun was a weird contrast with the faux toughness of the punks assembled, but I loved it. There seemed to be an unofficial uniform, and even the kids from my school who didn't dress like this normally wore plaid pants and sharp hair, unlaced combat boots, and the stereotypical studded belts, whereas I had gone out of my way to be as inconspicuous as possible—jeans and a blank white T-shirt. My hair messy but not *defiantly* so. Converse sneakers, but nothing written on them—heaven forbid I drew the wrong band logos.

At around nine thirty the first band, Legal Weapon, went on. They weren't very good. They were loud. I'd been to rock concerts before, but this was different than seeing, say, the Go-Go's at Radio City or Weird Al at the Beacon. The sound bounced violently off the walls of this much smaller venue. Orange County's Doggy Style were next. They played ridiculously fun, sexed-up hardcore befitting their name.

But it was coming up on midnight. And the place was filled with mohawks and gritted teeth. I never saw any violence—any real violence—but there was that undercurrent of menace at shows that made them alien and exciting, like corny horror films. When the Dickies finally took the stage, it was safely past midnight. My mom was waiting outside for us and could not possibly have been warm out there on 11th Street in late January. Thrilled and scared to be there, I leaned over the railing and screamed along with the Dickies' songs. They did "She's a Hunchback" and "If Stuart Could Talk," which was about the singer's penis! It was loud but melodic, snotty but sweet. Halfway into their set, I felt a very insistent tap on my shoulder.

"Stay. Right. Here," my mother said. She had bought a ticket (thirteen bucks or thereabouts), come in, and somehow found me among the hundreds of teens and twentysomethings—my bright white T-shirt had, ultimately, made me quite conspicuous. She then proceeded downstairs where there was a little more room and smoked while the band played. I saw her down there tapping her toes occasionally, to her credit, but I was furious and humiliated. I got to stay to the end of the Dickies set—no encore, they were technically an opener for England's Toy Dolls, who were going on *even later*—and then Abe and I were taken home in a cab by my extremely angry mother, who said nothing until we got back to the apartment, at which point she very softly demanded we go straight to bed. Abe was kind in that he never mentioned this incident, ever. It was years before I forgave her; now that I have kids of my own, I can't *believe* she didn't call the cops.

I was cordial with the demonstrative punk rock kids (studded belts, torn Exploited T-shirts, the occasional mohawk) at my school, but we never went to shows together. There was no obvious place where I fit in. There were kids who were into Van Halen or Madonna who looked at my shirts or my meticulously decorated notebook and scoffed, "The Dickies? What, like, little penises?" Punk rock was my secret; it was the thing that made me different, gave me a quirky identity, but not necessarily one that matched with the punks who had discovered weed and turnstile-hopping. The Izod-clad Van Halen fan would look at the song titles on my cassettes, roll his eyes, and hand it back to me. "Sounds *great*, John."

But this defiant weirdness allowed me to shift from the weak "me, too" that had not asked out the little red-haired girl into a more vibrant, self-actualized "me." There were the long-haired metal guys, the nerdy science kids who were still hanging on to Members Only jackets that their moms had bought them three Christmases earlier, the hoops players—and then there was young John Ross Bowie, coming into his own, wearing a vest over a T-shirt (often hand-designed with a slogan like CHILDREN SHOULD BE OBSCENE BUT NOT HEARD)* with a Douglas Adams book and/or *Village Voice* under his arm. Pretty smug, but he might make you laugh.

Punk rock didn't become my tribe, but it let me find my tribe. This crazy music made me feel less crazy, and in turn I found a certain social footing of my own. I felt less and less like I was blending into the crowd, less scared to be seen. My anger subsided a little; there was less to be angry about when you felt you were being heard, even if it was just by the bands you were listening to. And I eventually found other weirdos, kids who weren't easily classified, who kept scraping up against the confines of their boxes. Not all were into punk rock—they were mostly hippies and neo-beatniks—but they all seemed to appreciate that I was into punk. It was something that was mine that I brought to the table.

Then, suddenly, I was doing theater. I'd watched the school's production of *Oklahoma!* and been struck not by the actors—over-made-up fake yokels doing a pretty wholesome show, despite being pretty hard New York City kids (some of them allegedly did blow at the cast party!)—but the people scurrying around backstage, running up to the light booth to fix problems on show night. Not *on* stage (still terrifying, still the source of a throat-closing anxiety, even though it looked so appealing and fun) but involved anyway, engaged with the production. I would be responsible for something, for something entertaining no less, but with zero public speaking requirements. I meekly approached the stage crew's faculty advisor, Mr. Kelly, maybe even with my hat literally in hand, and by the next fall *I* was scurrying around backstage,

---

* Which was not only corny but wasn't even that original—I recently saw a seventies novelty T-shirt that replaced "children" with "women." I must have unconsciously plagiarized it.

building sets for *Fiddler on the Roof* and designing light cues for the winter talent show. The stage crew also set up mics for assemblies, and that did lead to students screaming "Nerd!" when I came out on stage, but this mattered less and less.

It was backstage that I met an adorable Dead Milkmen fan with huge brown eyes and a similar shyness. We found ourselves hanging out more and more, walking around the Village, where she lived, and as the fall air of my fifteenth year grew colder and colder, we walked closer and closer to each other, eventually linking arms for warmth. Kissing until our lips hurt. First hickeys, first everything. Correlation is not necessarily causation, but within two years of buying my first Ramones record, I had a girlfriend and had lost my virginity. It was way too soon to be having sex, of course, as July 1987 was only about a month past my sixteenth birthday. But the sex was really fun, and then we broke up temporarily. I was sitting there, weeping on our cigarette-burned couch, when my mom asked point-blank if I had been having sex, and I said yes. She forbade me from seeing my ex-girlfriend again, so of course my girlfriend and I got back together and the sex got *incredible*.

I dealt with our inevitable and final breakup by setting off fire-crackers with Abe and a couple other kids in a schoolyard in the east teens, the way sexually active grownups do. I was shattered about the breakup, visibly depressed, and not much fun to be around when I saw my dad for dinner. He, too, asked me if we were "sleeping together." I told him the truth, and he got quiet and smiled wistfully: "You beat me. I was eighteen and she was a hooker."

"Oh."

He elaborated. "They took all the pledges to a place near the university. She lay on her back and said, 'Fuck my cunt.' Real tender moment." He sipped his beer. "You're lucky."

I pushed my plate away, done eating for a while.

Dad had remarried in that summer of 1987—Carol, the choir mother from church—and they'd had a small, lovely wedding where I volunteered to be the best man, not realizing that the best man was required to make a toast. I kept it strikingly short—I remember telling the newlyweds "to live long and prosper"—but was genuinely happy for my father's new life. He was, too, even though he got a little too drunk at the reception.

Carol was/is great—smart and cultured with a streak of midwestern nice that was a welcome change of pace in the acerbic Bowie family. By age sixteen, for better or worse, the heavy lifting of childrearing is kind of done, so she never really felt like a stepmom per se—she was my dad's wife and was exemplary at that.

The other big milestone that came with turning sixteen was that I could finally set foot in CBGB—which was much stricter than the Ritz about checking IDs, even for their misnomered "all-ages shows"—which was everything I'd heard it would be. It was curfew-proof, to start, as the hardcore shows were all matinees. They started around three P.M., and you could see your favorite band and very conceivably be home by seven P.M. No need for parental supervision or custodial care. You entered off the Bowery and stepped right in front of the bar, which stretched into the club and led you to the stage, except the stage was at an unusual angle, vaguely facing the north wall. The bathrooms were all the way in the back and then downstairs and were as fucking gross as history has told. I don't know anyone who knows anyone who ever had a bowel movement at CBs. The men's room was a horrifying petri dish that seemed to prove herpes was actually airborne.* It had no stall, just a bare toilet on a platform and three urinals with no dividers between

---

* The bathroom was so notorious that a joke meme circulated during the nightmare summer of 2020 which promised that if you had used the bathroom at CBGB, you were likely immune to the novel coronavirus.

them. If you desperately had to take a shit, you went up the Bowery to Phebe's restaurant and hoped to God they'd let you in.

The matinees were always packed, and if people said "excuse me" you certainly couldn't hear it. At all. The sound at CBGB can't be overstated. If you stood near the speakers, they literally blew your hair. But the sound was clarion clear; all the money in the place apparently went not to maintenance or an exterminator but to keeping the sound system state of the art. You could hear every single string and every single drumhead. Kids were still doing circle pits, and I let the centrifugal force of slamming youths push me away, sometimes shoving a stray dancer back into the fray. It looked very dangerous, and I already had a bad back at sixteen. Fights broke out occasionally, and there was no room to avoid them, so you just had to sort of squeeze yourself through the crevices between sweaty bodies toward an egress.

Setting foot in CBs after hearing about it for years was a sort of punk rock Hajj, and I was incredibly excited to hear music at the place that birthed the Ramones et cetera. But once you got halfway into the tightly packed venue, which was almost all hallway, and saw the unusually angled stage, you had three concurrent thoughts:

1. This place shouldn't be laid out this way.
2. I should not be in here.
3. Oh, sweet *Jesus*, it is so exciting to be in here.

The scene out front was a well-lit version of the inside, just with more places to run, and run you wanted to as the Bowery was in full homeless-junkie swing under Ed Koch at the time. But for all the tough-guy posturing, I was finding a lot of the kids out in front of the club to be approachable—eager to explain who the band on their shirt was, what the political slogan on their leather jacket meant. (It was here I first heard of vivisection, found out what the African National

Congress was, and learned about the antinuclear proliferation protests that would clog the streets around the United Nations, forty blocks north.) Right above CBGB was a flophouse called the Palace Hotel, and sad old drunks would wander around in front of the club, glaring at the youngsters who were making all that ruckus. Next door they eventually opened up the CB's gallery, a record store and performance space that tried to do too much, even booking lame stand-up comedy some nights ("I tell ya, this new guy I'm dating? He's a plumber. Which sucks because he lives all the way out in Flushing," said one comic in a sundress. "Let's see. What else . . ."). The place was a microcosm of the city: ominous, educational, and funny for the wrong reasons—but you'll be okay and you can stay.

And I stayed for show after show. The Adolescents. Government Issue. Dag Nasty. D.I. Countless New York hardcore bands, including rougher, faster, and less melodic outfits like Youth of Today, Gorilla Biscuits, Token Entry, Breakdown, and the hilariously named Altercation, some of whom took hardcore and morphed it into Krishnacore, which is exactly what it sounds like: hardcore punk founded on Hare Krishna principles.

At the time, I was straight edge (a term coming from DC hardcore legends Minor Threat's anthem of the same name), meaning religiously sober from *any* substance. Straight edge as a movement was so self-righteous about itself that the term even has "edge" in it. As if to say, *I'm better than you because I'm not altering my mind, and if you tell me I'm not better than you, I'll cut you with a "straight edge" weapon. And I'll do it with scary precision because I'm sober.* Drinking and smoking were tools of the man, the establishment, tools of my father. I would get angry—wildly angry—when any of my friends smoked or drank, when my punk rocker role models tried to be like my dad by smoking or drinking. I would scream and cry a little. I took it as a betrayal. This sort of behavior would really only be addressed and quelled years later, when I started drinking myself. Once I saw the appeal of a numb escape, my anger softened. For a bit.

Pathological self-righteousness aside, being straight edge was a terrific bargaining chip with my mom. ("Yes, I might be out for a while, but I will return stone cold sober. Ask your friends if *their* kids can say that.") Ultimately, I fell in with the agnosticism of most punk rock, but I was nonetheless intrigued by working class toughs from Queens suddenly dotting their foreheads, chanting in front of CBGB. There probably have been musical subcultures weirder than Krishnacore, but none that I have seen up close.

The New York hardcore stuff wasn't really my genre, but I loved live music, and what those bands lacked in melody they made up for in incredibly loud and crunchy guitars. The music didn't *make* me angry; it just *responded* to a deep anger I was trying to cope with, that I was trying to burn off like excess body weight. The din was inside my head already. This was music made for little kids who didn't know who to yell at after a divorce. This was music for kids who had been robbed by people who would never be caught—by people who had snuck in through the old, quaint dumbwaiter in the apartment and stolen a television and your mother's jewelry and ransacked your room, so you had to lie in your bed that night and ask yourself if the burglars had sat on that same bed while they were going through your stuff.* This was for the kids who weren't sure how to talk to girls or stand up to bullies and as such screamed back at stereo speakers. This was for the kids who had back issues so bad they had to bring a back brace to summer camp (as I did). This was for the kids whose dads didn't understand why we hated physical education but who also weren't great academic students (it really shouldn't be an either/or situation). This was music for kids

---

* Given my druthers, I'd rather be mugged than burglarized. After a mugging, you can return to the safety of your home, whereas after a burglary your home feels markedly less safe. My wish for you is that you never have to form a preference.

who thought the standard American Dream—get an office job, advance within, support family thusly—seemed flawed and soul-crushing, not just boring but selfish. You were making money—that was it. It was a paycheck. What were you putting into the world? My father worked in the paper industry. Paper kills trees. Yes, we need it, but how much of it? Also, that paper he helped traffic? They printed the *New York Post* on it. At sixteen, I already held that pun-happy rag in contempt. *Fuck that*, I screamed into the speakers.

On the second to last Dead Kennedys record, *Frankenchrist*, the lead track is called "Soup Is Good Food." It begins with an itchy, psychedelic guitar underscored by hiccup-y drums. The song is so bleak, it's barely sung—just spat out—and it doesn't rhyme. The lyrics:

> *We're sorry—but you're no longer needed. Or wanted. Or even cared about here.*
> *Machines can do a better job than you—*
> *and this is what you get for asking questions.*

It goes on in this fashion about a world in which the only God is the bottom line. The song's narrator asks the listener:

> *How does it feel to be a budget cut?*
> *How does it feel to be shit out our ass*
> *And thrown in the cold, like a piece of trash?*

How would it feel? Is that, I wondered, what adulthood would hold? Is that what it meant to get a job? I was only a year away from submitting college applications, and I had no clue what I wanted to do with the rest of my life. I had given up the idea of acting (publicly anyway, though I still harbored weird thespian ambitions deep down inside, in a compartment that might be similar to where gay kids keep their true feelings), because a career in the arts seemed too dangerous, but Jesus, was anyone safe . . . ever? All important things to think about, but hell, I was still in high school, so let's pogo.

My approach to punk rock probably *did* make me a poseur. I avoided the pit, and this was back in the days when it was still one of those relatively chill circle pits (everybody sort of run-dancing in a prescribed motion, often clockwise to encourage a safe predictability), instead of the every-man-for-himself anarchy that cropped up in the nineties. I loved the bands that weren't just punk but critiqued punk, like the aforementioned Dead Kennedys asking, "Who'd fix the sewers?"—making very clear the limiting principle of anarchy with "Where Do You Draw the Line?" Or Hüsker Dü wondering, "Is it important? You're yelling so loud" in "Makes No Sense At All." Or 7 Seconds coming after toxic masculinity before we had a name for it in "Man Enough to Care." Punk rock had that self-criticism baked in in a way other genres didn't—heavy metal very rarely makes fun of heavy metal.

My fandom came to an apex on Halloween 1987 when I was standing in line in front of Irving Plaza. The night was chilly, and I wore a large tweed overcoat, because 1987. I'd had my hair teased to a spectacular height of four inches by my friend Eris (an almost aggressively interesting girl with two moms, a nose piercing, and what struck me as a premature fondness for William S. Burroughs) and was waiting for the doors to open for the Dickies with special guests Murphy's Law. The ticket I held in my hand stopped me: the name Murphy's Law, a "drunk-punk band" that was popular in New York at the time, was printed larger than the Dickies. The Dickies were the headliner, they were going on later, they had briefly been on A&M, they were better songwriters, and they had easily five or six years of seniority on Murphy's Law. My friends seemed nonplussed about this nontroversy, but something deeply upset me about it. I felt that the Dickies—ten-year punk rock veterans, refugees from a major label who were now hopping from indie to indie—deserved better. As I was articulating this to Eris, who should walk by but Stan Lee.

No, the other one. Stan Lee was the guitarist for the Dickies, a short, slightly chubby shredder who played fast and well and was responsible for a lot of the band's delicious hooks. He and the lead singer, the gangly and charismatic Leonard Phillips, were the two founding members and the only ones remaining in the current lineup. I recognized him immediately. So much of my adolescence was spent poring over lyric sheets while sitting on the ground next to the record player. In a very real way, unbeknownst to him, Stan Lee had spent a ton of time in my bedroom. He was not being swept past the line by security in front of Irving Plaza, and he was not walled in by an entourage. He was walking into the club where he was about to play a gig. He was going to work.

"Stan!" I yelled, because I thought I could. "Come here."

He walked over and said, "Yeah, what's up, man?" As if he knew me. This might have been that technique that people employ when they've achieved a little bit of fame—afraid to offend anyone, they say hello to everyone, often replacing "Nice to meet you" with "Nice to see you." I occasionally do this myself now. Or it might have been the sheer accessibility of punk rock. You hang out. You listen. You try not to be a snob or a rock star. Either way, I had, for the moment, the full attention of the Dickies' guitarist.

"What's the deal with this? Why are you guys in a smaller type-face?" (Yes, I would have said "typeface," as my mother worked in book design and we didn't yet say "font.")

"What the fuck?" said Stan Lee, who seemed profoundly annoyed at this slight. He gestured at me with the ticket. "I'm gonna be right back. Thanks for showing me this." And he headed toward the club. With my ticket.

He turned suddenly and hurried back to me and handed me something. "Collateral," he explained, and vanished into the club.

What he had handed me was a pair of sunglasses with tiny blinking
rainbow lights around the frames.

"What did you just do?" Eris asked. All my friends were at best
amused, at worst disgusted. I had traded my ticket for cheap novelty
sunglasses. "Dude," said Abe (back for more after the embarrassment
of the previous year's show). "You are never seeing that ticket again."

Minutes passed. We stood in the autumn night air, wind tunneling
down 15th Street. Cheerful punks on all sides of me, all of them about
to go see the most fun band in the genre, and all of them—all of
them—actual ticket holders. *What have I just done?* was running in a feedback loop through my head. Probably the best thing to do now would be to
cut my losses and head home, rather than walk my friends to the door and
let them proceed inside without me. *What the hell is my problem?* I thought,
pulse quickening, an unseasonal sweat breaking out on the back of my
neck. Was I that easily misled, that easily starstruck that I would just—

"Hey, man, thanks," Stan came trotting back from inside the club,
holding my ticket. "They gave us a couple hundred bucks as a sort of
settlement. We're supposed to be the headliners, man!"

I was so relieved I could barely talk. "You . . . you came back," I
managed. "They said you wouldn't come back!" My faithless friends
laughed nervously.

"And lose these?" said Stan Lee, taking back his novelty sunglasses
as he handed me the ticket. "Are you crazy? Hey, man, thanks again.
Enjoy the show."

And he was gone, back into the club, where the doors were finally
opening to the public and the horde of chilly punks were being let into
the muggy, paneled walls of Irving Plaza.

I turned back to my friends. A bigger man than I would not
have shoved his returned ticket in the faces of Eris and Abe. A

bigger man would have been gracious and satisfied just by being proven right.

I was not a bigger man.

"See? I fucking told you assholes that Stan would come back. *I fucking told you.* But no, you thought Stan was going to fuck me. Well, surprise, surprise, he came back and he thanked me. Man, I should have bet money on it, you motherfuckers."

◆

My dad didn't like punk. Punk didn't like my dad. This music was mad at the world, a world embodied by my father, who registered his dissent with my school renaming itself the Bayard Rustin High School for the Humanities by muttering, only half in jest: "Terrific. My kid goes to a school named for a [n*****] fag commie." (Bayard Rustin, a gay communist African American man, would probably not have been a huge fan of my dad's, either.)

My dad was from an older world. I'm not necessarily making excuses for him, but in his adulthood you still could tell ethnic jokes at work (under your breath, so the guys from the mailroom couldn't hear you) and receive no pushback. You could flirt with your secretary. You could get drunk at lunch and return to the office red-faced and smoke at your desk. Still, there were rules. One did all this while wearing a tie. One showed up promptly, deferred to management, and understood that the customer was always right. This was the contradiction of my dad's increasingly archaic existence—the rules seem arbitrary, but the focus is on profit over treating people decently. Punk was new—even ten years after its birth, when I was first getting into it in 1985—and my dad was old. The hippies preached tolerance, but dropping out was easier than engaging, and punk rock engaged—it didn't turn on or drop out, and it had specific issues to address: the military industrial complex, sexism, racism, exploitation of workers, the numbing quality of so much mainstream entertainment. It has often been said that punks are nice people pretending to be bad people, and hippies are bad people pretending to be nice people and while I eschew such sweeping generalizations, holy shit has this been repeatedly proven to me. Punk didn't have the above-it-all cynicism that I heard even in Dylan and other sixties icons, although my father didn't care much for him either. Punk was a warning shot to people like my dad, a distorted death knell to a generation, but my dad never even heard it until it was way too late. It caught me just in time. Punk told me there was something more, and it was loud and funny and disrespectful and insightful and a lot of other things that they wouldn't let you be at the office.

My father was born the day after Christmas (lots of people, including me, forgot his birthday in the post-holiday haze) in 1937, the only child of Scottish immigrants, in Midwood, Brooklyn. His father had come to this country in the early 1920s and had met my grandmother at the department store where they both worked. Both were from Glasgow but didn't meet until they were both in New York City. My grandfather, my namesake, John "No Middle Name" Bowie, the more working class of the two, apparently had a thick Glaswegian accent, and would pepper his speech with the exclamatory "Och!" But that was *Scottish* working class—it came from a deep, profound connection to the land, to the work ethic ingrained in a people who'd fought against an empire with whom they were landlocked. New York working class would not do, so my grandfather worked in an office, and the second his young son Bruce innocently asked if he could have a "hamboiger" it was decided that the Bowies would move out of Brooklyn. My grandfather would make the commute into Manhattan, come home after work in the offices of McLellan's department store, and listen to Scottish folk music over a couple of Rusty Nails or the odd gin and tonic. My grandmother Janet was a stay-at-home mom, increasingly scared by her husband's drinking. She thought about leaving—about taking her son, Bruce, back to Scotland—but her relatives back in the auld country said, "Nae. Stay and make it work, Jan." And she did.

My father grew up in New Hyde Park—shallow Long Island, not too far from the Queens border but a little suburban, in that he lived a block from the busy Jericho Turnpike but also had a lawn to maintain—and went to college upstate in 1956. His high school yearbook is peppered with references to his aspirations to be a lawyer and to his excessive drinking ("Bruce Bowie—a judge on the bench with a bottle!" writes one far-too-encouraging classmate). He was a foreign language major at Colgate, a school that has been termed "almost an Ivy" by people like, well, my dad (the school was denied entry into the league in 1973). He partied a lot while getting a degree in foreign languages (his Spanish was impeccable, his French wasn't bad, and he had picked up a smattering of Yiddish growing up on Long Island). But Colgate was a serious school for serious young men, and while there was certainly a lot of drinking, it had a strangely mature character to it, and my father fit in quite nicely with his peers. As youth culture become the only culture, he was rapidly aging out of it. He was an adult by the time Bill Haley and the Comets announced that they would like to "Rock around the Clock" and in doing so commodified youthful rebellion. He was thirty when it was declared, as a general rule, that you should not trust anyone over said age, and then thirty-one for Woodstock and its malevolent cousin Altamont. He served in the military, drafted right out of college and sent to Bangkok in that sweet peaceful spot between our conflicts in Korea and Vietnam. It's important to understand that my dad was *way* too young to be part of the "greatest generation," but also just a hair too old to be counted among the baby boomers. It was very recently that I heard this generation called the silent generation. They were never represented in the presidency during my father's lifetime; Joe Biden will likely be the lone silent generation chief executive. While dad served in the army, he never saw combat. "Get it straight," he was fond of saying. "We were in Thailand to send Uncle Ho a message." But according to my father's other stories of the service, the message was more to the effect of "Our soldiers can catch venereal disease at an *alarming* rate." I don't remember a time when I didn't know about my dad catching crabs from a prostitute in Bangkok and having to treat them himself because he was, after all, a medic. His biggest conflict in the military was with a drill sergeant who noticed how poorly he was scrubbing the barracks: "Private Bowie! You are doing a motherfuckly job on that floor!"

Laughter.

"What is so fucking funny, Private?"

"Nothing, Sergeant, I've just never heard that word used as an adverb."

WIPE CUT TO: My father enjoying extra kitchen patrol.

My father always had a deep passion for movies, TV, theater, and opera. He had amazing stories about his time as an NBC page at 30 Rockefeller Plaza for *The Tonight Show* with Jack Paar in the early sixties—watching Paar from the wings while the host interviewed Jonathan Winters and William F. Buckley, showing a young cabaret singer named Florence Henderson to her dressing room, promising dumb tourists tickets to a *Wagon Train* taping as a prank,* sneaking out in the afternoon to see a matinee of the original Broadway production of *West Side Story*.

His father died on New Year's Eve—falling asleep in 1964 and being found dead by his wife an hour later in 1965. The death certificate says 1965. Janet never remarried and went to work as a medical secretary to support herself until retiring in her seventies.

---

* *Wagon Train* shot in Los Angeles and had no studio audience. I still find this funny.

My dad was not at home when his father died. There's no reason he should have been, as he was twenty-seven, but he was left with a guilt he could never shake: "I was shacked up with a girl when my dad died." He promptly left the NBC page program—what he later claimed was the only job he ever loved—and found work at the World's Fair in Queens during its second season in 1965. While serving as a docent at the Ford Pavilion, he met a pert midwestern college dropout and wooed her away from her fiancé. Family legend holds that my uncharacteristically forward mom—Eileen Bryan, daughter of an alcoholic used-car salesman—ran under my dad's umbrella during a fervent Queens rainstorm. Two years after this cinematic meet-cute moment, they were married.

By the mid-1960s, my dad had gotten a job in the paper industry, and that industry had landed him and my mom in Coshocton, Ohio, near a paper processing plant. How law school got eliminated—and how a job in entertainment was taken off the table—was never clear to me. Coshocton is a very small town that I have only ever heard referenced by my parents. How small a town? My mom told this story about Coshocton: "Your father and I were driving around one afternoon, right after he'd taken the job, right after we'd moved there, and we saw this house up on the hill. And there was something chained up in this house's backyard. We couldn't get close enough to see it, and we kind of didn't want to, but it wasn't a dog . . . it was a person, a child? A child who was kept on a chain or a thick rope and was running around the backyard."

So in 1967 my parents moved from New York City to this *Deliverance* landscape, yet they still found a theater there. The Coshocton Footlight Players was in its twentieth or so season, and among their fall shows that year was the charming Adler-Ross trifle *Damn Yankees*. My mom sewed costumes, and my father ran lights. In case you don't carry my burdensome musical theater knowledge around, *Damn Yankees* pivots on a middle-aged baseball fan selling his soul to the devil to become a young, healthy Major League prospect. How to present this special effect in a large theater is a problem every director must deal with, and the director of the Coshocton Footlight Players production passed the buck to my father.

"So what I did was kind of interesting," he would say, with a light in his eyes that his work in the paper industry never ignited. "I plunged the theater into total darkness—which was against the law in the county, I even turned off the EXIT signs—and when they came back up, the old man had turned into the young man. The audience gasped." As fun as that was, he was really looking forward to the next production, that family-fabled staging of *The Haunting of Hill House* in which he was to play the town ne'er do well (MY MOTHER: "Typecasting") and my mom was to play a cruel domestic servant (MY FATHER: "Typecasting"). These were meaty roles, particularly my father's: a scene-stealing wiseass with a drinking problem. Any actor knows these are the parts you want—you show strength and vulnerability in equal measure. But it was not to be. Less than two years into my parents' stint in Coshocton, my father was called back to work in the New York office of his company, and as far as I know, neither he nor my mom ever set foot on a stage again.

I may never have seen my father on stage, but I imagine he was a commanding presence. What a voice he had. For all his Celtic temper, his voice was calm and measured, deeper than mine and devoid of any noticeable regionalisms. I have a little trouble with a sibilant *s*; my father had no such impediment. All sorts of people—actors we knew, my mom's flirty gay friends, the women my father dated after the divorce—told him he should look into getting a voice-over agent. Getting a voice-over agent is not cake, but they're out there, and they need clients. My father never followed through, never took up an actor friend of his from church on the offer: "You need a voice-over agent, and I'll introduce you to mine."

My dad's aforementioned job in the customer service department of a large multinational paper company was a source of no joy. He worked in a windowless office, on and off the phone all day with clients, making sure their corrugated cardboard got there in time, trying to persuade a newspaper to buy more newsprint. He smoked constantly and shared his office with men who smoked, so even when he wasn't smoking, he was smoking. He could be quite charming, spoke a couple languages, and knew a ton of jokes, some of which were even tasteful and genuinely funny.

In 1985, when I was in ninth grade, he took me to see Derek Jacobi as *Cyrano de Bergerac* at the Uris Theatre (now the Gershwin) on Broadway. Here's a man who wants to be loved but is reduced to being admired for just his wit and his swordplay. Sure, there's the nose, but there's also this fear he has that keeps him from telling Roxanne how he truly feels. His life is words, honor, and panache, but never love, so he sends young, handsome Christian in his stead to speak his heart. Jacobi was larger than life, barely confined to the cavernous theater, yelling and spitting and massaging the audience, all of whom sat safely in the palm of his hand. Not a particularly subtle performance, but good luck looking away. To watch all that life slip out of Cyrano at the end of the play—he is held by Roxanne, who cries that she has "only ever loved one man and has lost him twice"—was almost too much for my father. He barely spoke afterward, and it was one of the only times I ever saw him cry. My father had a couple of channels—caustic, funny and caustic, temporarily cheerful—but there were only a couple of things that made him cry, and they were booze and the occasional tragedy.

Here's a story that didn't make him cry: An overcast spring day in 1989, I came home to my apartment to meet my dad, who was there to take me for our weekly Thursday night dinner. Usually we'd just go to the diner on Ninth and 43rd that we called George's for its avuncular Greek owner. There was no better place in Hell's Kitchen to eat a cheeseburger deluxe under clinically awful lighting. But before we left, I could see something was weighing on my dad. He had recently stopped smoking and had put on weight. His jet-black hair was still very shiny and combed, and his Brooks Brothers suit, while tight, still looked pretty sharp, but he looked tired and weather-beaten. His serious blue eyes gave a look that said, *I need your full attention*, a look I had not seen since he announced the separation some ten years earlier.

"Sit down, John."

I did.

"I quit today." *Quit?* He'd quit smoking the year before, after a diagnosis of chronic obstructive pulmonary disease, so what could he . . . oh, wait.

"They promoted Eddie past me—he's better with computers—and I left. I never liked that job, anyway."

"Wow," I said. My dad had worked at that company for more than twenty years. "Good for you."

"Really?" He seemed surprised.

"Yeah. You sat across from Eddie for years, the office had no windows, it was filled with smoke, you hated the job, you've always said it was just a paycheck."

"Yeah," he said, nodding more confidently. "Yeah. Fuck it."

We skipped George's that night and went to dinner at the Italian place on the corner, a little nicer than usual. He told nightmare stories of co-workers yelling, of viciously insecure bosses, of Ivy League superiors incessantly mentioning their advanced degrees, of having to constantly entertain clients by taking them to mediocre Broadway shows. (My dad, it turns out, must have seen *The Best Little Whorehouse in Texas* a dozen times.)

It was a nice moment of triumph—local man breaks corporate shackles, ventures out on new life—but my father never quite recovered. He was fifty-one when he quit, had years of experience but no computer skills, and had a bachelor's degree in foreign languages, not in business or marketing or finance. He went on job interviews throughout the paper industry. No bites. Looked into customer service positions in other businesses. Ran into a friend of mine at a job fair at Madison Square Garden, which couldn't have been easy. Nothing.

He even applied to the neighborhood video store. Maybe he could finally cash in on years of being a movie buff, he figured, and it would be something to do. But they weren't hiring, and besides, my father's movie expertise kind of faded out around 1970 and was almost exclusively American, aside from the affinity that all men his age had for David Lean and the samurai films of Akira Kurosawa. "Dad, have you ever seen *Ikiru*?" I once asked him.

"No, what's that?"

"Kurosawa drama from the early fifties. Takashi Shimura from *Seven Samurai*, but it's a totally different role."

"Oh. Uh. No," he said, looking kind of melancholy about it. "I've just . . . I've never seen any of the non-samurai films." It was becoming clear that I was taking all the stuff he'd introduced me to and going deeper—not just listening to the hits but finding the deep cuts and learning how they all fit together. How one thing led to another—how the ethical dilemmas in *Seven Samurai* were made richer and more nuanced in *High & Low*. Being in college, I had the luxury of thinking through these things while my dad searched for a job.

There was a Picasso print that my father had had since college—the famous drawing of Don Quixote, the windmill in the distance—and he had hung it in every house in which he'd ever lived. Don Quixote. Cyrano. Kurosawa's samurai. Rick Blaine of *Casablanca*, to a certain extent. Knights errant, born at the wrong time. Followers of a dead code. Lone wolves who give of themselves for ideals long extinct. Never fully appreciated in their time, they hope to leave some sort of legacy behind them. And they love swords.

It took me decades to connect these dots. I'm not entirely sure if my father ever did.

He finally landed a position supervising a media storage warehouse, where he got to use his Spanish as an interlocutor between the manager and his mostly Puerto Rican staff, at what had to have been a significant pay cut from his office job. He stayed put for a few more years before quitting *that* job impulsively, announcing his retirement and his plan to live off "the market" and Carol's modest salary from—like my mother—publishing.

It reminded me a little of that Dead Kennedys song, except my father had shit himself out of his company's ass and, to clumsily extend the metaphor, tried to crawl into another company's. I was proud of him for quitting—still am—but there was something "too little, too late" about his disgust with the dehumanizing corporate life. His moment for a fierce, anticapitalist middle finger to white-collar America had been years earlier, maybe before I was born. He had, in a way, missed his cue.

But there he was, something of a casualty of corporate America. A secure professional life, I realized, was a myth. You could give decades to a company, to an industry, only to fall victim to a bottom-line-conscious disrespect that left your dignity no recourse but to leave.

So why bother? I thought with Dead Kennedys lyrics and my father's sudden corporate departure fresh in my impressionable young mind. *Why bother with anything?*

And on that cheerful note, I went to college.

CHAPTER FOUR

TALKING TO
THIRTY THOUSAND PEOPLE

I t was the end of my freshman year at Ithaca College, 1990, and I had just endured a winter of my hair freezing as I dashed between buildings at lunchtime, a winter of swooning at the familiar bouquet of Milwaukee's Best and Tompkins County bud that meant someone's RA was out of town. Ithaca is the most picturesque location in the Northeast, with inviting Victorian houses peeking out from bucolic hills that are verdant in summer and quaintly snowcapped in winter. It was incredibly progressive for a very small city, boasting a socialist mayor that year and multiple vegetarian food options. The town sits at the edge of Lake Cayuga, the longest of the Finger Lakes, so named because when created they were so beautiful the great spirit reached down to touch them, leaving his imprints. Ithaca is, as I write this, the North American seat of the Fourteenth Dalai Lama and home to his library, but even back in the nineties there was a peacefulness I found almost abrupt, like the sudden silence of the 1978 blackout. It's the sort of hippie municipality that's charming on its good days, but on its bad days you think, *Put on some shoes, buddy, you're in a grocery store*. None of this takes away from how pretty the town is, its famous six-mile gorge gliding through its center as alternately a peaceful babbling creek or a robust waterfall.

As my friend John Dicker pointed out, however, Ithaca College looks like a chain of Pizza Huts, all spreading like a fungus. The bulk of the campus was built on South Hill in the early sixties and bears all the earmarks of that unfortunate architectural era. ("What if the entire campus just looked like one long box?" "Terrific! Can it be beige?") I was walking to an eight A.M. class (Intro to Poetry with Kevin Murphy) one morning, mentally penciling through a paper comparing Theodore Roethke's "My Papa's Waltz" and Sylvia Plath's "Daddy," when it dawned on me: I have zero idea what the fuck I am going to do.

Not with regard to the paper—that wrote itself. Two very different poets finding common ground in a deep disdain for/fear of their fathers: I was going to crack that theory wide open, clearly the first ponytailed freshman in college history to commit such an analysis to paper. But as far as long term, as in finding a job? As in making a living? I had the vague idea that I would be a writer; my stories were well received in my public high school, but that was my public high school, where the bar was so low that many teachers were grateful if you showed up at all. No, I needed a skillset, and I liked reading, so it occurred to me I should do what most English majors do: become a teacher.

"That's fantastic," said my long-distance girlfriend, my high school sweetheart, with whom I had started making out a week before leaving for college, because my timing is *incredible*. "It's a noble profession, and you love talking."

Both are true.

There wasn't a lot of money in teaching, but there *was* a firm, safe professional ground (missing from both acting and, apparently, corporate work) and, maybe more to the point, a certain nobility. The chance to shape minds. To teach a love of literature and maybe, just maybe, a love of life. Perhaps it will be vaguely filmic, and I will be held aloft by my students a la Robin Williams in *Dead Poets Society*? The problem, of course, is that I still feared/loathed getting up in front of people, and the slightest five-minute oral report sent me into spasms of shame, fear, and diarrhea.

So that would have to be addressed. I would have to punch past or, knowing me, crawl through this anxiety. I thought maybe I'd cut into the problem by taking a public speaking class, or maybe I'd burn my anxiety away through some *grande geste* like streaking, but dear God, what self-respecting man would go streaking in a town where it hardly ever went over seventy degrees? If only, I thought, there was a way to speak in front of people without actually speaking in front of people.

My high school record collection had grown substantially (first pressings that later netted me hundreds of dollars at the notoriously picky buyback counter at Los Angeles' famed Amoeba Music), and by the time I reached college, I'd seen literally hundreds of bands—the aforementioned hardcore matinees at CBGB, Public Image Ltd dodging nostalgic gobbers (spitters) while promoting their album simply called *Album* at the Palladium, the Pogues, Violent Femmes and Mojo Nixon and Skid Roper at the Pier on the Hudson. Herbie Hancock in an atrium down by the World Trade Center. The Who at Giants Stadium, the same week I saw De La Soul at a club in the old Studio 54 space. I went to a *lot* of shows by myself in high school—bless Abe's heart, but I just couldn't find the people who were into the stuff I was into enough to stand in the Ritz into the wee hours, drenched in sweat. The sense of community was illusory, sure, but I loved being part of a small crowd singing "Let's wig out at Denkos," a big crowd singing "May the road rise with you," or an enormous crowd screaming "Sure plays a mean pinball!"

Listening to music was only half the fandom; the other half was arguing about it—about the sounds, about the lyrics—with anyone who would listen. I remember a kid named Max calling me out in eighth grade when I said Bruce Springsteen was questioning blind patriotism with "Born in the USA." Max was furious. Probably aping his father, he defiantly told me, "Springsteen *loves* this country."

"I mean, sure," I'd said. "Me, too. It just seems like he lists these awful things the guy has been through, and then goes back to screaming the chorus. And it almost seems like the song is deliberately running out of steam at the end, until it rallies. I think there's some *irony* there," I'd said, testing out a new-ish word.

"He's singing about a guy who went to Vietnam and then came back a hero," Max was pissed. "That was what the DJ on WPLJ said, and I think he knows a little more than you, John!"

I was not convinced that the DJ on WPLJ did.

When girls left, when dad drank, when mom checked out and didn't want to talk about my anxiety or the quiet hostility that seemed to run through the family like the low static on a dead radio station, music stayed. Some of this pain was just garden-variety teenage heartbreak; some was darker, nastier, a deep discomfort at what I thought were some very keen injustices in the world. *It's not just that she doesn't like me; it's that she likes him, and he represents all that is wrong with this world, with his mullet and his disgraceful taste in music. What teenager enjoys Jimmy Buffet?* Music seemed to listen back to me, pumping out of that shitty stereo in my room. I could pull myself out of an emotional nosedive with an optimistic Bob Marley or Toots and the Maytals song that contradicted my sadness or a properly deployed Cure song that validated it. Any girl who dated me in high school—or, rather, any girl I tried to date—was subjected to an array of mixtapes, some of them even on the less-than-impressive 120-minute format (the sound quality was terrible, but not to worry: the tape would probably break anyway). Those mixtapes were self-consciously eclectic; each potential girlfriend-to-be found Sam & Dave nestled against Youth of Today and LL Cool J. It was my less-than-convincing attempt to prove that the eligible young man who slipped her the tape in social studies was fun and energetic and contained multitudes.

If only, I often thought, *there were a way for me to build on this unique mixtape-making skillset.*

WICB is not a college station in the sense that you usually think of a college station. You did not get on the air and wing it; you did not pick all your songs; you could be dismissed promptly for hosting your show while chemically altered. It was an offshoot of a reputable communications school and as such was a breeding ground for actual broadcast professionals. The station was on the first floor of the then brand-new Roy H. Park School of Communications building, which looked a lot—I mean, *a lot* (lighting so white it's green and cold lacquered walls)—like a hospital and could be just as intimidating. Ithaca College is best known for putting a lot of entertainment executives in the world, and a lot of them started in the antiseptic but very professional halls of the Park School. The radio station had birthed shock jocks like Washington, DC's The Greaseman; sports commentators like Nick Nickson, who does color for the LA Kings; and untold morning guys in untold smaller markets across the country. A WICB DJ followed a playlist of current modern rock favorites.* You picked about six songs out of fifteen that hour, you read the weather, you threw it to news and sports, and you conducted yourself like you were talking to some thirty thousand people, which, actually, you were—the station had a massive transmitter on the top of Ithaca's South Hill. *Thirty thousand*

---

*   The genre that, of course, came to be called "alternative." At the time it meant stuff like the Pixies, the Replacements, the Pogues, the Smiths, and other bands that didn't crack the Top 40 but commanded loyal followings, but eventually the term would umbrella out to mean "rock by younger people."

people. On a clear night you could even hear the station in Rochester, a two-hour drive away. A captive audience of thirty thousand people who couldn't see me and whom I would not be able to see. An audience of strangers who weren't actually looking at me.

It was perfect.

To get a slot on the radio station, you had to go to the sleek offices of the Communications Building, where the DJs hung out with their feet on the counter (thoroughly professional by radio station standards) and listened to the free CDs that came in the mail from record labels big and small. You asked whoever was working there—usually a vaguely slender but also out-of-shape nerd wearing record company swag (say, an official Charlatans UK shirt)—for the audition kit, and they coolly pointed to a cardboard box that contained a few records, a few prewritten announcements, a couple of CDs, and an application form. You booked yourself time at one of the building's audio recording rooms—strange little cubbies that smelled like body odor and looked like miniature radio stations themselves—and basically did an hour of airtime that only a couple of radio station people would hear. The powers that be—in this case an amiable guy named Dave who wore overalls and wire-rimmed glasses—didn't want to hear the whole song, they wanted to hear your "talkset," your introduction of the record, the beginning of the song. Then you could fade it out, fading it back in just in time to showcase your segue, your transition between songs, a sleight of hand for which I somehow showed a certain and immediate grace. The songs in the audition kit were mostly collegiate one-hit wonders: "The Beaten Generation" by The The, something by the Blue Aeroplanes, and a couple larger "hits." (PiL were in there, and maybe Depeche Mode.) I remember the whole process well, because (1) I was not partaking, as we used to say, in the reputably strong herb that grew in those parts, so my memory of everything from back then is pretty sharp; and (2) I had to make two tapes. I must have been audibly nervous in the first one, and I heard nothing back after I turned it in. I went to the station and recorded again, and a week later I found a scrawled note on the dry erase board that hung on everyone's door and predated texting.

Dave from WICB called. 607-etc.

I literally jumped up for joy.

Everybody who started at the radio station got an overnight shift. In my case, my inaugural graveyard slot was three to seven A.M., late Saturday night to early Sunday morning. On the one hand, cool! A weekend slot! On the other . . . Jesus, three to seven? I had about seven bowel movements the day of my first shift and stayed wide awake and terrified all the way to my final walk across campus at two thirty in the morning. You had to start the hour with a station ID: "Ninety-two WICB—Ithaca." This was an FCC regulation you had to comply with, and the manual made it sound like there was no avoiding federal prison if you skipped it, even once. After that, we were off to the races with my freshly changed voice (it had stopped cracking and had settled into the nasal tenor I'll have for life) announcing the sounds of the Clash.

My first show went OK. Not great. I had one amazing intro planned for one particular song, the beautiful "Alex Chilton" by the Replacements, a jubilant powerpop number dedicated to the singer of Big Star, a huge influence on the Replacements and countless other good bands. I read the weather and dove in: "So I was reading an interview with Bon Jovi the other day, because I hate myself," said the young music snob who was trying to sound off the cuff but was working off notes, "and Jon Bon Jovi was upset that *Musician* magazine named the Replacements the band of the year. He said he'd never heard of them! Well, that's fine, Jon Bon Jovi. There are plenty of people who have heard of the Replacements. And there are even a few people who have heard of Alex Chilton!" And I hit play on the CD player and . . . can a silence be churning? This silence was churning. I sat whispering "What is happening?" with dead air in my headphones as I realized, graaaaaaaaaaaadually, that there was just one more button that needed to be pressed for the song to, you know, play. I mumbled something, somehow not cursing, corrected the situation, turned off the mic, and almost crawled under the soundboard to weep myself to sleep. It was supposed to go from me saying "Alex Chilton!" to the jubilant first chords of that song, which punch through the speakers, perfectly mixed. Why did I think I'd be good at this? But a budding depressive doesn't stop here. The inner voice got louder, more piercing: Why did I think I'd be good at anything? I couldn't make it through an hour of college radio, but I wanted to teach high school?*

Someone joined me that first shift—Mancuso? Carson? Was it Leigh?—because I needed moral support. He or she talked me down just enough: "It's OK, everybody makes mistakes, you're doing great, you're a natural." True or not, this sustained me enough that I made it through those four hours. The sun was up at seven when the Sunday morning jazz guy came to relieve me. I shakily walked out of the communications building to find amber sunlight melting the frost on the fallen leaves. Deer scurried in and out of the woods near the school as I left the building and walked across campus. I'd never seen that many that close, and when a family froze in front of me, I responded in kind. We had a standoff, each of us terrified to make a move, me wondering if I should just surrender my wallet as any New Yorker does when trapped—and then they dashed up South Hill, bathed in sharp orange morning light. The deer at daybreak were the most beautiful sight I'd ever seen. At that point, I'd been up twenty-two hours. I

---

* Also, it must be said: I had just heard of Big Star and had really only been into the Replacements for about a year.

crashed for a spell, rousing myself before noon to stumble down to the dining hall. I found some friends at one of the enormous Formica tables and one of them—Mancuso? Carson? Leigh?—said, "Hey! I heard you on the radio last night!" And they had, I guess. I had spoken in front of them. And they had heard me. And if they had noticed the "Alex Chilton" fuck up, they kept it to themself. And I had not seen them. And it had gone . . . OK.

Over the coming weeks, the feedback got more intense and weirdly more welcoming. People had heard me on their car radios, or while they were pulling all-nighters, or while they were fucking in the laundry room while I spoke nearby on a transistor radio (that only happened once, as far as I know, but stories like that tend to stick).

My dad and my stepmother, Carol, visited one weekend when I had a slightly earlier shift. I was filling in for a friend who needed their midnight-to-three covered, and I insisted they come to the station. My dad had been pretty skeptical about college radio—after all, it wasn't my major, it wasn't a career I'd be pursuing, and it was a clear distraction from studies for a guy who was already easily distracted. They came into the studio after midnight and didn't take off their coats. He tired easily—in his fifties now, his lungs losing their elasticity as emphysema crept steadily through them. We sat together in a darkened room, my dad and Carol dwarfed by the massive wall of CDs behind them. They looked out of place, but Carol (a genuine boomer, ten years younger than my dad, actually had solid taste in music, and I had taped some Who and some Roxy Music from her record collection) smiled the whole time. I had an idea that I thought would be funny, which was also a weird, nefarious power play.

"Wanna read the weather, Dad?"

"Oh. Um. What do I have to do?"

I handed him a slip of paper, which had chugged off the AP wire in the radio station's office. "Just read the weather," I smiled. "At the end, just say 'the temperature on the South Hill right now is' and it will be right here." I pointed to a digital thermometer at eye level over the sound board.

He laughed a little nervously and shrugged, slipped on his reading glasses. He cleared his throat and recovered as the throat clearing turned into a damp cough. I told him to put on "the cans" and he started before realizing I meant headphones.

I turned up my mic and the other mic in the studio. "Ninety-two WICB with the Stone Roses, backing that up with R.E.M. and 'Pretty Persuasion.' It's twelve fifteen A.M., my name is John Bowie, and it's time for a new segment we're calling 'The Weather with My Dad'!"

I gave him the up and then down point—a universal sign for "you're on" that I hoped he would remember from his days as an NBC page. In an uncharacteristically halting tone, he read, "Tonight's weather: cold winds at nine miles per hour. Tomorrow, cloudy with highs of fifty, lows at thirty-five. The temperature on the South Hill right now is"—he peered over his readers to where I was pointing—"thirty-eight degrees."

It was not lost on me that for maybe the first time ever, my father was visibly nervous doing a thing I was good at. I nodded at him, a patronizing nod, a nod that said, *Not as easy as it looks, is it?* and then immediately backpedaled by saying into the mic, "Thanks, Dad. I guess the listeners can now see where I got my sexy radio voice." Dad laughed uproariously, pinning the needles until I swiftly pulled down his volume.

◆

Throughout my college years, I kept making these live mixtapes for strangers (lots of strangers at once), and it gave me the confidence to get more involved in class discussions, futilely charging at giants like my Shakespeare professor (who was right, of course: Brutus is not the good guy, not by a long shot). The effect was a sudden blast of confidence, followed by a humbling realization: Maybe academia isn't for me. Maybe I'm simply . . . not smart enough?

This was unmooring. I had been told from a very early age that I was gifted. I had even switched schools to accommodate my giftedness as a youth. "John is seven going on thirty," chuckled my mother, disproportionately proud of what I guess she thought was her own coinage. Before I moved schools in fourth grade, I sat proudly at the top of my class, so universally disliked that we had a Secret Santa thing one year and no one got me anything. I sat near the top of a lower-income school, filled with kids whose parents were too busy to read to them or take them to the theater, and I was relatively born on third base. When I moved into the gifted program across town, the correct response would have been to rise with the tide and welcome the new challenges, challenges I could easily meet due to my aforementioned gifts!

Instead, I had forgotten how to multiply. The skill just completely *Flowers for Algernon*'d its way out of my skull the summer before fifth grade. Work became a rising tide, sure, but I was boatless and my anxiety was growing. Everybody was gifted at this new school. So much had come easy to me that at the first sign of struggle, my brain threw its hands up and my grades plummeted. Math and chemistry continued to torment me throughout secondary school, and while I did take Advanced Placement English in twelfth grade, I skated by with the lowest possible passing grade on the year-end exam. I was doing better in college—the English major precluded math and most of the sciences—but there was this sneaking suspicion that a life trying to wiggle my way into the ivory tower was not for me. Academia was not for any of my immediate family, although my father would eagerly have let you know that he had skipped a grade in elementary school. I felt as if I was drifting away from not just my family, but my own conception of myself as a "smart guy."

But I was an education major, goddammit, and I was going to be a teacher! I spent the rest of my time studying educational psychology: Piaget (kids can only learn certain things at certain ages). Bruner (fuck that, kids can learn anything anytime; you can teach a seven-year-old string theory if you phrase it properly). Dewey (get the kids involved and stop separating thinking from doing). The reading was overwhelming, and if the summaries in the previous sentence strike you as reductive . . . again, I'm not particularly sure I was smart enough to be a teacher. Dewey's "Is Logic a Dualistic Science?" was a peak I could barely reach, clambering breathlessly up the side, rereading each sentence until it connected. I struggled to get through the literature I realized I was going to be teaching shortly. I took the full summer of 1991 to read *A Tale of Two Cities* and the full summer of 1992 to read *The Sound and the Fury*, another exhausting peak I called "climbing Mount Faulkner." I was a solid B in my major at a college with something like a 70 percent acceptance rate. But the ethereal beauty and operatic curse of being twenty is that these doubts don't last. What are you gonna be? A teacher! Where are you going to live? New York City! Who are you going to marry? High School Sweetheart—eventually, I mean; we just started dating about a week before I left for college, so, maybe, dunno, isn't marriage an archaic social construct? High School Sweetheart had no interest in marriage or kids, and so, OK, me neither; I have no interest in marriage or kids.*

I was crazy about her, and she was beautiful with skin like milk and eyes a deep blue that only existed in Caribbean waters. Also, she was smart as hell and unflinchingly honest with me. I was considerably less honest with myself. "You talk about yourself a *lot*," she pointed out, and she was right, I did. "You have some issues with women," she pointed out, and whoa, Nelly, was she going to learn more about me

---

* As of this writing, I have a wife and two kids.

in that arena. She was a student at Barnard who had always been more academically successful and more insightful than I had ever been. She was working in theater *and* maintaining her American studies major. She would eventually graduate Phi Beta Kappa. Myself, I made it into the English Honors Society, Sigma Tau Delta, which has the most unfortunate acronym of all academic organizations.

There was a lot of bad timing in that relationship—did I mention we started dating right before I left for college? Because we sure did. We gave in to a mutual crush we'd had for a few months. Even more ill-advised about this endeavor was the fact that Abe had been really into her but had been dragging his heels, and she swore up and down that she didn't like him back, so I eventually threw Abe under the bus and started seeing her. I apologized repeatedly to him, but Abe and I—friends since fourth grade—never really recovered. We follow each other on Instagram now, but we didn't go to each other's weddings. I had betrayed a friend, and was shifty and unreliable.

So on every front I felt less than qualified for my career path. The truth was, I enjoyed WICB more than I enjoyed feeling cowed by the literary canon. It was radio where I found myself growing, opening up, letting people in. People would introduce themselves to me at radio meetings or tell me they liked my show when I spoke up in class—some even specifically enjoyed "Weather with My Dad" and wondered if I would do it again. People either liked what I was saying (nothing too heavy, just fun trivia about the bands or a light anecdote about campus life) or they weren't listening, I was just on in the background, and I was OK either way. Speaking out, talking to strangers, was fine, and natural, and not deadly.

I looked up to the other DJs at the station like Mike Faloon and Michael Galvin—enormous nerds all, but terrific on the radio, and fanatical consumers of music. I met Faloon my first week on campus. He was taking down an Amnesty International booth on the quad, and I helped him carry all the literature back to his dorm room, which was decorated with the album covers of Elvis Costello's *My Aim Is True* and De La Soul's *3 Feet High and Rising*. He was a dash shorter than me with very large glasses and not great posture. His was a life of the mind, and he was socially aware and an insatiable consumer of music. He was, simply put, exactly the guy everyone should meet in their first week on a campus. We bonded over music and a mutual fondness for the then brand-new show *The Simpsons*. We take *The Simpsons* for granted now—it's an institution, like a comedic IRS—but at the time it was a secret handshake, just smart enough for a college freshman to really appreciate the references and congratulate himself. Yes, it was a hit, and some people just dug the anarchic spirit of Bart yelling "Don't have a cow!" but some of us flattered ourselves that we "got" the show on a deeper level. ("Ha!" We'd chuckle sagaciously. "This episode is called 'Homer's Odyssey'!") Faloon and I flattered ourselves thusly.

Mike Galvin (black-haired, funny and charming, somehow pro-miscuous even though he was, you know, a college radio DJ) tried to host as many shows as possible, even taking to the air on the morning of April 1, 1992, and turning the station into a right-wing talk radio haven, fielding calls from irate college students desperate to hear Midnight Oil, committing to the bit hardcore until announcing "April fools!" at ten A.M. Steve Reynolds had such a warm, conversational voice that he spent a few years as a classic rock morning guy in Utica after graduation. There was DJ Sarge, a fellow Manhattanite who handled the urban programming and played me "Scenario" by A Tribe Called Quest for the first time, deserving mention if only for that. The radio guys (and there were girls, too, but there were less of them, and that always bummed me out) were people who thought about music the way I did, had records that were friends, parents, confidantes, teachers. And dear God, what an era to have records who were friends. In my tenure at the station, we broke two new Pixies records, the underrated

All Shook Down by the Replacements, *Flood* by They Might Be Giants, *Out of Time* by R.E.M, and yes, sometime around the fall of 1991, Nirvana's *Nevermind*.

That was a tumultuous cultural shift. The music I had been mocked in high school for enjoying (aggressive, snotty, marked by fanged guitars) was now what Division III football players blasted to get riled up before a game. I don't like snobbery in myself or others, and I think music should be an inclusive thing, but the huge jocks I remember rolling their eyes at my Bad Brains shirt (that arresting logo of lightning striking the United States Capitol) were now using Nirvana (huge Bad Brains fans all) as a sort of fife and drum combo in the battle against SUNY-Cortland. There was no other way to put it: The ownership of the music I loved was slipping through my fingers. This secret subculture was no longer secret. As North Carolina's Archers of Loaf would say a few years later: "The underground / is overcrowded." The guy who was super into Winger could now expound effortlessly about Mudhoney. She who enjoyed Bon Jovi could easily find her way to the Afghan Whigs.

Time was (and here I lean back into my rocking chair and light my clay pipe and for some reason adopt an antique Southern drawl) a feller had to hunt for music that wasn't on the radio. You had to take chances. You had to blow your allowance on vinyl at Second Coming Records on 23rd or Bleecker Bob's (which was actually on 3rd, not Bleecker), or you had to trust a fanzine review or a friend's recommendation, or you had to sift through the chaff on your local college radio station. And now a band like Nirvana was riding the pop charts with George Michael and MC Hammer. It took nothing to find them; they were handed to you. WICB was just doing its job as the town's modern rock alternative (nestled to the left of the 92 on the dial, we were technically supposed to be there for educational purposes, like public radio), but the local classic rock station picked it up, and then the local Top

40 started playing it, then MTV went all in on this record that was a co-production of Geffen and Sub Pop, which made them labelmates with, yes, both Winger and Mudhoney. The music somehow felt less . . . special, less exclusive. We now had to share it with everybody; it could no longer be a part of our identity. The music with which I identified myself was no longer just mine. And maybe that was fitting. After all, I was supposed to be starting a brand-new phase of life. Maybe the music had simply done its job, and now it was time to move on. Music would always be there, but deep down maybe I thought it a childish pursuit.

Adulthood beckoned: I was about to turn twenty-one. It was time to cut my hair and pursue a career.

◆

My first day as a student teacher was in the unforgiving winter of early 1993, my final semester in college. The haircut took my nipple-length coif down several inches—above the ears, shaped back as I've been wearing it for nigh on thirty years. I was assigned a cooperating teacher at Ithaca High School and showed up to meet both her and my prospective students on a sunny morning. Ithaca High couldn't be nicer. It's the only public high school in town, well funded by the property taxes of the colleges that surround it but open to the children of professors and farmers equally—the school had literally graduated Carl Sagan's son the year before. My cooperating teacher was a lovely older Scottish woman with the Dickensian handle of Helen Spanswick. She introduced Mr. Bowie to the class, and I managed to performatively declare, "Hi, it's a pleasure to be here—really looking forward to working with you guys!" It was just enough words for a kid in the back with dyed Manic Panic red hair to shoot up his hand and say, "What's your first name?"

"Uh. Mister?"

"No, for real."

Sigh. I wasn't entirely sure what was coming, but the kid's boldly artificial hair color gave me an idea. "John."

The kid lit up and then lit everybody else up by asking, "The DJ?"

And that was student teaching. Three-plus years in radio had granted me the position of a modest local celebrity with a vaguely recognizable voice (an intriguing hybrid of "deep yet nasal"), teaching kids who were all pretty motivated and excited to be there. I had the same challenges any student teacher faces except that I was the one student teacher who had gotten to interview the Mighty Mighty Bosstones when they were in town, and yeah, they were super cool and yeah, I *did* get into the show for free.

I was twenty-one years old in a tie and the one tweed blazer I owned, and I got to teach *The Great Gatsby* and *Macbeth* and (in an ambitious move) *The Autobiography of Malcolm X*. (Was I the most qualified person to teach that text? Perhaps not. It was Mrs. Spanswick's idea, and there's no way in hell I would've suggested such a thing. But if memory serves, there were no students of color that year in Ithaca's teacher training program, so I guess the one guy who'd lived in New York and had walked by the Audubon ballroom would have to do.)* The semester went well. My challenging students were just that—challenging—but not disengaged, and if they sucked at English, it was OK, they were probably better at other subjects and comfortably middle class no matter what. The kids gasped when we talked about the way Fitzgerald just plum made up the word "orgastic" at the end of *Gatsby*, and the feeling at surprising jaded teenagers with that old novel was, well, orgastic. My parents were impressed that I was teaching one of the great American novels, although they were both hung up on the same small detail—Gatsby's books.

---

* This elicited a surprising grunt of approval from Dad. "Good man, Malcolm X. Not a hypocrite like King. Fucking philanderer."

"You're talking about how the pages aren't cut?" asked Dad.

"Yes," I said, acknowledging the moment when it is revealed that the books in Gatsby's library have not been read: the pages in the old tomes are still linked, the way pages were printed in one long sheaf and then it fell to the reader to cut them with a letter opener. "A little bit. We're focusing on . . ."

"It's a pretty important detail."

"No doubt. But there's so much to deal with—Gatsby's ambition, the work he *does* do on himself, the metaphorical difference between East and West, the green light . . ."

"Yeah, but to understand Gatsby you need to understand his pretensions."

Mom echoed this separately. "I trust you're going to cover the detail about the books?"

"*Yes*. It's a pretty dense text, though, so we'll spend a little time on that and focus more on how the book addresses the ideas of the American Dream and the rise of new technologies . . ."

"OK, but don't forget the pages and how they aren't cut."

This was a very quiet way for my divorced parents to let me know that they, as much as they disagreed, were in perfect harmony on one issue—they were smarter than Gatsby, and probably smarter than me.

I got an A in student teaching (though I don't think anybody got less than a B). The grade elevated my GPA handsomely, so I graduated with a modest but not terrible 3.1, good enough for the dean's list. I headed back to New York, visions of Robin Williams standing on his desk and inspiring students to stand on *their* desks dancing in my head.

◆

In the soup-like humidity of summer 1993, I was twenty-two and back in high school. Specifically, I was in my vice principal's office—but this time, instead of talking my way out of a suspension for fighting ("This wasn't a fight, Mr. Chandler. This was a beatdown. I didn't even throw a punch!"), I was asking for a job. Mr. Chandler wore many hats; he was in charge of both suspending students and hiring new teachers. I knew they were down a couple teachers anyway—one phys ed teacher and one science teacher had been busted having nonspecific but definitely inappropriate relationships with students (one had left a paper trail of love notes; the other had gotten caught when the student wore a literal wire and recorded him professing his affections).

I had my New York State teaching credential, above-average scores on the National Teacher Examination, and my trusty tweed blazer that aged me up a little bit but was also a terrible idea for New York City in August because, like most NYC schools built in the thirties, the Bayard Rustin High School for the Humanities had no air-conditioning. My resume was nonexistent of course, but Mr. Chandler remembered me. I had been a decent student. I had been affable and genuinely liked a lot of my teachers. I hadn't been a troublemaker in any real sense (yes, there was one time I tried to glue the school shut under cover of darkness on a Sunday night, but I didn't get caught and the next morning it was open as if nothing happened, so my one real attempt at vandalism didn't actually, you know, vandalize). I thought it might be romantic in a *Welcome Back, Kotter* sort of way to return to my old high school to work—and come to think of it, Robin Williams returns to his old school in *Dead Poets Society*—so I applied.

I had spent the summer working in retail at the old Shakespeare & Co. bookshop on the Upper West Side, selling books to neighborhood luminaries like Anne Meara and Betty Buckley (who, on my first day, entered the store and left her small puppy with me at bag check). Working retail, even right after college, did not impress Dad: "Don't you want something with a little more stability?" he asked one day when we met for lunch near his apartment in Chelsea.

"I mean, sure, but I just graduated . . . it's June."

"The money's not great in retail."

"No, but I'm still . . . I'm still back in Mom's apartment."

"I mean, you have a teaching degree . . ."

He had a point. I did have a teaching degree. I could do the Gen X thing and work in retail for several years and just hope that I could get a novel published, or I could dig in my heels and Use. My. Degree.

"It's an English certification, John," Mr. Chandler said. He was a short-ish, heavyset man who had mysteriously grown back a thick clump of hair since my graduation. "I'm set for English teachers. The whole district's set for English teachers. People who major in science can go work in labs, for pharmaceutical companies, in defense. People who major in English pretty much just go teach. Some go to publishing, but believe it or not, at first? The money's a little better in teaching. But I'm not sure I can hire you."

"All right. I guess I'll try my luck someplace else. . . . There's a gig up in the south Bronx."

"But . . . everybody knows you here. And people remember you and like you." He ruffled through some papers. "Okay. I have a long-term substitute gig that I can offer you, but it's off-license. And since it's a substitute gig, the money wouldn't be what you'd be making with a full-time, appointed position. We've got a guy who's out recovering from prostate cancer, it's gonna be a couple of months. You can pick up his classes."

"What subject?"

"It's a position in the Humanities Center," he said, and when my face betrayed confusion, he continued. "It's what we used to call Special Ed when you were here. We changed the name so it doesn't"—here, he rolled his eyes the slightest bit—"*stigmatize* the students. They're no longer segregated on the back of the second floor, we're mainstreaming them as much as possible."

"Mr. Chandler—"

"Ronald."

"Ronald, I have next to no experience teaching Special Ed. One kid had some, maybe, emotional issues up in Ithaca—"

"A long-term sub can teach things he's not licensed for *if* there's a dire need for teachers in that subject. That's what 'off-license' means. And we have a dire need."

This, I thought, was unexpected. This would not be *Dead Poets Society*. This would not even be *To Sir, with Love*. This would be . . . I honestly had no movie for what this would be.

This was certainly more noble than the bookstore gig. I was only ever okay as a bookseller, not great, and I only really distinguished myself by once jumping over the counter to give a shoplifter chase,* but this, *this* would be teaching. This was what I went to college for. This would be a job (more or less) in my chosen field. This was what men did. They went to college, and then as quickly as possible they got a job doing precisely that in which they majored. I mean, sure, it was a grown-up job and I still felt like an errant child, but there were guys my age who were in Bosnia serving their country, and who was I to protract my adolescence? Didn't I owe it to the children of New York to bestow my gifts upon them?

The money was such that the newly minted adult Mr. Bowie had to make the decidedly unadult move of continuing to live with his mother in his childhood bedroom.

I had a lead on an apartment, which would mean rooming with my buddy Michael Galvin from the radio station (he of the right-wing talk show prank). He was able to cover the rent as he was temping at a magazine publisher in the East 40s, pulling down a then astronomical

---

* What would I have done had I caught him? Shaken him down for the stack of David Baldaccis he'd just lifted and scolded him for his trespasses?

sixteen bucks an hour, but there was no way I could afford my share with this job, just by the simple metric of "one week's salary should go to one month's rent." It would be closer to two-and-a-half weeks' salary, and I didn't want to be the roommate who couldn't pay his rent—that was not a thing a man should do. Instead, I would live at home and work at the most mature job imaginable: shaping young minds.

Just after Labor Day, 1993, the first day of school, I woke up in a teeth-grinding sweat and discovered my mother had laid my clothes out for me. I was filled with resentment about this ("I can pick my clothes out just fine! I am a high school teacher! What's more grown-up than that?!") but put the clothes on anyway. Khakis, floral tie, and a chambray shirt, the building blocks of early nineties couture, and if they conjure Michael Steadman on *Thirtysomething*, well, they should. I wore Doc Martens lowtops to remind myself of my punk roots, a quiet bit of rebellion. I sat down on the trash can in our cramped kitchen to eat my breakfast of tea and scrambled eggs. *Nothing to be scared of,* I repeated to myself. *This is what I've been trained to do. This is why I did all that time on the radio. This is the endgame. It is time to be an adult. To be a man. Why does my ass sweat so much when I am nervous?* I apparently looked so scared, so ashen and broken bird-y, that my mother asked, "Do you want me to come with you?"

On my first day of teaching.

She was smoking nervously—lighting one off another—and I know she was trying to help, but I looked at her across the small table that separated us with complete disbelief. *How could she think that would help?*

"That won't be necessary," I said, but probably in a far ruder fashion than that. It must have been an odd view for my mother—her adult son, leaving for his adult job, but also still living with her and quivering so pathetically that she just wanted to help. I left the apartment, walked briskly to the subway as I had every weekday morning from ages fourteen to eighteen, and headed down to work. Work. My job. The job that I have because now I am an adult. It was hard to tell how much anxiety was normal; I figured pretty much everybody would be terrified into a bowl of nervous soup on their first day of shaping young minds.

Upon walking into the school, I was immediately stopped by a security guard who asked for my program card, the form of ID that all students at Humanities carried. "I'm a teacher," I said, probably for the first time. I majestically pulled my teaching certification from my pleather satchel. The security guard looked it over and handed it back to me. "Dios mío," he said. "Good luck, kid."

The one thing I will say for Humanities Center classes is that they were small. Twelve kids per class on average. Five classes, sixty kids. Compared to the 150-plus students the mainstream teachers were working with, I had it made, right?

I wrote my name on the board and explained how to pronounce it. The kids just stared at me, with the exception of the one kid who stuck his head out the window and yelled at the top of his voice at his friend down on the street.

There are a couple of different ways to handle an infraction like this on the first day of school. There's the theory that you don't get strict too soon; you talk to the kid on his level, not as a friend or a peer, but without the authoritarian condescension that he's used to hearing from teachers. The other theory is that you come in hard and disciplinary to set the tone, especially on the first day: There's an old teacher adage that you "don't smile until Christmas." You spend the whole autumn tough as nails, so the kids don't get too comfortable around you, so that they're a little scared of you, even.

That one. I should've done that one.

"Hey, man," I said. "Who you talking to?"

The student—let's call him Ernesto, a tall, handsome sixteen-year-old Latino kid a year too old for tenth grade—ignored me and continued yelling at his friend, very amicably, in Spanish. I caught every other word, and the gist was that he wanted to know what his friend three stories down on 18th Street was going to do with his day.

"That your friend?"

"Yeah."

"Does he go here?"

"Yeah."

"Then, why isn't he *in* here?"

"He's cutting."

Cutting school? On the first day thereof? Why, I never! I understood the need to cut school near the end of the year, but on the first day, well, this was simply unheard of, and also who cuts school only to just *hang out in front of school*? My friends who cut school would go up to the Sheep Meadow in Central Park or down to Washington Square Park, both literally and figuratively shady spots to buy street herb. But they didn't just stand in front of the school. I'll grant you my friends weren't in the Humanities Center, but still. This was a part of the school I had not seen as a student.

"Alright, well, that's his choi—"

"*Bitch ass n****!!!*" he screamed at his colleague down below.

I put my very overwhelmed Doc Martens'd foot down. "No, you can't. *No.* You can't use that word in here. There's too much historical context that you can't"—nope, losing them, different tack—"You can call each other anything else, but not that." I had no idea what I was trying to accomplish with this edict. I mean, it's a horrible word, and the times I used it in anger as a child still burn in my conscience to this day, but I'm still not sure why *this* was the very first hill I chose to die on. I knew the word got thrown around. I listened to rap music. I had gone to this school, for Christ's sake. But my outburst worked, kind of. Ernesto sat down, and at the very least, I had his attention. I had very few great teaching moments, and some were accidents, like pulling a rule out of thin air and using it to garner a certain begrudging respect from the students. And getting them to stop tossing a hateful word around. For a while.

It became very clear over the ensuing months that a lot of the kids in the Humanities Center—the vast majority in fact—were not there because of any cognitive delays, but because they fall under the incredibly large umbrella category of "emotional issues." The impulse control problems that Ernesto demonstrated on that first day, for example. Manny's temper. Carl's incredible mistrust of authority. Pablo's Horshackian tendency to be way too smart for Humanities Center but to stay put because so much less was expected of him than would be in a mainstream class. Priscilla's unsettling tendency to tell me I "look really good" in every outfit I wore. I was very much swimming out of my depth, not quite drowning but getting a lot of sea water up my nose. The school seemed different, but it was probably just from my new seat on the other side of the desk.

There was a weird beauty in Humanities when I went there as a teen. Maybe we didn't have the college admission statistics of a Stuyvesant or a Bronx Science, but the building was filled with smart weirdos who just didn't test well, beautiful girls who spent their lunch periods reading Tom Robbins, former child actors trying to get back on track and have normal adolescences, advanced sixteen-year-old couples who would break up because they butted heads on Palestinians' right to return, and budding fashion photographers who would grow up to date Kate Moss. There were massive parties at the Westbeth apartment complex, and when I didn't know what that was, it was patiently explained to me by an eleventh grade girl with serious eyeliner that it was "the building where Diane Arbus died" to which I replied, in one of my earliest and best performances, "Oh, yes, of course." In the four years since I'd left, however, it seemed like a bright, exciting light had gone off. It looked like a typical mediocre public school now, filled with a lot of children who would rather be anywhere else.

I taught the Humanities Center kids from specially designed worksheets for about three months. There were tiny flashes, moments I felt myself a successful teacher, but it was mostly a wet slog uphill. Cognitive issues aside, these kids were malnourished and easily distracted, and we'd cover something one day and then have to go over it again the next because nobody retained anything. ("Ugh. Sped," said one colleague, using a pretty derogatory term for Special Education. "It's fucking *Groundhog Day*. Just the same thing again and again, day after day.") My classroom got broken into at one point; a chair was broken and a graffiti writer who goes by REAL 6 tagged my desk. The culprit was never apprehended.*

There was one weekly respite: a group of grad students from NYU's Tisch School of the Arts who came in to play drama games with the kids every Wednesday. Some of the kids lit up at this prospect . . . and so did I. I hung out and joined in on their games, albeit a little timidly. I vividly remember one improv game. To play, you left the room, and when you came back, you had to guess what famous person you were based solely on the questions they asked. I stepped out, came back in, and after an excruciatingly long inquisition realized the kids had made me Steve Urkel, the enthusiastic nerd from *Family Matters*. *Ugh* was my first thought, followed by *Fuck these kids* and *Fuck improv*. Just one more thing to make me incredibly anxious. Still, though, the playfulness of the theatre games appealed, the very term "theatre game" suggesting

---

* Years later, I was watching the Meryl Streep film *The Hours*. Meryl goes to visit Ed Harris in his apartment on 14th Street, and as she opens the building's door, there's a moment where you can clearly see the tag REAL 6 emblazoned in paint marker. In an arthouse in West Hollywood, I hiss "That mother*fucker*!" to a chorus of "Shhhhhh!"

an extra distance from actually acting—you weren't playing; you were just playing at playing.

Some of the kids were reachable, though, and I was eager to talk to the parents when parent-teacher conferences arrived in October. That morning, full of school spirit, I gave a pint of blood in the school's blood drive and carried through the day, optimistically telling the kids I would see them and their parents that night.*

Five parents showed up. I taught sixty children. All the parents thought I was another student, and their kids had to convince them otherwise. ("He mad young," said one girl, fifteen and taller than me. "But he mad smart.") Four of the kids represented didn't even need conferences; they were actually doing pretty well and were good listeners climbing over their individual challenges. One kid just didn't belong in a mainstream school, and teaching him to read had proven a Sisyphean challenge. Even the department head agreed. But the mom would hear none of it. Those special schools cost money that she didn't have. Her kid was going to stay put. As for everyone else—the kids whose parents didn't show up—they were seemingly on their own. They were mine for forty-five minutes a day. There was a pervasive sadness and anxiety that sunk into me at that moment—the world was broken past repair, and some people were going to slip into the chasms that careless people left. Some would be able to jump over, but some were just going to be eaten by the earth. To my great shame, there was very little I could do for them.

Or that's how it felt anyway. Could just be some parents couldn't get the timing right and weeknights are tough. At the moment, though, the future looked beyond dire.

The conferences mercifully ended at eight P.M. Mr. Kelly, my old art teacher, swung by my room. Kelly had a breezy way about him.

---

*   My blood type is O negative, the universal donor. I do my part.

Kids either loved him or just didn't show up for his class at all, because, fuck it, it's art. As his student, I had been firmly in the former camp. "We're going for a drink. Wanna come?"

This decision took some mental gymnastics, but I was nothing if not limber at the time. I was not my father, after all; I was, in fact, nobody's father, so me getting drunk, and quite drunk at that, would affect no one. Yes, I was still living with my mom, but she would likely be asleep before I got home. My time being straight edge had been a valuable chapter in my life, and perhaps it kept me from some awful decisions in college. But perhaps there was more to life than abstention. After all, am I going to define myself by what I *don't* do?

"Yes, Stefan," I said, calling Mr. Kelly by his first name. "I would like to have several drinks."

And so began my first evening getting drunk.

This milestone was achieved at the cheesy West Village horror-themed restaurant Jekyll & Hyde, a corny tourist trap staffed by waiters dressed as zombies, pumping standard theme restaurant rock with a little "Monster Mash" or "Dead Man's Party" just to stay on brand. Up a small staircase was the private room that, if memory serves, was called the Secret Lab. I sat surrounded by Stefan Kelly, my old English teacher (Ms. Axelrod, sweet, an easy A), and my old science teacher, who had allegedly fucked one of my old math teachers during his first year on staff (scandalous!). We were joined by a couple of other teachers who had joined the faculty in the four years I had been gone. I was heartbroken over the turnout at conferences and also, as I quickly and queasily remembered, down a pint of blood. Needless to say, the bottom shelf vodka and cranberries they were serving up in the laboratory were buoying my spirits.

Teaching in New York City was not what I expected. It was not what student teaching was in Ithaca, and it was not what I had seen on television—even bad television. It had quite literally driven me to drink.

But I had the camaraderie of adults who understood the job, and the war stories were flowing freely. This was being a grown-up. This was maturing. Drinks with colleagues after a hard day of real, occasionally meaningful work. Wasn't this adulthood? Wasn't this the sort of thing that would impress my dad? Was this not . . . a job for a man?

"Does anyone have Katie McNamara in one of their classes?" I asked.

My question was greeted by a bunch of knowing chuckles. "Boy, is she fucking stupid," said my science teacher, an easygoing hippie who spent every vacation scuba diving.

"Oh my God, it's remarkable," I was feeling loose. "She comes into my class, easily fifteen minutes after the bell. I say, 'Katie, you're late.' She responds, 'I'm not late. *I just got here.*'"

Kelly looked up at the ceiling, his brow furrowed in concentration—he'd heard it all, but this was new. "'I'm not late. I just got here.' Huh."

I drank deeply. "I mean—what? Is that some sort of fucking Zen koan?" This got a huge laugh.

My old English teacher, Ms. Axelrod, reasoned, "Well, maybe she means she's not late to just your class, she's late to the entire school day." She made a "does that seem plausible?" face. This rational explanation undercut my joke, even though it made a certain amount of sense.

"Maybe," I said, taking another tug and ordering another. "I've been thinking about it for weeks."

Ms. Axelrod got up to use the bathroom, and my science teacher waited for her to get out of earshot before he lurched forward. "Who invited Vicki?" he hissed.

"Oh," I mumbled "I did."

"Ugh. John. Can't stand her."

"I'm sorry! I ran into her in the hall on my way out and she asked where I was going."

Eyes rolled all around the table. I had been invited into a cool clique and had promptly blown it by inviting a not-cool kid. High school was the same, even from the other side of the desk.

"She's so fucking boring, and she's a terrible teacher," my old science teacher said. "Never again."

◆

The teacher with cancer became the teacher in remission and returned in November. Swiftly, as if on some sort of weird cue, another job in the building opened up—another long-term sub gig in the English as a second language department.

The objection I *almost* made was "But my Spanish is terrible." That was a completely useless point, though. If I was really going to communicate directly in the native tongues of my students at Humanities—the most diverse school in New York City—I would have needed Spanish, sure, but also Cantonese. Some Creole. Mandarin. Hindi. Farsi. And some German wouldn't have hurt.

Those couple of months were a blur. The first day, I walked into a classroom—I didn't have my own; I kind of bounced around from room to room depending on which class I was teaching—and I wrote MR. BOWIE across the board as neatly as I possibly could. I offered a little pronunciation guide but also assured the kids that I would be perfectly content being called Mr. B. We went around the room that first day, got everybody's name, got everybody's country of origin (all the languages I listed above, plus a few others). Playing to my strengths, I tried to mention a band from every country that came up. Sometimes this fell flat (*mostly* this fell flat), but it was worth it to see a young Japanese kid named Ryu get excited that I'd heard of the Tokyo-based punk band Blue Hearts.

I did this routine five times that day.

Thanks to another long-term absence among the faculty, I was also responsible for a homeroom, thirty tenth graders crammed into a steaming hot space about the size of half a subway car to have attendance taken and "listen" to the morning announcements. I'm all of five foot eight, but I've never really felt as short as I did in that homeroom. Those kids were up and about, they were not ESL, they all knew each other, and for them, homeroom was fifteen minutes of hang time. There was only so much I could do to get those kids to sit down (except for the pregnant student who sat very willingly and treasured the relief from her sciatica). Plus it was just homeroom, so who gives a shit? Three months in and I was finally picking up on some tricks of the trade. I was learning to pick my battles.

My ESL kids had a textbook they worked with, simplified stories of sports heroes or retellings of ancient myths, all broken down into basic English vocabulary words. But they were also absorbing English everywhere else—TV and advertisements especially—and as such, the "Legend of Atalanta" got translated into the "Legend of Mylanta" by one young lady who confused an early Olympian with a diarrhea medicine. Some kids were so eager to get better that they stayed after class to talk to me and ask me questions—not even about the work but about me, just for the sake of practicing English. "Do you have girlfriend?" Yes. "Where do you meet her?" Here, actually, at this school. "Will you marry the girl?" I don't know. High School Sweetheart was always exhausted and stressed because of her boyfriend's job and her senior year at a very demanding local college, plus marriage is a big step; it's like Advanced Placement relationship. "Oh. Do you do the kissing on her?" Occasionally, but we both live with our moms.

The head of the department, a sprightly twenty-five-year-old who dressed in long skirts and prim blouses and was doing everything she could to age herself into "matron," told me I was doing OK, but I was going to have to speak slower. And use smaller words. The school had already been incredibly diverse, but when I was a student, I hadn't communicated much with second-language speakers. As a teacher, I learned from grading papers that Chinese doesn't use verb tenses, at least not the way English does. You tell when something's happening by the words that surround it. Hence, when I had a sick day, Xiao Chi asked, "Where are you yesterday, Mr. B?" This bumpy translation seemed to fit—the workload was insane, I was constantly planning lessons or grading papers, treading water still felt like my only option, and I'd lost all sense of time anyway. Where *am* I yesterday? Where am I today, for that matter? Seriously, though—where am I tomorrow?

◆

Before I knew it, it was January 1994. A new year, a new semester, and the lay of the land had shifted so that I finally got to teach two whole classes of tenth grade English. Teaching in my field! I had finally arrived! This, this was why I had gone to college, pursued college radio, and studied literature. I had just a bit more bounce in my step as I popped a Breeders cassette into my Walkman and headed down to school every morning. My dad came down one day to see me at lunch. He'd had emphysema for a little over five years, and it had slowed him down a little, but we snuck out to a diner on 8th for a cheeseburger deluxe to celebrate what was, essentially, a promotion. "My son, the teacher," he said, so emotional he adopted a faux Yiddishkeit to hide behind.

Of course, a professional teaching load is actually five classes, so the remaining three were what we euphemistically called consumer math. Kids from the Humanities Center were put in this class against their will to pick up *just* enough math to function in society.

To consume.

Somehow I found the term "remedial math" less depressing.

So in between preparing my lesson plans on *Cyrano de Bergerac* (because who loves Edmond Rostand more than a bunch of tenth graders? Can I read a room or what?), I was frantically reviewing multiplication and division and all the things I, as an adult, am supposed to know. *Cyrano* was not in any curriculum, but I loved it and my dad was dazzled by this fact. "The kids will love it!" he said, echoing my own naïve thoughts. The head of the department (a tall, overly made-up woman we'll call Mrs. Philo) did two annoying things that first week during a faculty meeting: She identified herself as Dr. Philo even though everyone knew she didn't have her PhD, and she introduced me as having gone to Cornell, even though I had gone to Ithaca. She apparently believed I had said "Ithaca" the way Yalies say they went to school in "New Haven." I found myself clarifying this credential for the rest of the school year.

The days pivoted back and forth: one section of tenth grade English in the morning, reading *Cyrano* aloud, painstakingly slow, followed by three sections of consumer math, teaching kids how to balance a checkbook, something at which I myself didn't (and still don't) excel. Then back to tenth grade English at the end of the day. Some of the kids were so openly defiant it really tried my patience, and no one seemed to care that I was spending a chunk of my meager wages making sure the kids had pencils and running to Kinko's to copy poems for them to read because we were short on books. This was also the dawn of the joke construct that went:

"Hey, Mr. B? You know that kid Bofa?"

Which I fell for exactly twice.

Some of the kids loved learning and were engaged with the material (there was a young man also named John who read *Cyrano* like he meant it), some loved learning but not as much as they loved starting shit (a young lady who adored reading and also showed up tipsy to class), and some would have rather been anywhere else. One kid announced rather loudly that I looked like a "broken-down Tom Cruise."* The con artist kid who insisted that he, as a Muslim, had to pray during my class. A reasonable request, but I had just taught *The Autobiography of Malcolm X* the year before; the kid was praying toward New Jersey, when he should have turned around and prayed toward Queens. *Bluff called, Mansoor!* That class at the end of the day was secretly my favorite. By eighth period, the students who didn't want to be there just took the F and cut, and I was left with students who either actually wanted to learn or sat quietly and didn't give me any shit. I was able to get some of these kids a little excited about *Cyrano*. About William Wordsworth. About Alan Paton's heartbreaking *Cry, the Beloved Country*, teaching a seriously integrated group about Apartheid when it was still very recent history. It was, for about forty-five minutes a day, the closest to real teaching that I'd ever experienced. Some of the kids were really engaged, leaning forward, arguing with each other about the text. This was electric—until the nasty shift late in the spring of this, my first and only year of teaching.

I hadn't seen the kid before, but he was huge. He had just stormed out of a classroom down the hall and was walking toward the staircase at the opposite end, kicking every single door he passed. I remember I was in the middle of teaching something really delicate and not particularly accessible—maybe Keats—to fifteen-year-olds in 1994 Manhattan, and I was furious that someone was interrupting my *Dead Poets Society* moment. When the gigantic kid came to my door, he kicked it so hard the panel at the bottom of the old wood cracked. This, I decided at the height of my pedagogical passion, would not stand. I stormed out of the classroom and followed him. "Hey!" The hallway was empty except for the two of us. Huge ceilings with fluorescent

---

* Ridiculous, of course—history has shown that I look like a broken-down Ben Affleck.

lights looming above. Our footsteps were the only sounds as I rapidly gained on him. He kicked another door, and I let out another "Hey!"

Nothing. *"Hey!"* I came up right behind him. *"Hey!* What the hell do you think you're doing?" The kid kept walking. Kept kicking doors. I reached my hand out and, in the dumbest move of that academic year, possibly my life, I grabbed his backpack. He turned fluidly, and I saw a rather large fist coming straight at me.

I could tell you that I dodged the punch, and maybe I was dexterous enough that I did, but I'm pretty sure he was just trying to scare me. If he'd really wanted to hit me, he would have. Following such a blow, things like talking and writing a book would likely be very difficult for me. Either way, he didn't connect, but a warm breeze brushed my face as his fist whizzed past. I was so shocked at how close I'd just come to being seriously hurt—by a high schooler, no less—that I just stood there in the hallway, capital-D Dumbfounded as the kid turned and took off down the stairs. Another teacher stepped out of his classroom. He was tall and Italian with a salt-and-pepper moustache. I'd never had him, but he'd been at the school since it started.

"What the fuck are you doing, John?"

"What the fuck am *I* doing?" I sputtered. "The kid just tried to deck me!"

"And you weren't in your classroom where you're supposed to be. If that kid had hit you, you'd be fucked. You're not where you're supposed to be—*in your goddamn classroom*—so the union wouldn't be able to do anything for you. You had to come storming out here for no good reason. You let your machismo get in the way of your common sense. Get back to your students." And then he, too, left me alone in the hallway, his door slam giving off a dramatic echo.

I was so ashamed—and struck by the fact that no one had ever referred to my "machismo" in any context ever before. The teacher with the moustache, I realized, was 100 percent right. I'd let my temper get the best of me, and I'd almost been clobbered because of it. I should have let the school's security guards deal with the kid or just let him go. That was my dad, rearing his head and stepping out through my id. I'd had a temper as a kid—flipping over desks, punching walls when I didn't get my way, but age and four years in the peace and quiet of Ithaca had calmed me, or so I thought. But now, in a flash, the temper was back. This school, I realized with an incalculable amount of dismay, had pulled me back into my past. Maybe it was being back in the building? Maybe it was the fact that I was not going to punk shows to burn off energy anymore? Maybe it was budding resentments that would fuel harder drinking later in life? Either way, I couldn't go right back into my class, as those kids had heard everything. As angry as I was at that kid, I was even more furious with myself. I was flushed and irritable. I had to catch my breath for a second, lean against the wall in the hot empty hallway, and then return to class and not speak of what had just occurred.

"Probably for the best," my mom said over a bland baked chicken later that night. "Just pretend it didn't happen." She stubbed out her cigarette, and we watched *Frasier* before I fell asleep in my childhood bed.

A report emerged that spring of 1994 on "incidents" in New York City secondary education—either the *Post* or the *Daily News* jumped on the report, citing our crime-ridden schools or some such. I read the paper in my homeroom class as the children milled about, and Ernesto took an interest in what I was reading.

"Yo. It says Humanities has a lot of incidents, Mr. B."

"Yeah, I noticed that." I squinted. "More than I would have guessed. More than King? More than Morris? A couple kids just got *shot* at Morris."

"More than Stuyvesant?" mused Ernesto. "Fuck Stuyvesant, nothing but white n***** at that place."

"Ernesto."

Ernesto put his hand on his chest as a sincere gesture of apology. "No offense, Mr. B—you're my favorite white person."

I wasn't sure what to say, but I managed a "thank you."

Later on I asked Mr. Kelly why our incident report was so god-damn high.

"Because we report them," Kelly answered, long past jaded to a place of benignly serene acceptance. "Everything that happens we report. Kid gets a pair of shoes stolen out of his locker, we report it. Kid gets shoved into the wall, we report it. Those other places don't bother." He shrugged. "Bigger fish to fry." Then he added, "I bet you felt safer at Cornell." And we chuckled.

◆

And then it was June again, maybe two months after the flare-up of my "machismo." The heat was stifling, and I was sweating through whatever cheap Van Heusen dress shirt I was wearing. Some of the older teachers could grow facial hair, and as such they could wear polos or even T-shirts, but if I did that I'd just look like another student. So for me it was shirt and tie and even a blazer if it got down below eighty degrees. I sat in the faculty cafeteria late one afternoon (where the food was no better than in the students' upstairs) when Mr. Chandler walked in.

"John."

"Ronald?" He sat down next to me. We were at the same long tables they had in the student cafeteria, speaking peer to peer.

He said he'd tried, but there was no way he could make it work. He couldn't offer me a full-time position next year. All the first-year teachers were getting let go, this Giuliani guy was making massive cuts, public school funding was always the first to go, et cetera. This might have actually been true—it might have been a simple budget issue—or I might just not have had what it took. He might have been letting me down easy. I was quick to reassure him. "It's okay. I might be too young for this job. Or too angry. Or too . . . I don't know. Thank you, though. For letting me try."

We shook hands.

I had two more weeks left of school, and then I'd be paid through the end of the summer. I didn't know whether to be relieved that it was over, sad that I'd essentially failed, or terrified about what I would do next to make rent, to get out of my mother's apartment. I caught my reflection in the window. My girlfriend said I looked green and tired. She was right. I was exhausted. I wouldn't know this level of exhaustion again until I had children of my own. Don't ever let anyone tell you teaching is an easy job. Yes, the union—if you have one—makes it hard to fire bad teachers. Yes, you're technically done by three P.M. and you get your summers off. But if you're any good at all, you take the job home with you, and you spend your own money buying supplies for your students, and you bust your ass trying to invent ways to make poetry relevant to kids who aren't entirely sure where their next meal is coming from, and you watch a girl in your homeroom go through her last trimester and then bring her daughter to school, her daughter who is just fifteen years younger than her mother, and you don't know what else to say, so you smile tightly and shrug and say, "Congratulations!"

CHAPTER FIVE

WILL ROCK FOR FOOD

My mom was upset that I was moving out. She didn't say she was, but she was tight-lipped and very short when discussing it. She would have to change our listing in the phone book, she said—we had been EJ BOWIE for years, a decision she made to keep it from looking "like a woman was living here alone." This portmanteau'd us—Eileen and John Bowie—into one close-knit, gender-nonspecific entity.

I had to get out of there.

In the summer of 1994 I moved just a few blocks north of my mom in the still vaguely affordable Hell's Kitchen, near a two-dollar movie theater and a Chinese place that would serve you free plum wine with your cheap sesame chicken so you could go home sated and shitfaced for inside of ten bucks. I also started doing temp work to pay the bills, eventually landing a long-term gig at legendary children's publisher Scholastic.

The dress code at Scholastic wasn't that strict. You could get away with a simple collared shirt, or even a T-shirt on Friday. If you were feeling really ballsy, the T-shirt could even have a band logo on it! A T-shirt sounded like sweet relief to me. I'd been temping for months, doing data entry in a windowless closet at MasterCard, where they insisted I wear a suit and tie. Even in a windowless closet. Granted my suits were comfortable, double-breasted, and baggy, it being 1994, but still . . .

Teaching had spit me out, so I had to find work somewhere, had to do something. There was something Yojimbo about temping—a ronin, armed only with above average typing skills and a working knowledge of Excel, wanders into a town to offer his services. Some jobs were at crushingly dull places doing crushingly dull things, but Scholastic felt like a decent transition from teaching. It was a company I'd grown up with, a company people had heard of and didn't resent like they did MasterCard. The pay was low, but so were my expenses. Scholastic was where I got my first email address (the now dormant hate666@aol.com), given to me by a twenty-four-year-old co-worker who made me laugh.

Said co-worker was the office manager, which meant he sat at the front desk, ordered office supplies, and made sure there was always fresh coffee for the editors, interns, marketing team, and entry-level office temps like me. He was tall with a sort of cheerful glow about him. He claimed to be losing his hair, but I didn't notice because (a) he actually wasn't yet and (b) he was easily four inches taller than me. My mancrush was pretty instant. He also had a lot of downtime, so he'd often read at that front desk. One day, before I knew him very well, I walked by on my way to the copy machine and saw that he was reading *The Godfather*. I really wanted to impress this guy. He was hilarious, he was charismatic, and there was a big playfulness about him that said, *Follow me, this will be fun*. I had gathered from overheard conversations that he was an actor, and I wanted to know more about that, so I thought I'd say something clever and witty. Something that suggested that I, too, had read the book, not just seen the movie. What came out was, "Ah. Returning to the text."

The office manager laughed. His name was Rob Corddry, and years later he would tell that story at my wedding.

We became friends pretty quickly. Rob was an actor, living with two roommates to a railway apartment in the East Village and performing Shakespeare in ninety-nine-seat theaters, or doing rewritten melodramas in the back rooms of bars. He was magnetic on stage and deft with Shakespearean verse, but like every other actor I'd met, he was having a tough time. Paid work was sporadic and not lucrative; he temped to make ends meet. And as I would go see him play Lucio in a rickety production of *Measure for Measure*, he would come see Egghead., my band.

I'd dabbled in a band in college—a couple of gigs, nothing too serious—with Mike Faloon (the guy from the radio station, the guy you should absolutely meet during your freshman year) on drums and a physical therapy major named Travis on guitar. It had been a hobby, a distraction from the stress of my senior year. I had purchased a $100 bass from a very serious music major and taught myself some basics by listening to that first Ramones album, the one where all the bass is in the left channel—with a flick of the balance knob on an old stereo, you could isolate Dee Dee and follow along to some of the greatest punk songs ever written. It reminded me of what I loved about punk rock: You could start doing it before you really knew how. But it was just a hobby, and we broke up the night I graduated, even playing our final gig in our graduation gowns.

After a year of teaching, though, a year of what I took to be failing at adulthood, the band seemed like a good, perhaps even great, idea. And now Mike Faloon was living in Queens! And Mike Galvin was still living in Brooklyn! We could try the band again, we thought, but this time with three guys who had all done college radio together. There was a shared vocabulary that could not have been assumed had we met through the musicians wanted ads in the *Voice*. ("Galvin, this

should break down like the bridge in that Throwing Muses song."
"Got it. Like this?" "Yes, *exactly* like that.") Galvin arrived at our first
rehearsal armed with a surfed-up cover of Stephen Sondheim's "Send in
the Clowns" (no one else had ever merged my fondness for showtunes
and punk rock so seamlessly) and a three-chord garage rave-up called
"She's Coming Back (But Just to Get Her Stuff)." Said song featured
the verse:

> *She's hooking up with a guy from her gym.*
> *I might stick around, but she might bring him.*
> *I bet he's an ape, he's gonna haul off the couch.*
> *The thing weighs a ton, it's a sofa bed.*

This coupled well with my original "Will Rock for Food," a holdover
from the college incarnation of the band, which contained the verse:

> *They all turn a profit, have savings accounts that last.*
> *They get all of the groupies they want and they don't even pay*
> *for gas.*
> *But our contract rider—has a slightly different deal.*
> *We'll set up and play at your deli if we can scam a few free meals.*

This felt good. This felt like a cohesive unit. At five foot eight, I
was the tallest member of the band. All of us wore corrective lenses.
The name Egghead. fit these guys—we were small and smart and
presentationally nerdy. My students had just made me Urkel the year
before—why not lean into it? Over several post-rehearsal band meetings, we discussed how we wanted the band to be an entity, akin to
Devo or the Ramones, with a unifying aesthetic. We wanted, in terms
that weren't yet common, a unifying "brand." Faloon hunkered down
and created a mythical backstory for the band: We were the "punk rock

division" of a larger conglomerate menacingly named Gentech that was vaguely involved in defense contracting and genetic engineering. We produced a Xeroxed zine called *Go Metric* that contained record reviews, a couple of interviews per issue, and weird manifestos like Faloon's confrontational "Bands with 5 Guys Suck.'"* Gentech and the zine, like the period at the end of our name, might have amused only us. But God, how they amused us.

◆

Teaching had rushed me into adulthood. To be twenty-two and called Mr. Bowie was jarring, and I really had, like the old hack joke, found myself looking over my shoulder for my father. It's completely within your rights to expect me to be an adult at twenty-two—again, Bosnia—but I wasn't ready. I knew myself; I'd seen what teaching took out of me, I saw what a grown-up job had done to my father, and it put me off of adulthood in general. I enjoyed my time at Scholastic and made some great friends, but I found myself fucking off at work way too much, setting up fake accounts to send prank emails to other employees. The only place I exhibited a true work ethic was after five P.M. in the smelly little rehearsal studio in the West 30s where Egghead. made its magic.†

The lads—we took to calling ourselves the "lads" way too quickly—cobbled together a thirty-minute set list of originals and a medley called "Metal Memories," which gave me the once-in-a-lifetime

---

* A brief highlight from that piece: "Still not convinced? Styx, Journey, Kansas, Boston, Eagles . . . Not enough you say? Toto. Need more? Toto. (Yeah. They sucked *that* bad.)"

† It was New York City. No one had a garage or a basement or a living room big enough to accommodate even a power trio. A lot of the bands that have successfully come out of the city have come out of the deep, more suburban boroughs or have had a lot of disposable income.

opportunity to play the riff from Ozzy's "Crazy Train" on my bass. Our first show was at a bar on the Lower East Side called Street Level. We had to borrow a snare drum from accomplished funk group the Piranha Brothers because we all thought (wrongly) that the club provided an *entire* drum kit, when in reality they provided everything but the snare, the most abused off all drums. We wore matching shirts for that unifying aesthetic and also, we joked, so people could tell we were all in the same band (our musicianship sometimes suggested otherwise). The crowd was packed with friends from college and work—High School Sweetheart was also there (we were closing in on five years together)—and we went over just well enough to convince ourselves that we really had something. Even accomplished funk group the Piranha Brothers liked us.

We were going to gig more. We were going to rehearse more. I was going to need a new job, one that paid better than publishing. I left Scholastic and started temping elsewhere. All over the city, in every possible industry, each of which seemed to be doing its own special kind of harm to the world. Engineering: a firm whose lobby greeted you with their greatest accomplishment, a photo of a sleek highway gashing through a Hawaiian rainforest. Pharmaceuticals: a company that had rushed an angina drug onto the market only to find that it could have a side effect they termed "total mortality."* Finance: a couple bleak months at Goldman Sachs, which I knew was fishy, as nobody in that building made eye contact, and they all had Dole/Kemp stickers in their cubicles. A good day looked like this: Get into work around eight thirty or nine A.M., drink coffee, look busy, drink more coffee, sneak off to the restroom with a copy of the *Times* to deal with the aftermath of all that coffee, wait for someone to ask me to do something, hopefully type a letter for the boss (some of these guys were so old school they didn't have a computer and referred to someone like

---

*   "Death," to the layman.

me as a "typist"), submit the letter to the boss for a signature, send the letter off, book travel for a boss, try to save the company money, get yelled at for giving my boss a layover at Chicago Midway (in retrospect, a legitimate grievance), eat lunch, make a stack of copies and distribute them to the office, set up a meeting for the Clinical and Scientific Affairs Department, and then hit the pavement at five to make my way over to the garment district to rehearse.

A bad day was all of that, minus the rehearsal. All of this—the bad coffee, being yelled at by millionaires, booking trips I would have loved to be taking myself—was worth it to pay rent and fund my punk band. And yes, a band is an expensive venture if you take into account equipment, transportation, and our growing collection of matching shirts, which eventually became matching outfits. The band was starting to become a very pricey hobby, but then, so is golf. Our songs were getting better, we were getting tighter, but we couldn't honestly call ourselves a punk band until we had—to appropriate corporate lingo—checked one particular "action item" off our list.

That summer, 1994, I stepped back into the cool yet stinky vestibule of CBGB and asked for a gig. We had submitted a rehearsal tape (which included a new ode to New York's ethnic enclaves called "Neighborhood Palm Reader" as well as "She's Coming Back" and "Will Rock for Food") and were told we had to talk to the club's booker, Louise, the most notoriously unpleasant woman in a city that still held Leona Helmsley. Louise did not disappoint, glaring at me like I had walked into her niece's bat mitzvah and taken a dump on the bimah. At the time, I feared and loathed Louise, but hindsight has made me realize the job of booking bands for CBGB was a Geneva-convention-violating punishment I wouldn't wish on anyone. "Uh, hi, we sent in a tape?"

"Name?"

"John?"

It became immediately clear that I was already trying her patience. "The band's name is John?"

"Oh, heh, no, we're called Egghead."

She stared at me for a moment with a level of disgust I feel should be reserved only for people who clip their nails on a city bus. I almost took the tape back and apologized for everything, and then she flipped through a notebook, glanced at a huge calendar, and spat out a date. I thanked her profusely and backed out of the venue before she incinerated me on the spot. I had survived the initial gauntlet.

That Monday, at the required audition showcase hurdle we had to clear, friends from college came out to drink and support us. Both of my parents came, and they might have even sat near each other. The night is a blur to me, but I remember we played early enough that from the stage I could see a white patch of sunlight coming in through the front door of the long hallway that made up the club. We played fast and enthusiastically, tearing around the stage, jumping up and down to land on the final crashing chord of a song. People whooped and applauded.

After the show, my father said, "You keep jumping around like that, you're gonna owe a royalty check to Pete Townshend. When are you going back to teaching?" My mom said, "That was incredible! Great show!" and helped me carry my monstrous Peavey amp out to a cab.

Louise was pleased enough at our turnout that we graduated to Tuesday night. Corddry came to that show, along with a bunch of other people from Scholastic. That gig led to other gigs, at small clubs around the city, and after a couple months of this, some strangers—not family members, not co-workers, but total strangers—stopped us outside in the damp summer of 1994 and said we were great, did we have any merchandise? We did not, but God, what a sensation of pride. We had made a thing. People liked the thing—people who didn't even know us personally—so much that they wanted to take some small part of the thing home with them and then wear that small part, ostensibly in public. We were getting a footing. We found ourselves in the CBGB print ad they placed every week in the *Village Voice*. In the same block letters where it had said Dag Nasty or Government Issue or Gorilla Biscuits or even the Ramones or Talking Heads, it now said Egghead (they forgot the period).

Here's the thing about Egghead.: We were not great musicians, or, rather, we were not consistently great. We were fun, poppy songwriters with a sense of humor. The matching aesthetic would often just be the same T-shirt, but sometimes we'd invest in something more ridiculous, like identical NASA flight suits. Maybe an Egghead. show wasn't a bucket-list-worthy experience, but even if you caught us on a bad night, we had a certain sloppy charm, stumbling through the set, cracking jokes throughout, congratulating ourselves for ending a song at the same time.

If you caught us on a good night, you didn't want to be the band that followed us. The local scene in New York City at the time was very local. Nobody was getting signed to big labels, and it would be a few years before the Strokes would change that. Circa 1995, there were some likeminded funny punk bands that were fun to gig with, like the Sea Monkeys, who would cover the jingle for the local supermarket Food Emporium, and Furious George, a snarling trio whose closer was a song called "Gilligan"—the lyrics to which were, in their entirety:

> *I wear a white hat.*
> *I wear a red shirt.*
> *They all think I'm stupid.*
> *One day I'll kill them.*
> *I!*
> *Am!*
> *Gilligan!*

At most we'd make forty bucks a gig playing the cozy Continental,[*] barely enough to cover cabs, but we put it back into the band's minimal coffers, which fit in an envelope in my living room.

By 1995, we started doing mini tours, sneaking up to see old college friends in Upstate New York, one night playing a show in Auburn. There, we opened for a local band who had done that kind of lazy thing where they name their band after a song by another band they like so as to signal to their audience, "Hey, you know that band you like? We sound a little like them." We'll call them Blood & Roses, and they had to follow an Egghead. gig in which we played our hearts out and left sweat and even a little bit of actual blood on the stage of the bar. Blood & Roses were shamed. Their lead singer tried to look cool by chewing gum on stage, and the guitarist looked scorned and pissy but not in a badass Keith Richards way, just like a petulant child, but nobody was paying attention to them anyway, and they had to play over the chit-chat of a disinterested venue. I was otherwise engaged because of a local woman at the bar who loved Egghead. so much she wanted to trade shirts with me, even going so far as to begin to unbutton hers. I declined her weirdly specific offer out of deference to High School Sweetheart, but something had changed that night. Egghead., we realized, would have to be reckoned with. With a little hard work, and a bit more luck, it might even be, I dared to think, some sort of . . . job?

There was a certain whiplash in destroying a couple of shows during a weekend tour and then returning to a steady temp gig as an office drone. "File it yourself, dude," one wanted to say. "I was a fucking rock star this weekend." The sloppy antiauthoritarianism of punk rock slipped over to the stern corporate environment of most of my office jobs (don't call the partners at the firm "dude," and "casual Friday" does

---

[*] A sign over the bar warned that calling out "Free Bird" would result in the caller's immediate expulsion. I never saw a single soul test this.

not mean wearing a Superchunk T-shirt over jeans), but the disconnect was a sort of two-way street—the corporate jargon of my day life crept into my punk rock dealings as well. A show promoter could expect an email from me that went like this:

> Dear Skizz,
>
> I hope this note finds you well. With regards to our gig on this upcoming 6th of November at the converted funeral home known as the Mansion please advise as to whether a drum kit will be provided or if we will need to bring one, as this will necessitate the renting of a van. Thanks in advance for your prompt attention to this matter.
> Yours warmly,
> John Ross Egghead.

◆

Apparently the good nights of Egghead. were rare enough that we couldn't get signed to a label, so Faloon suggested we be genuinely punk rock and *do it ourselves*. We pooled our money from our collective temp jobs and, over two weekends in the spring of 1995, we recorded four songs at a strange little studio in the Meatpacking District, engineered by an amiable pothead who would mic the ceiling to create a bigger drum sound and gave the guitars a refreshing sparkle of anger. It took us two weekends to record and mix the seven-inch EP we called *Knock Off That Evil!* from a shouted slogan in the cartoon *The Tick*. Our friend Dave Palmer (whose grown-up job involved drawing the titular dog for the then new children's show *Blue's Clues*) drew a cartoon version of us screaming defiantly at the foot of a giant robot pointing a ray gun at us. This was the aesthetic—silly, carefree, unpretentious. I took a long lunch from my temp gig to go to the pressing plant and watch the physical creation of our record: the needle cutting our songs into the glass master that would then be used to mold one thousand seven-inch records. Watching music become tangible like that is incredibly moving—it puts you on the continuum of wax cylinders and Victrolas, and it marked what, in hindsight, may be the dusk of physical media. I was teary for the rest of the day while answering phone calls and returning emails.

The critics—other amateur punk rockers who happened to be writing for zines—dug it. The zines I read in high school, *Maximum Rock-N-Roll* and *Flipside*, both found it funny and hooky and every-thing we'd intended. Our set was now a catchy little miasma of surf and punk and garage and hardcore, and occasionally we'd cover the Kinks. We had turned a corner as a band, and around that corner was a tour of these United States.

Well. Some of them. Like, eight. In those early days of the internet, I sent off a flurry of emails and set out to book a tour of small clubs, hall shows, and house parties down the Eastern Seaboard. You would think that small clubs should be the order of the day, the preferred venue for the touring punk band, and you would be horrifically, almost comically wrong—clubs have massive overhead and famously shady, coke-addled management. House parties would charge a small fee for entrance and pay the bands, often saving the largest compensation for the band that came the farthest. We booked a slate of shows over one week in November 1996, rented a Ford Aerostar, got what was called a TripTik from AAA (a customized map that was handy in those Amish pre-GPS days), and headed out on a Friday morning for Eastern Pennsylvania. Galvin had a gorgeous bit where he would deliberately give every city the wrong nickname, thus proclaiming Honeybrook, Pennsylvania, "The City of Light." This makes me giggle to this day.

Hall shows ran much the way house parties did and are as old as American popular music itself. Somebody young would rent out a VFW hall, or a community center or, in the case of Honeybrook, Pennsylvania, a Quaker meetinghouse. Once you secured some sort of PA system, you were good to go. The bands played in front of a couple hundred kids from all over whatever county you were in, and the bands divided the door. That first night of the tour we shredded—Faloon taking us into choruses with determined fills, Galvin attacking his guitar like he had caught it in bed with his girlfriend—*and* we made an astonishing $100, sold a bunch of seven-inches, and were flirted with by an untold number of small-town punk girls. Thoughts of High School Sweetheart (we were now sharing a tiny mini-loft apartment in Hell's Kitchen, infested with cockroaches, two blocks from my mom) kept me from following through with any of these opportunities, aside from hugging this or that heavily mascaraed girl in fishnet stockings a mite too long. I was, quite sincerely, high on music, swept up in the romance of being a touring musician. For this I had walked away from a long-term temp job, and I had been absolutely correct to do so. For that one night, at least.

Sure, it's easy to say, "John, you went over big, but you went over big at a Quaker meetinghouse in Honeybrook, Pennsylvania." But a crowd is a crowd, and this crowd's applause and rapturous cheers had been buoyant and validating. We were rock stars in Honeybrook. A kid in the terrifically named band Third Year Freshman drove us back to his folks' house in his band's RV (which he, mockingly I hope, called "the Bitchgetter"), and we spent the night sleeping in their finished basement. If every night had gone like that night, the story of Egghead. would have turned out very differently.

Baltimore was a club show, but with popular local bands like Sick and the Jennifers in town, there was a receptive audience and a congenial air about the greenroom. After playing a dimly lit Quaker meetinghouse with bad sound, it was nice to be on a stage with a pro lighting system and decent acoustics, even though we didn't get paid much more than gas money.

Richmond, Virginia (GALVIN: "The Motor City!") had been the capital of the Confederacy. At the time, Monument Avenue was dotted with statues of Southern generals—and on the day we pulled up, a small but enthusiastic group of Civil War reenactors who let us take a photo with them. The photo is amazing. Faloon and I look embarrassed to be seen with Confederate nostalgists, but Galvin is all smiles to be *this* close to *that* level of crazy. The "rebels" scoffed a little when they found out we were a touring punk band from New York, but an even less welcome reception awaited us at the ska bill we were playing that night.

The club was huge and in a hip area near Virginia Commonwealth University. It was filled with sharp-dressed teens and twentysomethings very excited to dig the two tones of the Skalars, who, like us, were from NYC. I'd seen some amazing ska shows in high school, during New York's third wave of the genre populated by terrific live acts like the Toasters and the Boilers, but the ska scene in general had gotten pretty repetitive. I know that sounds like arch hypocrisy coming from a guy in a punk band, and it probably is, but I was quickly tiring of middle-class white kids telling me to *pick it up pick it up pick it up* while just tarting up stuff that was going on in Kingston, Jamaica, in the late sixties.

And Jesus Christ with the ska puns. Mephiskapheles. Ska Face. The Ska-Skank Redemption.

By the mid-nineties, the Mighty Mighty Bosstones had played Lollapalooza, and the ska-punk merger had injected some adrenaline into the genre. The promoter reasoned that a pop-punk band would fit in nicely on an all-ska bill.

And then the Skalars canceled. It's not great when the headliner cancels, and it poisons the mood pretty nicely when the promoter informs you that *you* must announce this cancellation at the beginning of your set.

We walked onto the stage as the house lights dimmed and strapped on our instruments. I took a sip of water, looked out at a sea of suits and porkpie hats, cleared my throat into the microphone, and said, "Uh, hi. The Skalars canceled?"

BOOOOOOO.

"Yeah. It's a bummer. But we're Egghead.? We're also from New York?" And we launched into the set, which was well played and fierce and met with a disregard that bordered on hostile.

In the van later that night, it was quiet. We were bummed. We stared at the headlight-illuminated blacktop until Faloon said, "The Skalastic Book Club."

Snickers all around. Galvin offered, "This Ska May Be Permanent."

Laughter. I took it home with "George Bernard Ska."

We lived to fight another day.

We arrived in Chapel Hill, North Carolina ("so nice they named it twice!") late the following afternoon, a Tuesday, and pulled up to a bar called Molly's to find the place was empty and the bartender had no idea there had been a gig scheduled for that night. He pulled out the phone from behind the bar, and I called the promoter. She had forgotten the gig as well, was studying for a test, and said it should be fine—as long as we had our own PA.

We did not. Gig canceled. We had a cooler in the van for snacks and hit up a grocery store, where Faloon and I had an argument. All bands argue—*Where's my blow? That's my song! You fucked my wife!*—and this tiff was no different. Faloon wanted orange juice without any pulp. I don't mind a little pulp in my juice. "If I wanted pulp," he said, not raising his voice, which actually made him sound more terrifying, "I'd eat an actual orange."

"Great. Let's have some nice smooth orange juice that won't affect your delicate palate." We were always on about this. Faloon liked what he liked, and he did not like ethnic food. We'd go out for Indian or

Italian or Chinese after shows sometimes, and Faloon would sit and eat bread. Apparently, pulpy orange juice was a little too ethnic.

GALVIN: *Guys.*

"It's fine. Whatever," I murmured, my passive aggression never more acute than at that moment.

But other than occasional juice aisle disagreements, the band was a united front. There was no blow, there were no disagreements over intellectual property, and none of us were married yet. We had forged a strong relationship that could only be fissured by the outside world—which was working on doing just that.

We sat in the hotel room that night watching local North Carolina political advertising (yikes) and then switched over to MTV. Some one-hit wonder alternative band was guest DJing—one of those bands that got swept up in the post-Nirvana major label buy-in when every conglomerate decided they needed their own Nirvana yet did not realize that Nirvana was pretty special. As such these bands put out one album on, say, Warner Bros., charted a little bit on college radio, got some rotation on MTV, and then were dropped quickly and viciously when they didn't sell a million records. So one of those bands was on MTV that night, introducing their videos, introducing other bands' videos, just hosting an hour of programming. And they looked like they'd rather be at the dentist. No joy, no enthusiasm. Three college radio DJs, all of whom enjoyed sharing trivia and banter with their audience, watched with withering contempt.

"Next up," said the singer, barely suppressing a yawn, "is Bush with 'Swallowed.'" And then with what amounted to a petulant shrug: "Check it out." Cut to video.

"Ugh," said Faloon, munching on Chex Mix. "Fame is wasted on the wrong people." I mentally scribbled that down and tucked it away in the dusty file cabinet of my mind.

The next day we drove down to Georgia as both Jesse Helms and Bill Clinton were reelected. We watched the returns in an Athens laundromat while we tried to get the smell of cigarette smoke out of our clothes. I had lost my voice—maybe psychosomatically? Maybe with a keen understanding that it would not be needed?—and was unable to speak above a wheeze. Luckily, it came back just in time for the well-attended house party just off the UGA campus. The "venue" was known as the Dead Body House, so named because the titular noun had been found there years ago. The story might have been apocryphal, but God, how the locals spoke with such incredible reverence. Our hosts, a band simply called Tres Kids, sandwiched us between themselves and another local band, so we were guaranteed an audience. At twenty-five, we were already the elder statesmen—out in the workforce (sort of), living with girlfriends, and now watching twenty-year-old kids tear through their sets with an abandon that was already getting scarce in us. We had a good show that night, though, good enough that a young lady invited me to her car afterward to "hear a new band that she really liked." I shrugged, said sure, and was walking to the car in the darkness when I realized I was heading down a dark passage, and I did have High School Sweetheart waiting for me at home. I sat in the young punk rock lady's passenger seat, with the door open and one foot on the ground outside the automobile. Generic northeastern hardcore—the kind I grew up on, chunky riffs but amelodic vocals—blasted from her stereo. "These guys are good!" I murmured, not making eye contact.

"I guess they're OK," she said. "It's my ex-boyfriend. He's kind of a dick. I can't tell if they're really good or if I'm still into him."

"Wow. That's, uh . . . that's complicated." Then, unable to help myself from flirting a little bit, I added: "In that case, the band is only OK."

She laughed. "He's a dick, right? Anyone in a band like this? Is a dick. I think I like funny bands."

I looked at her. She had a bob haircut and wore a choker, and I remember thinking she was really cute. But I was living with High School Sweetheart. And even though that was not going especially well, it was still going. There was a part of me that resented not having the opportunity to take advantage of the rock star/groupie dynamic I never dreamed would be available to me, and I'd love to tell you I never think about it, but I'm writing about it more than twenty years after the fact.

"I should check on the guys," I exhaled.

"Oh?" she asked, but I was already gone, walking quickly across the lawn of the Dead Body House, the first chill of Georgia autumn misting down.

◆

Egghead. didn't make it any farther south than Georgia—my Talla-hassee contact never returned my calls—which meant we broke north for Knoxville ("City of Big Shoulders!") on Thursday, arriving early enough to wander the ghostly remains of their World's Fair—completely worth a visit and great for dystopian photographs. The show that night was in a smoky bar/laundromat, opening for local faves 30 Amp Fuse, so the turnout was good. We'd just washed our clothes in Georgia, but we couldn't turn down the free detergent that was part of our compen-sation, so we washed one day's worth of laundry before the set. When you're four shows into a tour and your band is in good shape, there's a shared intuition that makes the songs sound exactly the way they should, maybe better. We refused to do the same set twice—and never did, over the course of a hundred shows—but we had a solid repertoire of originals and a handful of covers that we could rip through very ably, and that chilly night in Knoxville was one for the books. Fun, spirited, exciting. 30 Amp Fuse were so tight and so popular with their hometown crowd that they just *destroyed* after us, but let it be said the crowd had been thoroughly warmed up by the warmup band. We had no designated place to stay that night, so the guys from 30 Amp Fuse drove us over to another band's house (Superdrag were out on tour). The Superdrag house seemed specifically designed for band living, replete with multiple couches, a beer-stocked fridge, and various other accoutrements of guy life. We left a thank-you note on the foosball table.

Lexington, Kentucky, was a wash, despite Galvin dubbing it "The City That Never Sleeps." Phish was in town that night, which didn't directly affect our audience, but that plus rain plus a freak local distillery fire that filled the autumn sky with dense, Revelation-esque black smoke meant that we played for the bartender and the other two bands. A cheap motel would have to do that night. It was quiet. Morale was low. Questions were asked testily, answered briefly.

We met a band in West Virginia that lived on the road, out of a van; they called ahead for gigs but didn't really have a home base. They were a ska-punk outfit called One Eye Open, and there was something just so goddamn . . . romantic about them. There was nothing tying them down; they were literal troubadours, wandering punk rock minstrels scraping together enough money for the dollar menu at McDonald's, hiding their weed in their deodorant so the cops wouldn't find it and playing so tightly that one song slammed into the next, lurching the set forward like a beautiful daisy-chain car wreck. *That* was what it took—complete commitment. No girlfriends, no rent, nothing but the band and the van. We opened for them at a sparsely attended coffee house in Charleston. *We* played like we were in a sparsely attended coffee house. One Eye Open played like they were in a bursting, sold-out arena.

The tour finished at a house party in Pittsburgh ("Beantown!" proclaimed an exhausted Galvin as he drove us across Liberty Bridge at twilight, a gorgeous urban view that actually makes Pittsburgh look like the Emerald City), once again at a punk rock house. They had a modest PA, and I mean *modest*: in lieu of a mic stand, the microphone was duct-taped to a broomstick, which was in turn duct-taped to a bucket, which was held steady by a ten-pound hand weight dumped inside ("There!" said our host, upon securing this hastily MacGyver'd sound system). A local band played, and then everyone took a break to go upstairs and watch *The Simpsons*. (The episode was "Homerpalooza," which features one of the series best exchanges: "Hi. Billy Corgan, Smashing Pumpkins." "Homer Simpson . . . smiling politely.") *The Simpsons* continued to be a universal language: antiestablishment, almost anti-everything, smart, and even though at the time we had issues with Hank Azaria playing every ethnicity, the show was a beacon of what TV could be. It was wild. Absolutely everyone we met on tour had a favorite episode, and there were some conversations that seemed to consist solely of *Simpsons* quotes (the show was in its mid-nineties golden era). Then we played—to a crowd of the people who lived in the house, a couple of locals, and a buddy of mine from college who had moved back to his home city.

It's a long drive from Pittsburgh to New York City. You travel the length of Pennsylvania, which is speckled with some beautiful mountains and many more sad coal towns. "Our first tour is on the books," said Faloon over breakfast, raising his orange juice at a diner that Sunday morning. Galvin was quiet. I had a persistent ringing in my ears—from time to time it still comes back, twenty years on, if I'm stressed or overtired. I was going to have to find a new temp job when I got back.

"I am beat," I said, seeming older than my twenty-five years. "Amazing to think people do this for living."

"A few," said Faloon. "There're guys like One Eye Open. But I think a lot of people have to hold down day jobs." Faloon was getting ready to go to grad school to be a teacher.

"No, but I mean the bands we like, like Boris or the Queers."
These bands—Green Bay's Boris the Sprinkler and New Hampshire's the
Queers, fun, hooky bands that Egghead. admired—seemed to me
like the endgame. Bands that released records regularly, toured a
lot, never got huge, but this was *what they did as a job*.

"Joe Queer owns a restaurant."

"He does?" I was flabbergasted. It had never occurred to me that
the guys in a silly punk rock band that released songs like "Kicked Out
of Webelos" and "I Can't Stop Farting" were unable to monetize such
an endeavor into full-time employment.

"And doesn't Norb from Boris do web design?" Galvin spoke up.
"Or something?"

"Layout for a magazine, I wanna say," continued Faloon, picking
at his hash browns.

Again, I was stunned. The band that brought us "I Wanna Get to
Third Base with You" and "Screamin' Demon Martians Riding Go-
Karts in My Head" didn't just do those songs for a living? This will
seem wildly naïve to most readers, but the idea that these guys were
anything other than total full-time punk rock stars seemed completely
foreign to me.

It really appeared that there was no punk rock middle class. Your
choice was Green Day or day job. We got the check.

The tour, for all its myriad pitfalls, was a highlight of Egghead.—
and my life, if I'm being honest with myself. I saw a huge swath of the
country I'd only ever read about (good luck finding another New York
liberal as thoroughly enamored with Waffle House as I am). I learned
about collaboration and performance and discovered a huge truth: For
me, a fucking miserable gig in Kentucky beats a good day at the office.

High School Sweetheart greeted me at the door when I staggered
into our little apartment on 9th Avenue at around nine P.M. on a dark
November night. The ground floor apartment was what had been

termed a "mini loft" in the real-estate ad. It was a privacy-free large studio with a loft bed, and its proximity to a restaurant right next door made it a haven for cockroaches. There was a hug, but it was not a passionate reunion; I smelled like a hockey team and was grumpy from the eight-hour drive from Pittsburgh. I showered and we went straight to sleep.

We were communicating, sure, but when we were honest with each other, we ended up angry. So, too often, we sublimated this by drinking (especially me) and going to movies and theater whenever we could afford it.

"You ever think about getting married?"

"Uhhhh. *Fargo* is playing at the cheap theater on 49th!"

And so on. It's not that she was some sort of eye-rolling killjoy, viewing her boyfriend's expensive hobby as a ridiculous time and money suck. She came to gigs. She even sold merch for us a couple of times. Some of our better songs were about her, after all. But it was never really her thing—she was a folkie, a northeastern college woman who listened to a lot of Donovan and reggae. They also have their charms, don't get me wrong, but if she had a choice between listening to "Will Rock for Food" or "Sunshine Superman" at skull-shifting volume, her choice would be clear. To say nothing of the fact that High School Sweetheart thought the tour would lead to a bigger reputation—a label that would sign us, maybe a larger band that would take us out on tour as support, defray the costs somehow. Maybe we'd make a little money. I thought this might happen, too. We broke even on the tour, just barely, and largely because of that first night in Honeybrook. Her disappointment mirrored mine and might have even been a little more acute, as she was always the more practical one.

The band carried on for a little more than a year after the tour, and there were a couple more short trips: a squat in Philadelphia where the electricity was stolen from a nearby lamppost; a benefit for Ithaca

Rape Crisis, where we followed a heart-wrenching testimonial from a victim;* a show at a packed New Jersey bowling alley the night before Thanksgiving 1997. We recorded an EP at a punk house in Central Pennsylvania that made the Dead Body House in Athens look like the Ritz-Carlton—the inhabitants stuck their tattoo bandages up on the wall like trophies, and the bandages stayed there, adhered to the wall with ointment and blood and lymphatic fluid. It was like a whole building made of hepatitis. We were not making a real dent in New York, however. Louise refused to give us a coveted weekend slot at CBGB, and we were not getting any sort of reliable high-profile gigs at larger clubs.

On January 8, 1998, I was sitting in my cubicle at the Firm, a multinational consulting/accountancy company with huge, gorgeous offices in Midtown Manhattan. After our tour had sent me spiraling into debt and unable to find further temp work, I'd accepted a job as a marketing copywriter, full-time and replete with benefits. I had achieved financial solvency for the first time in years. I still owed a lot of money to the steadfast student loan corporation, but there was generally less penny pinching, and High School Sweetheart and I even talked about going on vacation. That's what we needed! A little alone time! Get out of this cramped apartment and go to a cramped hotel room! But someplace else!

With this solvency and freedom came a health plan. I went to the dentist and got a cavity filled. I spent money on booze and put vodka in a milkshake, because I'd heard that famous New Yorker writer Robert Benchley had done so. This was numbing a little of the foreboding doom that was starting to creep up my back, but I could tell that there was volcanic activity somewhere between my lungs and emotions and

---

* Literally. A woman told a horrible, heartbreaking story about her assault, and then it was "Thank you, Deborah. That was very brave. Please welcome Egghead.!"

it was going to burst, and soon, so I decided to find a therapist. High School Sweetheart had been going to one for a bit, and it was helping her process some issues with her parents, and she seemed to be generally less upset. So I thought, *Hey, the Firm is paying for it, might not hurt to look under the hood, kick the tires,* whatever sort of automotive metaphor I could summon to take away the nagging fear that talking to a professional about my problems was somehow very emasculating. My dad went to a shrink, but my mother rolled her eyes when she talked about the fact that my dad went to a shrink. This was something that was done by people who were either crazy or were so weak that they thought they were crazy. But . . . again . . . the Firm was paying.

So a few months earlier, as Faloon was getting married to a veterinary student who brought a lot of stability to his household, I found myself sitting on a floral upholstered couch near Central Park West talking to a PhD who wore a cardigan and leaned very far back in a La-Z-Boy. At first I just sat. Then I lay down, as people do in the movies. That felt abhorrently clichéd, so I sat up again. Eventually I stopped worrying about the staging and just found myself talking about the Firm, my parents, and High School Sweetheart, and how my life had suddenly gotten much more stable and much less . . . weird. And how very weird that was.

It was weird working for a massive consulting/accountancy firm while still booking shows for my punk band. It was weird leaving work and changing into a T-shirt and jeans in the men's washroom in order to go see Fugazi at NYU. It was weird fronting the band for T-shirt money using my company's Diners Club card. I told myself that this desk job was temporary, and after all, it wasn't technically a corporation. The Firm worked *for* corporations, handling their internal audits, implementing new software, "restructuring their human resources" (a lyrical euphemism for "laying people off"), and that sort of thing. This wasn't working for the *man*. This was working for the *guy* . . .

who worked for the man. It was a necessary hair-splitting that got me through some long days. I mean, look, I was *in* management consulting, I was not *of* management consulting. This was clearly just a money-making venture, here to support my life as an artist. Until January 8, 1998—Elvis's birthday, which I found oddly significant—when Galvin called me at work and said he was moving to Los Angeles to be a screenwriter.

A novel he'd written in New Mexico had actually been adapted by him into a screenplay and then filmed—a staggering achievement, no matter how small the budget—and he had an agent and a place to live for a bit, and while, yes, he did love being in Egghead., he had come to realize that "not enough people like us."

This was true. Our turnouts had plateaued. People seemed less interested in our matching shirts and goofy songs. He'd been smoking a lot of pot and it was affecting his playing, no question—even OG Egghead. fan Rob Corddry, the Scholastic office manager, had noticed—and it was hard to tell who had lost interest first, our modest group of enthusiasts . . . or Galvin. We'd played to a packed house the night before Thanksgiving, but most of those kids were there to see the headliner, a terrific Pennsylvania band named Weston. I kept thinking about bands far more established than us who still needed day jobs ("the guys in Sicko write code? What does that even *mean*?"). It was looking less and less like we would ever be able to make the band our day job, even for a bit, and maybe Galvin was the first person to really realize it.

"So yeah," he said. "I think I can make a living as a screenwriter."

"Well, good luck," I said, stifling a cynical, Han Solo–ish *You're gonna need it*.

We hung up—it would be months before I'd talk to him again—and I turned to Sharon, the fiftysomething who was in the cubicle next to mine.

"My band just broke up," I said.

"I'm sorry," she said. I could tell she meant it, but she also used to listen to Yanni at her desk.

Although it may have seemed like a stupid, youthful, money-sucking lark to my father, I regret very little. I don't regret inhaling paint fumes while we silkscreened T-shirts at Galvin's apartment off the Fort Hamilton Parkway stop in Brooklyn. I don't regret postponing my student loans to watch a record plant press the glass master of our first seven-inch. I don't regret opening for the Figgs, Sicko, Furious George, or Discount. I definitely don't regret opening for the Dickies. I regret that we didn't execute every dumb idea we had—an album called *Michigan during the Renaissance!* with a song called "Smoking Makes You Cool!"*—but I'm grateful we got so much dumb stuff accomplished. I am bound to Faloon and Galvin the way some people are bound to brothers, and we have since seen each other through death, divorce, and worse. The breakup of Egghead. felt like a real breakup—it knocked my life off its axis, first in a little way then in a very large way. The lesson I took—at that moment, as the band dissolved—was that it was virtually impossible to do something you love and get paid for it. Galvin was going to try, but the odds seemed insurmountable. So I sat in my cubicle, turning his phrasing around in my head. "I think I can make a living as a screenwriter." In other words, *I can do something I enjoy, and it can be my job.* Which was great for him—he loved screenwriting, was very good at it†—and yes, maybe I could try, too.

What the fuck else did I love?

---

* The album title came to me in a stress dream wherein I was working my old work-study job at the Ithaca library and someone came in and asked me for a book called *Michigan during the Renaissance.* I searched fruitlessly for what felt like hours and then woke up sweating.

† *Freak Talks about Sex* was released straight to video in 1999 and contains great work by Steve Zahn and Josh Hamilton. I'm not just saying that. It's really good. It's like a Gen X French New Wave movie set in Syracuse.

CHAPTER SIX

LEANING TOO FAR BACK
IN YOUR CHAIR

*D*epression is not sadness.

You're thinking of sadness. Sadness is sadness.

Depression is a chemical imbalance that will make your brain look different on an EEG or an MRI. Depression takes the lives of over forty thousand Americans a year[*] and conservatively costs the United States economy $236 billion per annum.[†] Depression is a black hole of feeling, a "storm of murk" according to William Styron, who wrote one of the great depression memoirs, *Darkness Visible*. Depression can come at you when things are great, when things are bad, when things are mediocre, or when you are standing knee-deep in perfect, turquoise water, a just-strong-enough mai tai in your hand and the clear, white Jamaican sun shining down upon you.

---

[*] Centers for Disease Control and Prevention, Data Brief, April 2016.

[†] P. E. Greenberg, et al. "The Economic Burden of Adults with Major Depressive Disorder in the United States (2010 and 2018)," *Pharmacoeconomics* 39, no. 6 (May 5, 2021): 653–665.

By April 1998 or so I had accrued some vacation time and, absent a band, finally had disposable income. High School Sweetheart and I decided we should take that much-discussed trip, someplace far away, someplace relaxing. Montego Bay, Jamaica, for instance. She worked for PBS at the time, at a really noble job that didn't pay super well, and I was still plugging away at the Firm, working on a newsletter that would serve the entire change integration practice of the East Coast Division. (I had proposed "Ch-ch-ch-Changes" as its title, and, when this was roundly vetoed, settled on the much more vanilla "Eastern Standard Times.") I was starting to settle in at work; the food in the cafeteria was excellent, and if I craned my head in my cubicle and leaned back I had a staggeringly pretty view of lower Manhattan. I was making more money than I ever had before, and while it was still a struggle to afford a place in Hell's Kitchen (my fourth apartment in the neighborhood, counting the one I'd grown up in), I had received a raise late in the previous year, right before Egghead. broke up. And to add to these riches, I did all my work on a company IBM Thinkpad souped up with Lotus Notes, the entire Microsoft Office package, Minesweeper, and a 56K modem that gave me the quickest and most comprehensive access to pornography I had ever known.

Pornography had always been just out of reach—and I do mean just. Feet away. I waited for the bus to school on Eighth Avenue right near two porn theaters (one gay, one straight). Growing up blocks from Times Square, it was omnipresent, surrounding me but also locked off. This isn't some sort of prudish anti-porn screed—adults are adults and can do what they want with consent—but there's no way being nine years old and waiting for the M10 bus in front of a marquee advertising *Beyond Shame* won't skew your perspective. As the bus crept north, you'd pass the Hollywood Twin Cinemas, which was a porn multiplex in the seventies, when multiplexes of any kind were still something of a rarity. You'd pass a couple adult boutiques, several peep shows, and if you got out and walked South, a strip club. And this was just Eighth Avenue—porn's prevalence famously grew if you went the one block east to Times Square. It was everywhere, and it pushed children toward an adulthood for which they might not have been ready. When I was in fifth grade, two fourth grade girls led me into a supply closet off the cafeteria and felt me up. Didn't kiss me, just groped my crotch and positioned my hand so that I could do the same to them. Which I did. It was thrilling, of course, but I had also just turned eleven. And what do you do with this information? Does it count as molestation if the predator is actually younger than you are? I told my mom that I had been felt up—carefully omitting that I had returned the favor—and if you can be alarmingly blasé, that was her. "Don't worry about it," she said. "You had fun, right?" And then she went off to bake some very bland chicken. Not a sexual libertine, my mom; in fact, the opposite was probably true, which made even discussing this stuff out of the question. I am fully aware that being groped by a curious classmate is not the same thing as having a priest violate his sacred vows to do something similar, but it definitely changes you. Does it give you a sort of hypersexuality? A sort of weird sense of entitlement? A pervasive need to have everything offered to you? It was not something I started really dealing with until I was in my thirties.

Trouble was, I was with High School Sweetheart in my twenties.

I was not a great boyfriend. I was inattentive, way too keen to spend New Year's Eve in a smoky rock club rather than considering High School Sweetheart's wants and needs. I was a champion mansplainer before someone could stop me with that neologism. I remember with a deep, purple shame her twenty-fifth birthday, when I gave her the screenplay to *Seven Samurai*, which is very much akin when Homer gives Marge matching bowling balls on *The Simpsons*. I could feel her moving away from me. Honestly, who could blame her? We had gone through so many shocks of our twenties together: Pasta is so versatile!

Jesus, mattresses are expensive! Whoever is up first should make the coffee! We tried to make it work. It was the nineties, remember, so hell yeah, we tried swing dancing lessons.

Therapy was for talking about the encroaching anxiety that kept me up late at night, pacing our very small apartment, convinced I had taken several fatally wrong turns in my life. Why hadn't I gone to grad school? Why hadn't I stuck it out in teaching (even though it was obviously killing me)? Why hadn't I done more writing? Why had I started dating a girl one week before leaving for college? By that spring I had sunk to the level of—ugh—cybersex with strangers in the cesspool of AOL's fin de siècle chatrooms (and God knows whom I was talking to, and thank that same God it was all anonymous). On a whim, unable to sleep one night, I had crept over to the computer, which we kept under our shared bunk bed, logged onto AOL under an assumed name, and hung out in rooms with names like "Hot Tub" and "Lonely Spouses." This had turned into a decidedly persistent habit that was relieving certain needs but also giving me a dark secret, which only made the anxiety worse. Our brothers and sisters in Alcoholics Anonymous will often say you're "only as sick as your secrets," and my secret was that I was a vile new breed of digital pervert who feared human connection but also was trying to fight loneliness. I had painted myself into a lovely corner of rationalization: it wasn't cheating, per se, the way working at the Firm wasn't working in corporate America, per se. It was a delicate, surgical bit of rationalization that no longer helped, and the guilt and shame was starting to burn.

I wasn't very social. I hadn't seen Corddry in a while and hadn't hung out with Faloon, who had started graduate school after the band went south. What I needed was a vacation, in Montego Bay, with no internet and my supposed girlfriend. I convinced myself that would wash all my worries and misgivings away, instead of shining a bright equatorial sun on them.

Which led to me standing in the water that April with a mai tai and a pervasive sense of dread, a sensation like someone sitting on my chest, cutting off my breath, a looming depression that made everything shitty. The blue sky itself, that universal metaphor for worthy goals and noble ambition and good cheer, was just a "pestilent congregation of vapours" as English literature's greatest depressive called it. Montego Bay and its environs contain the most incredible natural beauty I had ever seen—towering waterfalls, colors that defy description, the clean white sun plunging swiftly into an azure sea at day's end—and none of it seemed real. It was all just a vague bit of fakery meant to distract me from the fact that (a) the world was terrible and (b) I was very clearly part of the problem. My posture has never been great, but it got worse that week in Jamaica. Surrounded by nature's artistry, I could only stare blankly at the white sand. This wasn't sadness; this was the "storm of murk" that silences real emotion and replaces it with horrific, deafening white noise in your head. Nothing is good. Nothing tastes good, feels good, sounds good. Music is a deceitful charade. Food is a manifestation of love, and you don't deserve love, John, so stop eating. I'd had panic attacks as a child, debilitating dizzy spells that upended my world and sent me to the nurse's office, but this was something else, something far more disruptive. It was a steady feed of anxiety and guilt and shame that felt like constantly leaning too far back in your chair and never quite being able to get all four legs back on the ground. This was a cycle of repetitive thoughts telling me that I was garbage and a waste of space. This was a very serious contemplation of what would happen if I were to die—who would miss me (not too many people) and who would be better off (tons of folks, if you really think about it). I'd gotten a brutal hot pink sunburn in Jamaica, but even after my skin healed, the burning seemed to work its way inside.

By the time I returned to New York, I was really sick. High School Sweetheart knew something was up, but I wasn't able to give it a name yet, even with my biweekly therapy sessions. I returned to work and had to play a ton of post-vacation catch-up, a ton of expectant emails that I wasn't able to check while away from the office (1998!). I was eating less and less from the Firm's stellar cafeteria (Salmon with a horseradish and breadcrumb crust! New York cheesecake served so cold it was almost frozen but still creamy and smooth! Flavored coffee Friday!) and one day had to excuse myself from my cubicle to go throw up what little I had eaten. Deep down, I understood that I did not deserve nourishment. Anyone who thought that I did was a well-intentioned fool, but they could be forgiven, for only I knew the truth about how awful I and, by extension, the world, truly was. And it was the whole world, honestly. The media was mad at Bill Clinton for fucking around on his wife. Everyone else was mad at the media for basically killing Princess Diana. A drab thirty-year-old from Princeton had just made partner at the Firm and that pissed everyone off at the Firm, so much so that two other employees extracted their revenge on the world by cheating on their spouses with each other in that conference room down on four, the one with the fogged windows. Everything seemed to be going to hell.

The panic-ridden puking continued into the summer. I lost weight, abruptly. At night I lay in bed, my body on fire with anxiety, so filled with self-revulsion that I kept my arms over my head so as to not touch myself, even platonically. High School Sweetheart and I had already been sort of an old married couple, but our intimacy really flagged. When I allowed myself to masturbate, it was always followed by a profound shame that I hadn't felt since I had started doing it at thirteen. I would eventually drift off to sleep, just for a couple of hours, just long enough to sort of recharge my battery, wake up, and start panicking again. Music was not doing its job—it was no longer the blast of dopamine it had been in high school. Now that I had written songs, such as they were, my appreciation for songwriting was replaced with a deep cynicism: "Ah. They're doing the thing where chords climb to a fifth from the base note. That's supposed to cheer me up? Ha! Nice try."

I had reasons to be sad: no band, a job that loosely implicated me in the firing of thousands of people, guilt over the porn hobby. I had stopped frequenting chat rooms (High School Sweetheart had busted me after I forgot to delete one of my online pseudonyms like the master criminal I am) but had moved on to the vast wilderness of the web (and the slow loading amateur porn sites that were popping up internationally). But the creeping panic and blackening mood remained and were an untenable combination. The worst part of depression is the way it lies and tells you that everything else you've ever felt is bullshit, that this loud gloom is the only real truth, and you're in denial if you think otherwise. I started using my 56K modem to research this illness, this mud seeping into my life. There was something soothing in reading about the actual chemical imbalance that was happening in my brain: how it was burning off serotonin at an unprecedented rate, how I could treat it by mixing Western and Eastern modes of healing. Finally in the early summer of 1998, I paid my first visit to a psychopharmacologist, a very quiet man who wore a turtleneck and talked like a late-night NPR host, who prescribed Zoloft, the quickest-acting of the selective serotonin reuptake inhibitors (the class of drugs that also includes Prozac and Paxil) and Ativan, a mild benzodiazepine (a not-quite-as-debilitating cousin of Valium and Xanax). As sick as I was, this turn to pharmaceuticals felt like a defeat. Having temped for Big Pharma, I hated being on their teat in any meaningful way. These were the people, after all, who had brought us the phrase "total mortality." Why was I so weak that I needed pills to feel better? Why couldn't I just have normal emotions? Swallowing those pills was a white flag. Drugs were for the weak, an assumption I had long held. I was on drugs, so it followed that I was weak. I didn't tell my mom about this surrender, not for many months. She couldn't understand why someone would need therapy, let alone pills—never mind the fact that her husband was a drunk or that her father once went on a bender so severe he vanished from Ohio and turned up in Florida. One bucked up and soldiered through. So if my mom didn't need pills, why should I?

But then the medicine started to work: The light was bright and hopeful instead of just illuminating all the awful around me. Music was sincere again, not just an insincere mockery of people's delusions. The four legs of the chair settled back down to the floor, a true balance restored for the first time in months. I felt . . . not normal, but at least I felt.

There's a horrible misconception that antidepressants are happy pills, or some sort of Huxleyan Soma. They're not. They're like insulin, medicine that takes you back up to a baseline. They clear the storm of murk, but they don't make you happy—that's still up to you. The Zoloft turned the volume down on the white noise. I joked at the time that "it didn't stop the voices, but it made them speak one at a time and in measured tones." It was like those days when you get over the flu and you're happy to be outside, but you're still weak and tired and made of thin glass. Depression has never really left me since, not completely. It still shows up on occasion, like a racist uncle who comes by unannounced, sits on your couch, and spits slurs at the TV. His visits are awful, but he leaves eventually.

◆

That summer of 1998, I learned that healing depression would be a process, a lengthy (in my case, lifelong) process. The medicine takes you up to a level of normalcy, but that might mean that when you and your high school sweetheart go out for dinner for your ninth *(ninth!)* anniversary and you get caught in the rain—which should be really romantic—you will instead start weeping uncontrollably. You'll go home that night, and you'll feel awful, but at least you'll feel.

Again—there were very clear reasons to be sad. I was profoundly dissatisfied at work. I was resentful that I was twenty-six and had been in a relationship since I was eighteen. I was deeply, existentially bored with my life, which had set a course that looked, at that moment, very similar to my father's—my father, who, to my surprise, offered to take me to a diner during this existential funk, just as I was approaching twenty-seven, an age at which many musicians die, provided they've had the good sense to become famous. I had a bagel and coffee, which was all I could keep down. The diner was between our two apartments—a little aluminum beauty on 33rd and Tenth, passed daily by the trains that leave Penn Station, heading west to Jersey and points beyond. The menu is the same everywhere—way too big, way too comprehensive, and it's probably best to keep your order simple. My father had just retired—and by "retired" I mean he had once again quit in a huff, but this time it was for good, he was never to work again and now had ample free time to meet for bagels.

"What helps?" my dad asked, quieter, more thoughtful than usual, as we cautiously began talking about the cloud of pestilence hovering over me.

I made a sound, a sort of pensive exhale like *pssssssssh*. What felt better right now? "Accomplishing things," I said. "Small things."

My dad nodded solemnly: "Little errands. Small tasks that you can cross of a list." And it was here that I realized he'd been an untreated depressive for most of his life. There was no way a guy like this had ever been able to talk about such a thing. And to whom would he speak anyway? His army buddies? His Scottish immigrant father, who was definitely an alcoholic and probably also a depressive? His first wife, my mom, who was throwing up her hands at the idea that someone could think they "didn't deserve food"? No. He had been alone in this struggle.

"OK," said my dad. "What are some things that you can accomplish?"

This was the most punk rock moment my father and I ever shared. It was a relationship peak reached in an old school diner on Ninth Avenue. This was my dad asking how I could do it myself. This was not looking for a job or relationship to fix things—this was looking within. The depression—the medicine was working on that, slowly. The bagel would have to do for now. But what was going to fix the gloom, the emptiness, the storm of murk?

It was somewhere around here, during the first of several presidential impeachments to occur in my lifetime and with a mental health crisis seeping through my brain like tar, that I realized this moment was as good a moment as any to get into comedy.

CHAPTER SEVEN

THE FIRST UNUSUAL THING

I f I had anything to offer at a workplace—or at a school, or in a relationship—it was that I was funny. Or at least witty. Once on stage at CBGB with Egghead., I plugged our merchandise table. "We have T-shirts and seven inches!"

"You don't have seven inches!" said a heckler.

And, with a speed that startled me, I responded, "Sure we do—between the three of us!"

This is a dad joke, sure, but I got there quickly and it killed. Even the sound guy laughed, and sound guys are historically not an effusive bunch. Funny felt good. Funny felt right. Funny, at this point in my life, felt important.

I was one of those kids who stayed up late to watch *Saturday Night Live* and viewed it—as I still do—as a sort of sorcery, an incredible highwire stunt that mere mortals dare not risk. It's never been a particular dream of mine to do the show—it looks, frankly, like way too much pressure, and my friends who have since been on it have confirmed this—but I remain a fan and am in awe of even the lamest episodes. When I was twelve years old, my dad got me a book about the show and inscribed it "John—Enjoy but don't emulate. Love, Dad." There are a couple of ways to take that advice. One was, obviously, "Avoid cocaine unlike every third person in this book." The other way to take it—and I think the subtext was there—was to "avoid the performing arts in general. There be dragons, crazies, and narcissists."

Reading about the cast of *SNL* again in my mid-twenties, I was struck by how many of them—John Belushi, Bill Murray, Martin Short, Phil Hartman, and, by 1998, Mike Myers, Will Ferrell, and Ana Gasteyer—had gotten their start doing improv. And yet, improv fucking terrified me. Improv was dangerous, because if it went poorly, it wasn't just me up on stage; it was me up on stage looking stupid, which, even as I became more comfortable being in front of people, was still one of my deepest and most elemental fears. I dread looking stupid the way some people dread spiders—in a cringey, I want-to-hide sort of way. Egghead. had a deliberate stupidity about us that was so dumb it came around and became smart again—that was different. Improv looked like a perfect opportunity to look foolish while attempting to look smart. Disaster. So when a friend suggested I start taking improv classes, I very specifically said to him, "I fear improv more than I fear jail or the military." I'd played a couple of improv games with my high school students—you'll recall they made me Steve Urkel once—so this fear was sincere and based on hard experience.

But then the band broke up. And then the depression kicked in. And my job was terrible. A co-worker returned from a business trip in Ohio and said, with a dead-eyed smile, "I reduced that company's staff by 35 percent. That's good consulting." And then there was my nine-year relationship, which was suffering from my mood swings and was becoming less "high school sweethearts" and more "two roommates who resent each other." And then Rob Corddry came back from a year doing Shakespeare on the road with a small theater company. He was looking for a challenge, so we sort of dared each other to take the Level 1 improv class at Upright Citizens Brigade.

It was a rainy Saturday morning in May 1998; I was still twenty-six and would remain so for a couple more weeks. I had a blood level of Zoloft, but I had decided not to take a supplementary Ativan because I wanted my wits about me. While I was incredibly nervous, there's a difference between incredibly nervous and in the throes of a panic attack, and, at least for the moment, I was on the right side of that line. The theater where they held class was easy to miss—Solo Arts was in a shitty Chelsea office building, several stories up, and the elevator only really fit about four at a time. It was cramped and weird and felt dangerous, but then so did punk rock.

The UCB now has had several theaters and is an accredited institution—you can get honest-to-God college credit from their classes—and they've sent people like Donald Glover, Rachel Bloom, Ellie Kemper, and Kate McKinnon on to fortune and glory and steady work. Hundreds of students are taking classes at any time, and they compete for increasingly scarce stage time. In 1998, however, the Upright Citizens Brigade consisted of four scrappy twentysomethings who'd met in Chicago and were barely making ends meet in New York by teaching improv classes to the few dozen people who were interested in such a thing. The UCB had been teaching in New York for a couple years at that point, and they'd been doing their free Sunday night show *ASSSSCAT* for as long.

ASSSSCAT was incredible: a guest monologist receives a suggestion from the audience, tells a story, and then the UCB and their guests do scenes based on that suggestion. It wasn't the sort of short-form improv I had seen at the Village Gate, or on *Whose Line Is It Anyway?* These were freewheeling scenes that connected to each other, characters popping up in new realities, sometimes crass, often disjointed, but God, how funny. Scenes about a postage stamp that commemorated the rich history of anal sex would suddenly pivot as one player runs up to another and discovers that the stamp has arrived on a letter from his parents. The idea that such a stamp was so prevalent that your parents were using it just laid me out; I laughed uproariously, and it felt like a world that was eons away from the Firm. I wanted to live in that world.

The core four members of the UCB—Matt Besser, Amy Poehler, Ian Roberts, Matt Walsh—were no longer teaching the basics-covering Level 1 class. Instead they had brought in a recent Chicagoan with the incredible name of Armando Diaz, an improv teacher so legendary he had an entire improv form named for him—the Armando on which *ASSSSCAT* is based. Armando doesn't quite fit his badass moniker; he's actually a gentle giant, a sweet guy with not-great posture and an incredibly calm, patient demeanor. And thank God for that, because he had to sit through some terrible scenes that first day, mine included. The exercise was to get up two at a time, be given a situation that normally called for conflict (getting fired, fighting over a parking space, etc.), and find agreement using the storied "yes, and" rule that governs all improv. A guy named Ken and I got up, and Armando told us that we were both arriving to take the same girl to a date.

The scene was not particularly good, per se, and we broke a bunch of rules ("asking questions" chief among them). But something clicked up there for me. The theater smelled old and recently damp, like the 13th Street Playhouse just a few blocks south, the theater where I'd long ago been too scared to get up and be one of the seven dwarves. But here I was: on stage, no script, the risk of looking stupid dangling over my head. It was highwire thrilling.

"Where did you meet her?" Ken asked of our absent date, who had already been established as very promiscuous and heavily tattooed. "Seminary," I blurted out, and got a laugh. Not a big laugh, but a laugh. I had gotten laughs before, but always in situations where I was graded on a curve. ("Look, the teacher is kind of funny." "Look, the bassist in the punk rock band is kind of funny.") This moment felt pure—I got a laugh in a setting where getting a laugh was not just the point but the minimum requirement. The scene ended with the two of us wandering off to grab dinner on our own (with a vaguely homophobic "LOL, get it? They're actually gay!" vibe of which I am not proud). Armando nodded, smiled lightly, and warned us against asking questions. In a medium that requires you to add information, questions created a deficit of information. We were supposed to listen to each other instead, add to the details that were already there. Specifics were our friends. This I seemed to understand intrinsically, and I grinned when he gave us the perfectly fine starting critique of "good job." I had not embarrassed myself. I did not look stupid.

I sat down and a woman right in front of me named Celia Bressack turned to me and said, "So you're an actor?" And I quickly and emphatically and almost defensively said no. And then I thought, *Wait . . . why not?* The presumption in her question—not "Are you an actor?" just a clarifying "So you're an actor?" was electric.

This was what punk rock had prepared me for. From the moment Stan Lee came back with my Dickies ticket in high school, I understood the barrier between performer and audience was porous; he had come through to say hi, and now it was time for me to break through from my side. I didn't say anything to Celia, High School Sweetheart, or anyone else, but that was the moment I knew I had to at least try to be an actor.

The four core members of the UCB were performing once a week, and they'd started putting together improv teams that performed something called the Harold, a structured improv form that makes stories and scenes connect in a really fascinating way. You start with an opening where you deconstruct the suggestion—say, for instance someone yells out "penis"*—and you perform an opening, some sort

---

* And in a world with no guarantees, I feel comfortable guaranteeing that someone *will*, at some point, yell "penis."

of verbal montage, almost a piece of performance art. You kick around ideas inspired by that word—sex, intrusion, procreation, fragility, gravity, masculinity, toxicity—all the themes that "penis" might evoke. That exercise, in turn, inspires scenes that float on and off the stage, and if it's working well, the scenes will dovetail gracefully like a good episode of *Seinfeld*. I would voraciously watch teams do Harolds, observing the smooth folding over of ideas and the less graceful instances of "Hey, how did all these characters wind up in the same Oval Office?" I would go to class on Saturday morning, go see another improv show somewhere in the city that night, then see *ASSSSCAT* on Sunday nights. On Thursday nights, Corddry and I would pile into Solo Arts, sometimes surreptitiously pass a bottle back and forth, and watch the first Harold teams get up and excel or fail. Gradually tribes formed. We were getting to know the people in our classes, like a lanky Marin County expat named Seth Morris who claimed to have gotten high for the first time when he was eight and would eventually do a one-person show with the brilliant title "Dude, I Am So from California You Don't Even Know." Corddry's roommate Brian Huskey started taking classes, too. Also a refugee from indie rock, he'd been in the trenches of the Chapel Hill music scene (Had toured with Archers of Loaf! Knew Superchunk personally!) until he realized he was brilliantly funny and could transform on stage into a variety of weird personalities, including specific rednecks and dangerous nerds who say things like, "Good morning, my cock is a weapon." The four of us started to hang out and talk—and talk and talk and talk, carbonated by the shows we were seeing, full of ideas and questions and a deep need for exegesis. There's that old saying attributed to Jackie Gleason that comedy is "like a frog—if you cut it open, you'll figure out how it works . . . but it'll be dead." Not for us, this fatalism. We sat down at a diner on 14th Street and talked about the frog we had just seen, what worked (that moment when we thought Ali was holding a camera, but it turned out he had a backstage pass around his neck, a decision made for him, but for which he was totally ready, which hairpinned the scene into a fascinating dissection of fame and its traps) and what didn't, we discussed why things work, why things don't work, and resolving together that yes, the frog was dead, its laugh-blood running down the drain, but tomorrow we, based on what we had learned, would build a better, funnier frog.

And when we weren't talking about the craft of comedy, we were talking about mental health with a disarming candor that would have been really unwelcome at the Firm (despite the fact that the Firm was paying for my treatment). Work colleagues held views similar to my mom. Therapy? Drugs? Those were for weak crazies, and their use was an admission that life had beaten you. My UCB friends were different: These guys knew I was taking Zoloft. These guys knew about my suicidal ideation, about the dark thoughts that kept me up at two A.M. and made me want to crash at two P.M. They had them, too. My therapist had soothed me at the time with the adage "Hey—everybody thinks everything," but it was my friends at UCB who proved that.

When I told my dad I was taking improv classes, he made a sound that actually sounded like scoff. "What do you even do in improv class?"

"We practice."

"Practice? What? Improvising? But you're just making it up."

"Do you know how to improvise?"

"No."

"Well," I said, probably a little smugger than needed. "I want to learn."

It's hard to grasp the work that goes into improv. Done well, it looks choreographed. *That was clever; there's no way he didn't plan to say that,* you might think while watching someone pull a scene out of a dive by justifying someone's weird accent ("You'll excuse my uncle—he was born in Brooklyn but lives in Australia") or reveal themselves to have just the perfect hilarious occupation for the scene they're in (the incredibly polite assassin has a side hustle where he writes greeting cards). There are, of course, the standard rules for improv that any school will teach you, but what distinguishes UCB training is the emphasis on the "game" of the scene: how two people entering a space and responding honestly to each other will eventually lead to something unusual happening. A guy actually gets in a van with a stranger, or a woman on a date reveals that she specializes in human taxidermy, or a Seeing Eye dog is actually the Hound of the Baskervilles. That first unusual thing? That's the game. You play the truth of that moment—"Hey, nice van. I love the taped-out windows. Got any candy?"—and then ask yourself, *If that's true, what else is true?*

God, that phrase—if this is true, what else is true? What a way to make sense of the world, especially when it seems like the world makes zero sense. In this, I found a secret not just to comedy but maybe even . . . to life? If life itself was terrifying, and it kind of was at that time, then pursuing other terrifying things like improv didn't seem so terrifying after all.

◆

On my last day of my Level 1 class, deep summer 1998, a fellow student suggested I audition for her improv troupe, a collective named Amnesia Wars. The bad news: The audition was that afternoon, at a studio right in Hell's Kitchen, and I had no headshot, no resume, and also no experience and had only been ball-shrinkingly panic-free for a few weeks. The good news: It was an improv audition, and as such there was nothing to prepare.

Normally, after class, I would go get something to eat with a few classmates. But on this day, I decided it made more sense to wander around nervously for several hours by myself in the thick Midtown heat, letting my panic rear its head again. I pulled it together just barely after an internal monologue that sounded a little like the St. Crispin's Day speech from *Henry V* ("the odds are terrible, but wow, what courage, we happy few," etc.) and walked into a high-ceilinged, thin-hallwayed rehearsal studio on Eighth Avenue in the 50s, saw a couple of people from class, looked ruefully at their sleek black-and-white headshots and padded resumes, and signed in. I wore shorts and a T-shirt; I was worried about sweating too much. They were calling people into the room in groups of five, and the audition would be a series of short scenes based on suggestions given by the director, a stern, ponytailed guy named Rob Reese.

Reese wasn't a typical improv guy. I mean, yes, he was Caucasian and not particularly in shape, but there was also a seriousness about him that I hadn't seen elsewhere. He'd studied movement and "devised theater" with Anne Bogart and seemed intent on using improv as an actual theatrical tool—and if it was funny, then, hey, bonus. It would have read as pretentious if he hadn't known what he was talking about—if he didn't have a vision toward what he called "unscripted theater" that would bridge the gap between Anton Chekhov and Wayne Brady. I found myself on stage with a guy from my class and three other people who had seen the ad Reese posted in *Backstage*. I have no memory of the scene—at all, it's a total ellipsis—but at one point, an auditioner named Josh Cohen definitely got up with some really fit dancer guy who heard the suggestion "fire truck," pointed off into the middle distance, and said "Wow! Look at that fire truck over there!" and then mimed getting a hose and soaking Josh to the bone. Josh tried to get a word in edgewise; his scene partner was acting like a lunatic, and the best move for him was to bring things down, maybe interview this clearly crazy guy for a job as a fireman.

Of that group, Josh and I were called back for another audition the following week. Called back. *Oh, shit. A callback. I've heard of those.*

I went home and told High School Sweetheart that I had just gone on my first audition and had gotten called back. This, I knew, was so rare as to be absurd. A unicorn on a rainbow under an eclipse. I can't say she was pleased, or proud, but she was definitely surprised. I was honest with her: "There's a part of me that hopes I don't get it, I'm just . . . really overwhelmed and still not feeling sane all the time." High School Sweetheart, who had tons of friends who had worked very hard for a very long time and did *not* get callbacks on their first audition said, "Maybe it would be better if you didn't. You don't . . . you don't deserve it."

It hurt me to hear that, and I think it hurt her to say it. This wasn't a simple "girl wants to squash boy's dream" thing. She'd been trying to make it as a theater director for years, working on projects naïve, ambitious, good, and less so, and we had gone to see a ton of shows downtown of all stripes, from a site-specific Greek tragedy by Tina Landau to the stoic, breathing paintings of Robert Wilson, to avant-garde puppetry from Janie Geiser. While I loathed some of it, it all gave me ideas. It all gnawed at me and made me look at acting from new angles; the very presence of those performers on stage seemed to mock my cowardice for not getting up there and doing it myself. But High School Sweetheart couldn't possibly have known that because I'd never shared it with her or, indeed, anyone. What she saw was just a guy trying to retie the frayed knot of his well-being by stumbling into her world and immediately being rewarded. A very lucky dilettante who, one week later, after a callback, was invited to join Amnesia Wars for their fall show. The most instant validation—a small gig, to be sure, and no money, but a sense that I had wandered into the right room.

Meanwhile, back at the office: The drugs were working, I was keeping food down, and I was continuing my work on my newsletter that would change the way the Firm communicated ideas—except nobody could agree on the logo, and the partners were not enjoying my just-for-fun "trivia section" with such endearing inquiries as "Can you name the first film in which Clint Eastwood sings?"* A woman in my four-person cubicle space had painstakingly downloaded a *Titanic*-themed screensaver off the internet and it played whenever she stepped away from her desk for any significant period of time, and that cloying fucking tin whistle that begins *that song* began earwigging into my day-to-day. I had lunch in the luxurious corporate cafeteria, trying to make friends with people who said things like "I'm not at all racist, but . . . ," and "I liked *Saturday Night Live* before it got all political," and "You like music, right, John? You know who never gets old? Clapton," and variants on "Depressed? What do you have to be sad about?"

My mom, who had worked in publishing since the early eighties and inherited a small design firm from her late boss, had just driven said firm into the ground. Clients were leaving, work was drying up and, at fifty-six or so, she had realized that what she really wanted to do, what her dream was, was to be a "professional organizer"—help people pull their lives together, categorize their closets, et cetera—and that was going to require some startup money. Which I lent her. I was happy to do it—well, no, not happy; it kind of bummed me out that my mom had to ask me for money, which she did apologetically, almost choking up with the humiliation.

"This is not the way," she said, taking a drag of her cigarette (we were eating outside in Hell's Kitchen, and it was getting warm). "This is not the way this is supposed to go."

"I don't know, Mom," I said, not quite sure what else to add. "How is anything supposed to go?" I signed a check and handed it to her. She gave me a tight-lipped "Thank you."

---

* *Paint Your Wagon.*

But these were my parents: never quite finding out what they wanted to do until it was empirically too late. And now, hovering around sixty, both were unemployed.

Home life was not much better. High School Sweetheart and I were drifting very far apart. I announced that I would need headshots, and she sighed, "There's a reason I don't date actors." And I somehow kept myself from saying *Because you've never dated anyone but me*. Which wasn't entirely true, but she was seventeen when we got together. The longevity of our relationship was beginning to take a toll on me—and her—in the worst way. Questions were asked testily, answered briefly. She came to one of my first improv shows and didn't seem too surprised or impressed that I was relatively adept at it. There was a scene where characters were playing the board game Life, the object of which is to succeed and become a doctor, and I made the bold-if-hacky choice to become a crack whore. This killed—Armando was still quoting it to me years later—but High School Sweetheart was nonplussed. And yet, as we drifted further and further away, she made one last-ditch effort to right the course of the relationship—a beautiful gift certificate that she drew herself, offering $100 toward headshots.

I never cashed it in.

This uptick in good luck buoyed me, but it didn't keep me from my internet . . . hobbies, we'll call them, since "obsession" is an ugly word. I had stopped talking dirty to strangers on the internet, but porn websites—slowly loading pictures creeping across the screen—were becoming a little more common and easier to locate and navigate, and I was twenty-seven and in a celibate relationship. I would tell myself, *A man has needs*, and a man does, sure, but this was gross and time-consuming. This was before *Friends* made a joke of Chandler's porn habit, before a Broadway musical called *Avenue Q* contained a showstopper called "The Internet Is for Porn." As far as my conscience and I were concerned, I was a very sick man, a deviant who prowled the internet's off-ramps, perusing sites like Amateur Index (I tended to prefer the no-makeup, real boobs aspects of those channels). It was not a good feeling, and it was something I wanted to stop, which is probably why I got lazier and lazier about cleaning my computer's memory.

Late August, I came home one Saturday afternoon from improv class, and High School Sweetheart was sitting on our bed, telling me that she had checked my Netscape browser history (1998!) and had been disgusted by what she'd found. She had those beautiful blue eyes and had been crying, and while I had been shaking at my confines for years, I felt very much like I'd broken something kind of precious.

"You have to get out," she said. "Just go somewhere, I need to be alone."

I walked all the way up to Central Park, numb again, but now I could at least point to the source of the numbness. The city—deep into summer by this point, all sweaty bright colors—seemed gray. The sound muted. Weirdly two-dimensional. A couple of hours later, exhausted and wanting to get . . . whatever was waiting for me over with, I came back home. Walking up those five flights of stairs felt like the longest trip of my life. I was not looking forward to the shame that awaited me in the too-small apartment. This was going to be awful.

She was sitting on the bed, a box of tissues near her. She had pulled herself together somewhat. She had gorgeous posture, but now she was hunched over like I usually was, protecting her vitals. The phone was next to her. Oh, God, she'd been talking to people. Her friends? Her mom? Her . . . therapist?

"You have a pathology," she said (therapist, definitely, although maybe a couple of friends, too). "Or you just want to be a bad boy for once. I don't know." Her face was pinched as if she had just smelled something awful.

Maybe. Or maybe I just wanted to be someone else?

I turned to the chest of drawers, golden afternoon sunset pouring into our bedroom, and pulled open the top drawer. *Am I doing this?* I thought. *Nine years. I have just turned twenty-seven, so that's a third of my life. That's my entire adulthood up to this point. Am I really doing this?*

And as if to answer my own question, I grabbed several pairs of socks from the dresser drawer—and that's when it became real, I was packing up my socks—and threw them into the nice leather shoulder bag that had the Firm's stentorian logo embroidered into its side. "I have to leave," I said, grabbing a few more essentials before walking down Tenth Avenue to my mom's house. She was out of town, visiting her brother's family in Scranton, and I let myself in with the key, sat on the couch, and shook violently for hours before I fell into a fitful sleep on the couch.

The next morning, after not much sleep, I got up and looked around. My room was pretty much the same. My mom had put in a desk, and my punk rock flyers (this Dickies show, that Dag Nasty gig) had come down, but the drab white walls and small bed and tiny little bookshelf and the window that looks out on the building's backyard, where the garbage cans go—all was more or less the same, which was simultaneously comforting and depressing. This new world, post–High School Sweetheart, looked grimly like the old world, pre–High School Sweetheart. I went to Dunkin' Donuts on 42nd to get some coffee and a donut, then walked over to the cheap movie theater to see *Out of Sight* with George Clooney and Jennifer Lopez, a film so good that it took me out of myself for two hours. The decision-making process for seeing this film was disarmingly simple: *I am alone. I would like to go to a movie. This particular movie. This is when I will go, and I will sit wherever I want. I will get a large popcorn and an extra-large Coke, and when I am done with the Coke, I will chew my ice. This is new. This is a frontier. There is no law in this new world, and I will have to make my own. Also—God, the acting is good in this film.*

My mom came home late Sunday night, and I got to have a super fun conversation with her about internet porn, an experience I can't recommend enough—something to do ideally before thirty. It was cringe-y and humiliating, and it physically hurt to explain the circumstances of the breakup, but this was part of my self-flagellation. This was the depression talking—the need to let people know exactly how awful I am, in order to convince them that I'm garbage, in the hope that they might offer me the acceptance and forgiveness you couldn't offer yourself. I was her son, and she understood that nine years was a long time and that I was still young(ish), and she said I could stay as long as I needed. I offered to chip in on rent. She accepted, and it helped ameliorate some of my shame. Yes, I had moved back home, but I wasn't freeloading, right?

Right?

There were few sympathetic ears at work, though I spared them the details. I did not look well, but I was starting to put weight back on and maybe sleep some more. I was still in improv classes, still making new friends, still practicing the craft. I had started writing a little, trying out dopey ideas for sketches, one of which was set in the coffee/break room at the Reichstag, which operated like any other office, replete with people bitching about the coffee and petty office gossip ("Man, Himmler has been in a *mood* lately."). A funny sketch, and a clear cry for help.

I lived for the weekend—to be back in class, among people who thought like I did, and joked like I did, and understood that John Travolta didn't come back to life at the end of *Pulp Fiction*, which distinguished them easily from a co-worker at the Firm ("But we see him die . . . and then at the end . . . he's back up and around, like nothing's happened! I mean, what?"). I found office life deadening. I didn't love the idea of getting the partners richer and helping larger corporations fire people. There are people who thrive in that setting, and I saw them up close, and I don't view them with some sort of elitist contempt. I'd love to be happy in that line of work; it would make things a lot simpler. I envy them.

But they're not me. My people were waiting for me at UCB. I'd found my tribe again, but this time it wasn't in the confines of high school or college—those institutions were too finite. This could last. This could be a livelihood. This could be my life.

◆

The entire marketing department had left Washington, DC, a little late, and we were racing to catch our flight on a little puddle jumper that would fly into LaGuardia. We'd hit Beltway traffic and a crush of commuters at the airport, and we were racing down the hallway at Ronald Reagan. The guys from graphics, another copywriter, a couple of event planners, all of us were leaving after the huge annual meeting of the East Coast branch of the Firm that took over a Hyatt or a Hilton somewhere in DC every year around October. Everyone was incredibly annoyed with everyone else. Everyone wanted to get home. But I *needed* to get home—Amnesia Wars was doing a show that very night, in just a few hours, at eight P.M. The show was a pretty complicated sort of super Harold devised by Reese that was going to be held in a five-story walkup theater in Tribeca. It was improv; worst case scenario they could do the show a man down, but I really wanted to be there. This was going to be my first show with the group.

This was going to be my first non-student show.

We got to security and there was, no joke, a crowd of some twenty Boy Scouts ahead of us in line. They all look overwhelmed; you could tell they hadn't flown before as, one by one, they walked through the metal detector. The first unusual thing: twenty Boy Scouts, all about to go through security.

"Christ, this is gonna take forever," I said. "They've all got pocket-knives," and the laugh that blasted through the team from the Firm was genuine and real and warm. My newsletter was a shambles. I had been useless at the meeting, sullen and depressed and antisocial (save for inviting a co-worker to join me in my hotel room for a bottle of wine; she politely declined and *thank God*, good for her) and was not contributing to the work being done. *The work*. The work was taking money from corporations and funneling it to a limited liability partnership. Along the way, people lost jobs and livelihoods. I was never going to be good at it and didn't want to be. But hey, at least I could make these people laugh. And quickly, too—the joke had popped out of me within seconds of seeing the Scouts. The improv classes had developed . . . muscles, there was no other way to put it.

We got on the plane to find that there was inclement weather over New York, the clear DC skies mocking me as I chewed my fingernails bloody, sitting on the tarmac. When we finally did get up in the air it was close to five thirty, and we flew through incredible turbulence for forty minutes to skid down at LaGuardia a little after six. The only place in New York where you can get a cab in the rain is thankfully at the airport, and the yellow car deposited me in front of the theater in Tribeca frazzled but intact at around 7:40.

My father came to the performance—no easy feat, as the theater was five stories up and the walk was brutal on his smoked-out lungs. We had a good show. We got laughs. Riding high from my dumb Boy Scout joke, I got several laughs. High School Sweetheart was there, curious to see what was next for me and mercifully eager to make this transition less painful than it easily could have been. Rob Corddry was there, all smiles, all encouragement. No one from the Firm was there. At the end of the show, my father looked at me like I had wings and gills—like there was a whole part of me that he had not been aware of and said, again in a strange, detached Yiddishkeit voice, "My son, the actor."

"What did you think?"

He shrugged, sort of wearily. "It was fun."

My mom was thrilled. Almost starry-eyed. "I had no idea you had it in you."

◆

October 23rd, 1998

To whom it may concern:

Effective two weeks from today, I am tendering my resignation from the Firm to pursue a career in improv and acting. Thank you very much for your time.

Yours,

John Ross Bowie

The sheer hubris of that email! A career . . . in improv? Holy shit, dude, do you know how fucking quixotic that sounds? You're a freshly single nobody with a mood disorder and no arts training and you want to be an actor at an age when most people are giving up on dreams like that? And you've set a silent goal for yourself that you're going to book a commercial within a year of this email or you'll . . . Well, you're not sure what you'll do. You've already tried a lot of other paths. You're heading into a business known for selfish backstabbing, which would be really terrifying if you hadn't also seen selfish backstabbing at *every other job you've ever had*. This whole venture is ridiculous!

And it really should have been, except it worked.

◆

"Fifteen hundred dollars to join SAG."

"Jesus, John."

"I know, Dad, it's a lot, but . . . here's what happened. They let you do one commercial, and you don't have to join the union yet, there's an exemption, it's called—"

"Taft-Hartley."

"Yeah! So. I did that. And then I booked another one right away, and that was also covered under Taft-Hartley. But now, I've booked a third commercial and *have* to join the union, or the producers *and* the union won't let me do it. But it's so soon, I haven't even seen the money from the first two."

"What's the new one for?"

"Sprint. It's for a cell phone that will get you on the internet."

"Oh, for fuck's sake."

"I know, right?" We were genuinely in agreement here. What could be more absurd than checking your email while you were out at lunch or, Christ, on a date?

This was August 1999, about ten months after I had quit the Firm. Everything had moved very fast. I had gotten headshots, black-and-white portraits of me lunging at the camera, begging to be let into some sort of party—again, ill-advised, but it kind of worked. A notoriously callous business had welcomed me with open arms, and I had gone from "that might be fun" to "working actor" in a very short time. And I was in the middle of a palm-sweating phone conversation with my father, asking not for charity but a loan, in order to keep this momentum going. He was quiet, and I was sitting in my dingy Queens apartment, a poster for a Hal Hartley movie hanging on the wall, Built to Spill probably playing softly on the CD player. I couldn't gauge his reaction to this request at all.

"If my father knew that I was paying—"

"I know, Dad."

"—for his grandson to join . . . a *union*." He spat the word out, the way all conservatives do. "And an actors union no less. I mean. Jesus. Remember what Spencer Tracy sa—"

"Dad. Listen. If this goes the way I think it's going to go, I will pay you back before Christmas."

"Be that as it may—wait, Christmas?"

"Yes."

He was understandably incredulous: "You're gonna have fifteen hundred dollars to pay me back in four months?"

"Yes. This is a national commercial."

"They pay that well?"

"They can, yes."

My dad gave a sincerely labored sigh. His lung capacity was really starting to slip. "OK," he said.

I met him at the Times Square SAG offices on a cool summer morning, and he greeted me with a cashier's check and a defeated look. I thanked him and acknowledged that, no, it can't be easy for a Republican to pay his son's union entrance fee.

And then I paid him back two months earlier than expected. We were both surprised.

When I started acting, I had several things going against me:

1. No experience.
2. No training.
3. Nothing resembling leading-man looks.
4. Clinically, diagnosably bad posture.

But what I had in my favor:

1. Regular opportunities to perform at an increasingly popular theater that seated ninety-nine people legally but was almost always over capacity and where you could be seen by a commercial agent (which is how I got into this whole "three commercials in a row" predicament).

2. The hook of being a new face at twenty-eight, an age at
    which a lot of people have been on the audition circuit
    for upwards of five years.

3. Years of critically watching actors and indulging not just
    in a lot of "I could do that" but also some speculative
    "If I did that, how would it look?"

4. Growing up in Hell's Kitchen, a neighborhood was
    still so filled with actors you could soak up advice just
    by paying attention. Case in point: I passed a pair of
    actors discussing technique on the street one day, just
    off Ninth Avenue. One said, "Another trick is you go
    through the script and copy down everything your char-
    acter says about himself, and everything *other* characters
    say about him." Incredibly solid, free advice, and I use
    it all the time.

5. It was 1999, the dawn of the dot-com era, and every-
    body needed nerds for their commercials.

The biggest thing going for me? I fucking loved it. I was at my
happiest practicing improv, rehearsing sketches, and running lines
before auditions. There was a risk, a dangerous exposure unlike anything I'd felt before. That year I had been asked to join a new sketch
comedy group, the Naked Babies (me, Corddry, Seth Morris, and
Brian Huskey), and they were very much my second band—a bunch of
like-minded dipshits who laughed at the same things but didn't have
to carry amps or drum kits. We made a mark early in the theater's run,
tirelessly promoting ourselves and gradually building sellout crowds.
The thrill of comedy was probably greater than the thrill of punk rock,
because even this early in my career it was clear that I was a better actor
than I was a bass guitarist. I'd be a Bible salesman—Rob Corddry
playing my boss—and we'd be selling Bibles in a fun, niche *Glengarry*

Glen Ross parody that Rob had written. The artifice of acting (we have agreed to this fiction, and we're using this fiction to make a point about the commodification of religion, and it works best if we really pretend it's real) was a crazy adrenaline rush. Right now, together, we are yelling—right now, we are cursing God like he's a low-performing real estate agent—right now we are transitioning into the next sketch. Our work doesn't necessarily belong in the pantheon of great comedy, but there was an honest rawness to the work we were doing. All of us were in therapy, and that introspection fueled our work. We had a terrific, weirdly crowd-pleasing series of sketches called the Emotional Stunts, wherein we put on crash helmets and performed feats of psychological derring-do (called an ex-girlfriend, looked at pictures of our parents fucking, read from our high school journal) and it used to kill. It felt right. All the things that embarrassed me and gave me anxiety—sex, relationships, communication—were now comedy fuel, and people were enjoying it.

That said, I was still on unsure ground, not steady on my feet at all, when Corddry and I went for coffee one cold afternoon in Chelsea. I felt out of place; I didn't have the confidence that seemed to come so naturally to Rob and others. I said as much to Rob, and he literally put a hand on my shoulder. "You're a natural actor, Bowie." The coffee that day tasted good. Earned.

This was what I wanted to do. This was what I loved. This was how I wanted to make a living.

◆

Of course, no one at UCB was making a living quite yet, though there was blood in the water at the brand-new Upright Citizens Brigade Theater on 22nd Street, in the sticky old space that had been the Harmony Burlesque. Casting directors and agents were funneling into the place, sending their nets out and bringing people in for auditions for voiceovers, commercials, even the odd film role. Corddry had started booking. After years of doing good work as a Shakespearean clown, it was improv that got him noticed, and he'd booked a Barq's commercial and a 1-800-COLLECT ad with Carrot Top. A lot of us were stepping away from temp jobs for extended lunches to sneak over to casting studios in Chelsea to do bite-and-smiles (it's exactly what it sounds like: You bite into a burger and smile without showing the food in your mouth and then they decided whether or not you can represent Burger King).

I'd booked the first commercial for which I'd gotten a callback—a regional spot for Cablevision, co-starring a young commercial veteran named Tony Hale (who went on to star on *Arrested Development* and earn an Emmy nomination for his work on *Veep*), and it felt validating and awesome and bone-chilling. They had put a camera in my face, put the slate between us, and its loud clap meant to sync sound made me sweat a little (dear God, they want you to act now—for *money*), and then, three weeks later, I was handing someone a muffin in a Dunkin' Donuts ad. Neither had paid anything more than the basic session fee—about 650 bucks each—and that had gone straight toward rent and utilities. The residuals that came from repeated airings had yet to arrive. Now I was running on empty, but this Sprint ad had come along, and my grace period with the union had run out. And my father had stepped up, put aside his political misgivings, and helped out.

I had done it. I had cleared three commercials before my quiet and self-imposed October deadline. I liked it. It felt good to be good at something. I walked taller, a working actor striding his streets, knowing that his gifts contributed to the local economy. So I immediately went back to something at which I was terrible.

They needed office help at the UCB—someone to manage the theater during the day. "You'd be perfect," said Katie Roberts, the wife of

UCB co-founder Ian Roberts, a smiley Virginian who was expecting her first child and was abdicating her role as office manager to go on an extended maternity leave. "You've got all this office experience, and you can still make time to audition."

I'd just booked my first film role—the cut-proof part of Waiter in Todd Phillips's *Road Trip*. (I say "cut-proof" because said Waiter tells Fred Ward that his credit card is maxed out, a plot point that sets act 2 in motion.) I was auditioning steadily for commercials and even a rogue pilot, *The Trouble with Normal*; the role went to David Krumholtz), and it looked like I was going to qualify for SAG's generous health insurance plan! I wasn't just making a living; I was making a living in my chosen profession. And it felt . . . unreal.

As in, literally, not real. *This can't be a job, I'm having too much fun, I like the people I'm meeting, so it can't be real work, real work sucks, and you hate it, and you resent it, and you drink to forget it. Right? Well, John, how about a windowless office—yes, in a theater, but during the day—making decent money filing and handling a ledger, even though you can barely balance your own checkbook? SIGN ME UP.* There was something self-flagellating about accepting the job, like I was having too much delight in my day-to-day life and needed—nay, deserved—to be punished.

◆

By the time *Road Trip* came out in June 2000, I had been working at the theater for about nine months. While I was there, I suggested we start advertising, which we did, placing ads in the *Village Voice*, the *NY Press*, and the like, and with that came an influx of interest that was quite overwhelming. People came at every moment of the day to drop off deposits for classes, and my job was to make sure they got their classes, but it became hard to keep track of the tsunami of checks, so some went into a cardboard box in the basement, to be dealt with later.

And later. And later. I made it look like I was on top of the scene and didn't ask for help, but I really wasn't on top of any scene and desperately needed help. A lost little boy with a real man's inability to ask for directions. I got this, I thought, even though I really didn't. Real men do the work, and they do the work without assistance is (I guess) the fucked-up logic that kept me from letting on how overwhelmed I was by the work.

The theater was growing too fast, for someone of my limited skillset anyway. Three Level 1 improv classes became ten, and new teachers had to be hired, and once in a great while students had to be expelled for either really not getting the fundamentals or showing up drunk to a Saturday morning class. I myself was treading water and drinking a lot. I had gone off my Zoloft because, "Hey, I'm not crazy, I was just in a bad place and now I'm in a better one!" but that abstention led to me napping at the theater a lot more than was appropriate and trying to medicate with cheap white wine and the weed that was *always* around the backstage area. Seth had introduced me to weed, which I thought offered a more holistic way to deal with anxiety, and it did. But I was not the kind of stoner who gets a ton of shit done while they're high. I was more of the "rent four Pam Grier movies and decimate some fried rice" type of pothead.

The auditions dried up a bit, slowing down to once a week from a peak of five or so a week (the dot-com bubble was already starting to thin). I'd hit a plateau that was normal but still striking, since I'd climbed so quickly. So again, I was the office guy. At a super cool improv theater, no question, but one where I was doing a really shitty job. My nights were buoyant—doing shows at UCB or elsewhere with the Naked Babies or with random pick-up improv teams, trying my hand at stand-up (at which I was only OK, and I realized early on that the world was actually all set on white guys who were only OK doing stand-up, thanks). The magic of improv was buoying me along handsomely and Christ, was it magical. A bunch of us were doing an improvised movie show called *FeatureFeature* (one suggestion leads to a breakneck thirty-minute movie): There was one really anarchic show where we were doing a sort of pastiche of Nora Ephron movies, and I played a kid who had lost his mother to a "debilitating disease." Only I fucked up, got tongue-tied, and said "decapitating disease." The saying in improv is that "mistakes are gifts," and I had just handed the rest of the team an enormous box with a picturesque red bow on top. Obviously, the disease was airborne, and obviously, no one was immune, not even the romantic leads, who were swiftly beheaded by the decapitating disease at the fade out. This is why nerds get into improv—there's a sense of camaraderie and mutual support that is usually just the purview of athletics, and it allows us to say the under-used phrase "I'm on a team," and our fuckups are as treasured as successful Hail Mary passes. And, of course, there's the other truth that draws the maladjusted and awkward to improv: When everyone is listening to each other and finishing each other's sentences and arriving together at the same inevitable ending, improv will make you believe in the Force.

◆

When *Road Trip* premiered in theaters, my parents stayed valiantly true to their brands: My mom took several of her girlfriends to see it opening night. (I have just the one scene, about a half hour into the film—blink and you miss me.) She gushed. She was so proud. The scene was so funny. Her friends thought I was the best part. Some of that may have been true. My father went to see it by himself at a matinee and, when called for feedback, said, "Well, you and the kids were cute, but it's no *Citizen Kane*." Which is brutal, because if ever a film had pretensions towards great art, it's the Tom Green starrer *Road Trip*, also featuring Andy Dick as a hotel clerk and Horatio Sanz as a waiter who farts on French toast.

Everything impresses Mom; nothing impresses Dad.

Later on, my dad would speak about the film in front of me but not *to* me. We'd be at church or at dinner with my grandmother, and he'd stop and smile. "It was nice seeing John up there, but what was really great was at the end"—and here he'd gesture, his raised hand imitating the crawl of the closing credits—"seeing the family name scroll up like that."

"That was weird, Dad. You didn't even look at me when you said it," I told him later that week on a phone call, when it was still bothering me. "You didn't even seem that excited about the movie when it came out."

"Oh. Well. I guess I'm just jealous," he said, with a nonchalance that one would use for a slight change in health: *I had a fever. My bunions are acting up. I am jealous of my son.* I was furious. This seemed like a betrayal of the social contract—you should want your kids to do well. This might even have seemed like a contradiction of the American Dream itself—you should not only want your kids to do well; you should want your kids to exceed your accomplishments. This was . . . this was unpatriotic is what it was.

"Well, don't be" was all I could muster.

And he said, "I'll try."

◆

I worked at UCB for a year and then gave notice in October 2000, and it was discovered just how behind I was in my duties—there were unaccounted monies all over the goddamn place. Literally boxes of cash in the basement. I quit before I got fired. I quit because I knew I deserved to be fired. I quit because I just couldn't live the lie that I belonged in an office anymore. The main four members of the UCB reacted as expected: Besser was furious, Ian was profoundly disappointed, Amy was forgiving, and if Walsh cared, he was *very* cool about it. Ian (focused, austere, so good at improv that he was often called "the Machine," and that earnest quality served to shame me pretty intensely, whether he meant to or not) took me into the theater, this place that had become almost a temple to me, and we sat in the audience. He shook his head in disbelief, looking down at the floor during one of the worst conversations I've ever had in my life (and I had just had that lengthy conversation about internet porn with my mom not two years prior). "This negligence is, it's just inexcusable," he said, as right as anyone has ever been. I was almost shaking with shame. "You can still perform here, but don't work in an office. Any office." I hung my head, thanked him because I didn't know what else to do, and stayed out of the theater for a few days. This was the dull, drab pattern of my life—I am unhappy, in either a job or a relationship, I need help, I don't get help, things blow up, I panic.

I'd let these people down, these people who had let me in, who had helped me find myself, and it hurt so bad I thought about walking in front of a car on Ditmars Boulevard—over being bad at an office job. This was the last time I seriously entertained suicide, and if it seems overwrought—it is, of course, but keep in mind that UCB had changed my life for the better, given me an extra opportunity, and I had blown it by any reasonable metric. I had been irresponsible and deceitful, all the while dating my assistant, a recent college grad who definitely deserved better. I was disgusting, clearly, and the world might be better off without me. After a tearful fit in a psychiatrist's office, I went back on antidepressants, switching over to Paxil. Just in time to really fall in love.

The secret to good comedy is timing.

Her name was Jamie Denbo. She was this beautiful, hilarious girl in my Level 2 improv class. The teacher was Amy Poehler, who was totally crushable as well, sure, but there was something very alluring about Jamie . . . I didn't start to fall for her until I saw her improvise. One Saturday morning in the fall of 1998, she got up on stage with a lazy male improviser who did a thing that lazy male improvisers do constantly, which is just heap abuse on their female scene partner in an unsightly id drainage that isn't funny and is hard to watch. There are a couple ways to handle guys like this—one is to just give as good as you're getting, but that can get very yell-y and violate the sacred dictum of "yes, and." What Jamie did was beat herself up. Literally. She just started punching herself, first in the arm, then eventually in the face until it looked very much like—*spoiler alert*—the scene near the end of *Fight Club* when we realize that Edward Norton *is* Brad Pitt.

I had just had a psychiatrist hold his head in his hands and say, "Wow, John, you really like to beat yourself up," which was totally true, and not something to celebrate, except here was a woman who was doing . . . this. Literally.

After class, I got to talking to her, and talking to her was the easiest thing in the world for me—despite being on antidepressants, which she openly owned, she brightly colored every room she entered. She was Jewish, from a little town just north of Boston, insanely funny and talented, an only child like me, and hell-bent on pleasing her parents and marrying a Jewish guy. I couldn't offer her that, but I could offer her a gentile who had picked up a lot of Yiddish from his father, and oy vey iz mir, was I fucking crazy about her.

She'd pass those cheesy novelty shops on the West Side where they sell T-shirts that say FUCK YOU, YOU FUCKING FUCK and announce, "*There. That* is the shirt I will wear to yoga." She held poker games in her apartment in Queens, which was decorated with a *Fish Called Wanda* poster and a CD collection that was small but included both Green Day's *Dookie* and the original Broadway cast of *Sweeney Todd*.

She cursed constantly and one time said she had a "fucking huge crush on Rick Moranis."

"God bless you, Jamie Denbo," I blurted out.

"Bowie," she said, putting a hand on my arm, "you know . . ." She didn't finish, but I did know.

Before the humid August 2000 night when we hooked up for the first time—in a cab on the way back to our Astoria apartments—she was in me, deep behind my eyes, in a very profound way. They say you only really know a language when you start dreaming in it. I had been dreaming in Jamie, waking up next to ill-advised hookups with other women, having just been hanging out with her in the casual pandemonium of my subconscious. The first night we were together I had occasion to take off my shirt, revealing a weird, sandpapery stubble across my chest and belly. "OK. I can explain this."

She touched it. "Ouch. I'm listening."

"I just did a bit on Conan, and the idea was different ways to shave your body hair so that it looks like a bathing suit? And I was supposed to wear a chest hair bikini, but in order for the bit to work, my actual chest hair had to go?"*

"Good bit. How'd it go?"

"It destroyed, actually. Got sort of a weird gasp and then a lot of laughs." And we started making out again.

It was a rocky first couple of months—she had just gotten out of a relationship, and I had thoroughly embarrassed myself at the theater where we both performed. I was just starting to step back into performing on the UCB stage. My moods were all over the place, and my body was adjusting to the new antidepressants, with the understanding that they were going to be a permanent part of my life. There was a huge

---

* *Late Night with Conan O'Brien* hired so many UCB students for little bits (a speaking role could cover your rent, if you spent wisely) that other comedians in town took to derisively calling the theater "Conan O'Brien University."

part of me that felt like I—a terrible office worker, still mired in student loan debt, shiftless, and dependent on Paxil—certainly didn't deserve to be happy. But I knew it was real one night around Halloween 2000. The theater was packed for the annual October 31 show *KILGORE*, a Grand Guignol homage that required the entire stage to be covered in white plastic so the fake blood and offal could be easily removed after the performance. The story—such as it was—was about an eccentric billionaire who kills unlucky travelers in his secluded mansion. My death? I got my tongue torn out and bled to death on stage along with the rest of my touring band. I scurried off during the blackout after my scene and ran into Jamie in the narrow hallway, right next to the theater's office where I had worked for a year, the site of the last great mistake I made in my twenties. I was covered in the thick stickiness of corn syrup and food coloring; it had even matted my hair down thanks to a puddle in which I'd landed. And she said, "Will you go out with me?" And I said, "Yes." And in my head, I continued, *Yes, and I will marry you and we'll have children.*

We had long talks about goals and mistakes, walking across the Brooklyn Bridge or in the narrow aisles of our local supermarket, which smelled like cats. We hashed through our old relationships and what went wrong, we laughed and confessed, and I was super candid about how my relationship with High School Sweetheart went south.

"The Amateur Index?" Jamie asked. "I don't know it. Is it like Persian Kitty?"

I was taken aback. "What's Persian Kitty?"

"Just a compendium of porn links. Not just photos, but videos, even stories. Amateur Index is just, what, amateurs?"

"Uh. Yes."

"I will make a note of it."

We walked across the Brooklyn Bridge, the sun turning everything a perfect orange.

◆

I had been living by myself in a dingy studio in Queens, so dingy that stepping out of my shower onto a mouse happened so often that I could authoritatively say, "Man, I hate stepping out of my shower onto a mouse." In dire financial straits, not able to borrow money from my parents out of pride or stupidity, I moved into Jamie's one-bedroom apartment in Astoria. I also put together a one-man show about my time at the Firm (I called it "Paid to Stand Around," from a Fugazi lyric), and a manager in Los Angeles saw a tape of it and signed me. New York was getting more expensive and feeling smaller and smaller. We both looked around the city and saw relationship ghosts, burnt bridges, and then, just weeks after we moved in together, actual burning buildings, smoke scarring the blue sky on an idyllic Tuesday morning. We lost no one we knew, but we could see the carnage from our roof. Jamie and I held each other a lot that week. As the city gradually began to return to "normal," we both got called in to do a dumb sight gag on *Conan*. We jumped at the chance to work and had a great time doing it. But that was the day somebody mailed anthrax to Tom Brokaw in the same building.

My parents and friends were safe, but the city was starting to feel like my Bedford Falls—a place where fate had stuck me. We did a lot of Ecstasy that fall, and honestly who could blame us? When the autumn air became choked with the smell of burning landmark, and I was thirty, and I wanted to be an actor but could not get seen for *Law & Order*, and I had a manager who had an office in West Hollywood but not one in Manhattan, it seemed clear that it was time to do something really scary again.

The line from the classic if overplayed Kander and Ebb song proclaims that if you "can make it there, (you'll) make it anywhere," and that's likely true, but there's another, less-discussed implication: If you *cannot* make it in New York, there are several other smaller cities that might be more your speed. No shame in that.

It's hard to leave New York City when you were born there—you feel like an ingrate. If you grew up in a small town, felt you had exhausted its possibilities, and then moved because you were restless, no one would blame you. It's your hometown. You're supposed to leave your hometown, even if only for a while. For example, Jamie had left her small town of Swampscott, Massachusetts, and that's fine. There are no songs that glorify Swampscott, Massachusetts, and no romantic comedies that make you say, "It's almost as if Swampscott, Massachusetts, was a *character* in the film." Nobody builds their career dreams around Swampscott, Massachusetts, and no one suggests that you see it before you die. If you leave Swampscott, Massachusetts, no one questions your decision. But if you leave New York? "How could you? You have Broadway and you can get pizza at four A.M. and look at Central Park in the snow! What more could you want?" But the answer was just "Something else."

CHAPTER EIGHT

ALL THE LOOSE OBJECTS

*T*he key to enjoying Los Angeles is to stop comparing it to other places. It's vibrant and occasionally insincere. The weather is so consistently nice it's easy to lose track of time, and by time I mean what *season* it is right now. It's an uneasy mix of suburb and urb, and you will have to maintain a lawn *and* ask a crackhead not to urinate on it. Most places it's just one or the other. But there are some things you can count on. Here's what it's like being in Los Angeles in your thirties.

It means you can find amazing sushi in a completely unprepossessing strip mall in North Hollywood.

It means you see Winona Ryder getting her prescriptions filled at the Rite Aid on Fairfax.

Being in L.A. in your thirties means you can tart up your progressive alcoholism by calling yourself an "oenophile" and discussing the bouquet of whatever pinot grigio you're guzzling.

You *can* surf in the morning and ski in the afternoon if you want, but if you do, we're probably not close friends.

It means you can probably try snuff for the first time (like you're some sort of eighteenth-century hipster fop) in the back of the legendary

Formosa bar in West Hollywood and spend the rest of the night sneezing your eyes out.

You will likely try stand-up again and bomb horribly in front of a small audience that includes David Faustino from *Married . . . with Children*.

It means you can get shrooms from a stand-up comic you know, not have anywhere proper to enjoy them, end up eating them before Hollywood High School's production of *Fiddler on the Roof,* and then find yourself weeping uncontrollably during the pogrom that closes act 1.

You will be able to see every movie you've ever been mildly curious about in a theater if you're patient. Even *Salò, or the 120 Days of Sodom* by Pier Paolo Pasolini, which will shake you to your nauseous foundations, but wow, the Egyptian sure got a nice print.

It means you can see Stevie Wonder at the Hollywood Bowl, which you should, because time is short.

You can gaze at the Giacometti sculptures at LACMA and then walk outside to some of the greatest food trucks of all time on Wilshire.

Living in Los Angeles in your thirties means you can immerse yourself in a city built on dreams and aspirations, many of them foolhardy, but you can still make a living in this huge multicultural city that has cheaper real estate and better Mexican food than New York City or San Francisco.

And it means you can read *Seize the Day* by Saul Bellow and feel the following quote kick you in the chest and then dust you off and tell you you're safe: *In Los Angeles all the loose objects in the country were collected, as if America had been tilted and everything that wasn't tightly screwed down had slid into Southern California.*

CHAPTER NINE

YOU GUYS THINK I KILLED HER?

he beginning of 2002 was a very weird time to drive across the United States. There was a lot of love and desperate partying—we stopped in Memphis and visited Graceland on Elvis's birthday—four years to the day after Egghead. broke up. I recommend visiting Graceland on Elvis' birthday: Play your cards right and you'll have cake and meet the mayor of Memphis, who told me, "In a time of national crisis, there's no better place to be than surrounded by Elvis fans." We ended up so hammered in a New Orleans strip club that I bought Jamie a lap dance so hot a random stranger tipped me! But there was a lot of dumb anger and fear along the trip, too—take, for instance, the roadside shop off Route 66 that sold decorative cow skulls, truck nuts, and swastika flags.

"Let's go. Now," whispered Jamie. "You look very Jewish. Move."

Jamie drove the whole way. I still hadn't learned to drive—I'd taken a couple lessons when we were living in Queens but failed a road test when I blew the parallel parking portion. So Jamie drove her boyfriend, a clinical depressive with comically heavy debt (including owing another grand to his father, just to get started in L.A.), a single film credit, and no driver's license to Los Angeles. We stayed for a

few weeks at Galvin's place—he had established a footing as a screenwriter and was, in fact, making a living—a great little duplex near the
famous Canter's delicatessen. Jamie and I quickly found our own place
and made a very common mistake that New Yorkers make when they
move to Los Angeles: We pounced on a big disgusting apartment just
because it was so big we were able to look past the disgusting. Terrible,
almost greenish lighting, wall-to-wall carpeting that barely concealed
all manner of sins, a picturesque view of a police precinct and a bail
bonds place but *holy shit, two bedrooms!* We lived cheaply at first, eating
breakfast at home in our strangely greasy kitchen or at the IHOP that
was a short drive right down Sunset. One time while sharing a Cinn-
a-Stack there she left her wallet at home, and while I had my wallet
with me, it was useless. There was literally nothing you could do with
anything in there. The credit cards were maxed and the debit card
connected to nothing, so, as I had no driver's license and therefore no
government-issued ID, my wallet was just dead pig flesh in my pocket
and might as well have been a paperweight. Jamie hopped in her visibly
exhausted Corolla and drove back to Hollywood to grab her wallet,
leaving me at IHOP as collateral.

I looked out the window on Sunset Boulevard, only a few miles
from where Norma Desmond lived. Not quite the fabled strip—that
starts down on Laurel or maybe Fairfax. I had not expected to be
welcomed with open arms by Los Angeles, but the sudden impatience
of Los Angeles was personified by the waitress. "Is she coming back?
Do you want more coffee? Do you want the check? Are you just going
to sit there or what? *What are you doing here? Do you think you can be
an actor without any formal training? Who the fuck do you think you are?*"

This was to be my first pilot season, and it was a deeply unusual
one—9/11's aroma seeped into scripts, even the comedies, and there
was a lot of material that took place in news stations, or in embassies,
or even, in the case of the first script that landed on my doorstep, in the

federal prosecutor's office in Lower Manhattan. The script—*A.U.S.A.*—literally landed on my doorstep, as we weren't sending PDFs around just yet, so you got the whole script as a hard copy with the audition sides tucked in.

Wally Berman, late 20s—overweight, not particularly bright but good natured. PLEASE SUBMIT ALL ETHNICITIES.

"Did you get the script?" asked Joel, my manager. Younger than me. Perpetually well-dressed.

"Yeah, I, uh, I haven't had a chance to read it yet—"

"Do not worry about the fat part, they've seen your picture, they still want to see you tomorrow."

I read the script; a young, naïve law school grad named Adam Sullivan goes to work as an AUSA (assistant United States attorney) in Lower Manhattan (it would shoot on the Fox lot in Century City). My character was the dim paralegal assigned to our hero. It was a single-cam comedy in the vein of *Scrubs*, and the scuttlebutt on the street (I heard, like, one other actor say this) was that it was essentially *Scrubs* for lawyers.

I would like that, I thought. I could watch *Scrubs* with lawyers. Shit, my dad loves *Scrubs*. What if his son was on *Scrubs* with lawyers? Plus, the show was written by a guy named Rich Appel, who had written for *The Simpsons*! (He had, it turned out, written some pretty amazing *Simpsons* episodes, including the one where Homer's mother (Glenn Close) returns, and we reveal in a flashback that Kent Brockman used to go by Kenny Brocklestein, which was one of those Simpsons jokes that could cause the viewer to hold his head and walk around the room sighing at the show's brilliance.) It got better—the pilot was to be directed by Michael Lehmann, whose feature debut was *Heathers*, a film so near and dear to my heart that I have since written an entire book about it. It felt like every one of my passions was converging on this one show. This job was so dreamy I could not wait to not get it.

I'd had an acting teacher named Caryn West, and she was terrific. As of this writing, she still teaches, and she's great for sitcom auditioning because she reminds you of a couple key points: one, sitcoms are rooted in the commedia dell'arte tradition, and as such the characters are broad archetypes—there's room for nuance, sure, and you can dimensionalize it all you want, but it goes back to the trickster Harlequino, the buffoonish Il Dottore, etc. The other thing Caryn reminds her students is that the producers have a problem (no actor for the role) and they need you to fix it (be the actor for the role). They are counting on you. They are, no matter how awful they act in the session, no matter how glued to their computers or salads they seem to be, rooting for you to come in and plug the Wally-sized hole in their show so it actually gets shot and then, God willing, goes to series.

So. Wally. Wally, on the page, is dumb. REALLY dumb. A paraphrased exchange from the pilot:

WALLY: I'm just a dumb guy. I even have a dumb name.
            Wally. See? Dumb guy.
ADAM: You know what's not a dumb name? Walter.
WALLY: *(Beat)* Hey, that's my name.
ADAM: No, I know—
WALLY: From my mother—Walter—
ADAM: I understand—
WALLY: Wally's like a . . . nickname.

And so on. So I figured there's only a couple of ways to play this role. One is to lean into the dumb and try to bring a bit of Joey Tribbiani into it, but *Friends* was still on the air, indeed on this very network, and Matt LeBlanc was very good at that, and as much as networks like more of the same, they don't really want their evenings filled with Xeroxes of other shows. So. Caryn would ask you to fill in this blank. "Wally is the most _____ person in the world." This would take you to the raw archetype at the core of the character, and you can build from there.

Happy. Wally is the most happy person in the world. An actor who lives with depression might equate "happy" with "dumb" more than is wise, but this was my way into the guy. This was how I would put my best foot forward and then lose the role to someone more famous or better-looking.

As much as producers want you to fix their problems, they also really want to cover their own asses, so you will go through several steps in order to actually book a pilot. The first—and this is unavoidable if you are new to the town (and indeed the business)—is called a pre-read. Rob Corddry drove me to mine (he was in town shooting *his* first major gig, the frat comedy *Old School*). A pre-read is just you, the casting director, and an assistant who's running the camera. It's an airlock, a security check—a gate kept by a gatekeeper to keep the crazies away from the higher-ups.

The 20th Century Fox lot sits in the center of Century City, a mostly industrial chunk of land just west of Beverly Hills.* It's all law firms and agencies and a couple of hotels and skyscrapers—and yes, that's Nakatomi Plaza popping up off the skyline near Pico Boulevard. *Die Hard* works because it's all businesses in Century City, and there are very few residences within its confines (and there were even fewer when *Die Hard* was shooting), and yes, it's very possible it would be dark and quiet at night, particularly on Christmas Eve. It was bright and quiet the day of my pre-read, a brisk Saturday morning in February 2002 (but an L.A. brisk, which is to say forty degrees warmer than Queens at that moment). Corddry dropped me at the gate on the corner of—and

---

* The show was a co-production of 20th Century Fox Studios and NBC network—a very common cost-saving measure that is still a little confusing. I don't know enough about the economics of it, but very few shows are owned and operated by the same studio and network. *The Simpsons* is one.

this is the God's honest truth—Galaxy and Avenue of the Stars, and I found the entrance. I submitted my ID—my passport. They handed me a pass and a map of the lot, which takes up a couple of city blocks, including the actual fake city blocks where they shot the exteriors on *NYPD Blue.*

The casting director, a thirtysomething woman with a cute short blond haircut, met me at one of the bungalows that line the western part of the lot and managed to be perky but also kind of distant; it was Saturday morning on the Fox lot, no one wanted to be there, and she was swimming through actors of various qualifications all morning. There were tons of us in the waiting room—anonymous to the casting director and to each other. She called my name, smiled politely, and led me into her office, where it was just me and her and a silent assistant running the camera. She sat on a couch; I stood across from her. I could feel my heartbeat in my eyes. We began the scenes, with her reading all of the other parts: Wally is introduced, we discover that he only has the job because his father knew somebody,* and then Wally has his dark night of the soul where it is revealed he is actually *Walter.* Since I was already pretty nervous, I used it: I incorporated a nervous giggle into the sides, even going so far as to discreetly wipe my lower lip in case I had drooled in my enthusiasm. The casting director clocked that, gave a sort of shocked laugh, and when we were done, she stared at me for a few of the longer seconds of my life before she said anything.

"I'm going to producers!" I announced to Rob when I got back in his car.

"Cool!" He exclaimed. "What . . . what does that mean, exactly?"

"It's a callback, I guess. That was just the casting director, now I get to meet the producers and read in front of them?"

---

* In the lengthy backstory I had devised for the character, Wally's father had been a secret lover of former New York mayor Ed Koch.

"Cool! Congratulations!" Rob said and then took me for sushi.

The producers session was the following week. Jamie drove me, and we got to park on the lot this time. This was striking—there was a different class of actor here. I recognized some of these guys, even knew a couple names. Guys who had been in the *American Pie* movies. Guys who had been series regulars before. Guys who were from England! This was profoundly uncharted territory. Here be dragons.

Here was Rich Appel, boyish, energetic, maybe a little shorter than me. He greeted me with a smile and a "Thanks for coming in." I did the sides again, and he laughed—a sort of surprised laugh. I had apparently approached a joke—a joke he had written—in a manner that he did not expect. It was probably the drool bit.

"That. Was. Great," said Rich. "Thank you so much!"

The casting director gave me an excited little smile, much like the smile a friend gives you when it's clear a pretty girl likes you.

At home in Hollywood a few hours later. Sirens often. Also black mold. But two bathrooms! My phone rang. It was Joel, my manager.

"They want to test you!"

"Oh?" I had a vague idea what that meant. At the very least I had cleared another hurdle.

"Do you have a quote?"

"Um . . . 'a decent actor who is easy to work with'?"

"John."

"No, I don't." A quote is a polite way of saying "a price"—literally how much you charge for your acting services rendered in a pilot, the same way a mechanic looks at your car and gives you a quote for how much it's going to cost to replace your catalytic converter. It's a little more abstract and inexact in casting; it's a number indicating how much your agents think you are worth. There is a union minimum for such things, but most people—even newcomers—are paid well above scale for a series regular role. I had no quote. I had no starting point. I was a blank slate. My manager said he'd figure something out and call me back. Jamie had been through this process before and explained what she could.

"Ugh. The way testing for a pilot works: your representation and the network's business affairs department decide on your quote—how much you'll get paid for the pilot, then how much you'll get paid for each episode. And for how many seasons—usually the contract is for three, and then you renegotiate."

"Like *Friends*?"

She smiled. "Slow down."

"Yes, obviously . . ."

"But yes. Then you sign the contract."

"After I get the job?"

"That's why I said 'ugh.' You sign the contract before you go and do the scenes in front of the executives from the studio. If that goes well, you then do it in front of the executives from the network. If *that* goes well, you get the job, and *then* the network signs the contract. If it does not go well, you don't get the job, and the network tears up the contract."

"So I know exactly how much money is at stake for possibly the next three years of life, and they have my signature and essentially all the cards."

And Jamie paraphrased the line from *Jerry Maguire* that an actor forgets at their own peril: "Is it called 'show friends'? No. It's called 'show business.'"

The amount of money settled on was, for me, at the time, astronomical. For anyone who's ever taught public school, it bordered on obscene. I gasped when I heard the figure. I was raised Episcopalian, so I simply can't go into numbers (Could you imagine? Dear God, how gauche) but my fee for a pilot could put me in a Mercedes-Benz C-Class, and my fee per episode could put me in a responsible Camry. Every week. Were I able to drive.

Now, of course, the dumbest thing in the world you can do with your pilot fee is go out and buy a new Mercedes-Benz—you will have to pay commissions to your manager, agent, and/or lawyer, and you will owe taxes on it in a year. Also, you always have to remember that show business is slightly more mercurial than most industries and that this money is not necessarily going to keep coming, so set some aside for the lean times to come. But still. Jesus. My pilot fee was going to be almost what I made in a year at the Firm, never mind what I made as a teacher. And if you multiplied it by an average network season of twenty-two episodes and then multiplied that by three seasons—there was an incredible amount of money on the table. A guilt-inducing amount.

I told no one. Not my parents—"LA's fine. Weather's amazeballs." Nor my friends—"A little weird. Still finding my footing. I saw Matthew McConaughey jogging shirtless at a place called Runyon Canyon!" No one needed to know what I was headed in for; no one needed to know what was at stake. I would just not get it and then mention casually, "Oh, yeah, I got close on a pilot, but they went with someone else," or better yet, I would just take the story to my grave. I showed up back at the 20th Century Fox studios for the studio test; the network was later in the afternoon.

"OK. These are executives—they're not always big laughers," explained Joel on the phone. "So don't get freaked out. This is gonna be fine. Just go in and do what you did at the first audition."

The walk to the offices is a blur. It was still February, but it was Los Angeles, so I was still perfectly capable of sweating profusely, from my pits, temples, and ass crack. Why did I wear khakis and a shirt and tie? Because the show takes place in New York City and my character works in an office, and I'm a goddam professional who's going to look the part that he's about to not get.

In the climate-controlled offices of the studio building—airier than the corporate offices of my twenties, the vibe closer to publishing than it was to consulting or pharmaceuticals—people seemed more relaxed, people were dressed more casually. It is *not* called show friends, it's called show business, but the business was telling stories, and the business was making people laugh. There was a breeziness in the office. A receptionist took me to a waiting room outside a corner office—warmly lit hallways and the occasional blast of laughter from a cubicle. Not even an office, a cubicle! People in cubicles were enjoying themselves! Everyone seemed in generally good—

"John!"

"Hi, yes, hello!"

We're ready, gestured the casting director with a warm smile. I walked past the other actor, a kind of doughy guy with a bad haircut that actually might have been a choice. *That's a good choice*, I thought, wondering if I, too, should have gotten a bad haircut before the test.

I'd love to take you through the process . . . but I remember so little. Everything was a very intense beige.

I was in a fugue state—I had run the scenes so many times it was like I was on autopilot, outside looking in, yet still unable to recall much of anything from that morning.

Or that afternoon, because shortly after the studio test, I got a call that I had cleared that gauntlet and was now on my way to network (the final obstacle). In one of the NBC buildings I read the scene again in front of different executives, one of whom was Jeff Zucker, then president of NBC. I did the scenes. Got some laughs. Made it through the whole process without having a panic attack. This felt like an achievement.

I had taken cabs to everything all day, but you couldn't get a cab to drive up to NBC—it's a weird intersection with something like five inroads and "no standing" signs everywhere—so I walked across the street to the Wienerschnitzel (a hot dog chain I'd only heard of in a particularly juvenile Descendents song) to get a nice cold soda when the phone rang. It was Joel. I flipped my phone open (2002!) and said, "Hey, man."

"Hey," he said, his voice emotionless. "How'd it go?"

"Um, good, I guess? I don't really know? I felt good about it."

"Well"—and on this I literally heard him smile—"you don't have to feel good about it, because *you got it*."

My knees buckled. I reached out and put my hand on the nearest car, and then immediately yanked it back because New York taught me that nobody likes strangers touching their cars. A flood of information and questions came at me: Wardrobe is going to call you; Rich Appel wants your contact info; are you going to be able to get to set?

The first table read was back at Fox, and the whole cast was assembled—the amiable Scott Foley, fresh off four years of *Felicity*, was playing our lead, Adam, the naïve young federal prosecutor; beautiful, doe-eyed, and classically trained Amanda Detmer (who had been hilariously killed in *Final Destination* the year before) was his romantic interest, Susan; guys' guy Eddie McClintock, who appeared to have been in every sitcom at least once, was the layabout roommate; and Peter Jacobson, a terrific New York stage actor whom I'd seen kill it in an off-Broadway play several years before, was our boss. The whole cast was great, but I had a blooming talent crush on Jacobson, a Juilliard grad who had done Shakespeare in the Park. To think that I was to be counted next to someone with those credentials gave me a weird thrill mixed with no small amount of imposter syndrome. And yet, he could not have been nicer or more gracious to this complete fucking imposter.

We shot the pilot in a week in late February. Still lacking a license, I took the subway and then walked through Skid Row to our downtown L.A. set, which terrified the producers. I'd seen worse devastation in New York in the seventies, but Foley gave me a ride home (he had the nicest car I'd ever seen; it was nicer than most people's houses), and then production arranged for me to get transportation to and from my apartment for the rest of the week. ("Do you understand me, John?" I was scolded. "No more subway. Ask for help if you need it.") The shoot was amazing; the show was not perfect—very few pilots are—but it was subtle and there were gorgeous flourishes of *Simpsons*-style absurdity throughout. (Jacobson played Foley's boss, a blue blood who wore two sets of suits throughout the day, one bespoke around the office and one shabby when he was in front of a jury because "you don't want these people resenting you.") My work made the crew laugh, which any actor will tell you is the highest compliment possible on a set—the focus pullers can be super jaded, and getting a smile from them is no easy feat. The resulting twenty-two minutes were sweet and sharp and set up some rich characters.

Jeff Zucker didn't like it.

He liked the idea, but he didn't like single-camera comedies, he vastly preferred shows where you could hear an audience laugh. His most recent innovation was taking "must-see TV" and "super sizing" it, so an episode of *Friends* would be a full ten minutes longer. The pilot he was really jazzed about that spring was called *Good Morning, Miami*, and it was about a young news producer who takes over a Florida morning show, which is very much what Jeff Zucker had done before becoming the head of NBC.

But *A.U.S.A.* was not dead! We were to reshoot the pilot as a multi-cam in front of a studio audience that summer, and then resubmit it for reconsideration. This meant getting paid again and getting to do the show again in a completely different format.

By this point I had *finally* learned to drive—much to Jamie's delight—and, being suddenly flush with cash, I paid back my father, bought a used Honda, and deleted my student loan with one extravagant flourish (a three-thousand-dollar check with a memo that read CHOKE ON IT YOU VAMPIRES). I was enjoying driving timidly around

Los Angeles, and took great pride in joining in generic traffic-related bitching with friends and co-workers ("Jesus, the 10 was a beast this afternoon. Just a parking lot all the way to Crenshaw.") I could not believe my good fortune, and I was learning a ton about the business. Shooting the two pilots—and studying the shift between two formats of television comedy—was fascinating.

"There's gonna be a tendency to want to go bigger in our performances," Jacobson said to me in a way that was informative but not condescending. "But I think that's a trap." We talked a lot about balancing acting for the camera and acting for the audience, and I all but sat at the hem of his garment and soaked in his wisdom. I was in Los Angeles making a living as an actor, working with *Simpsons* writers on a show that was, like *Rhoda*, set in Manhattan but shot in Los Angeles. Absolutely everything was going right.

And then, bit by bit, absolutely everything started to go wrong.

First: the conversion to multi-cam had broadened the tone of the show, and some of the subtlety was shaved away. The runner about Jacobson's suits was gone. A climactic scene near the end still included the Walter/Wally moment but now also included a bit of forced physical comedy wherein I brandished a stapler as a weapon against an aggressive FBI agent. It was fun to do, and the pilot audience really dug it, but it seemed a little . . . overdone to me. That said, someone told one of my castmates that we had a guaranteed hit, so that castmate promptly leased a Porsche.

A second red flag: We'd had a single person of color in the first cast, a deliriously handsome guy who'd worked on soaps and could not have been cooler. He was fired for reasons that were never adequately explained to me. He was replaced with a woman of color for the multi-cam taping, and she had two scenes and didn't make much of an impression. When we got picked for twelve episodes that fall, there was yet a third attempt at diversity, this time in the form of a stunning

Nuyorican named Ana Ortiz, with whom I promptly became good friends. But it was weird, this seeming fungibility of ethnic types, and the steady recasting felt like bullets whooshing past my head.

Jamie—who was having an almost exact opposite experience in Los Angeles, not booking auditions and getting audited by the IRS—was flipping out about her own bad luck but very sanguine about mine.

"Just keep doing good work. Head down, cooperate. You're killing it."

Wally didn't get the zingers, the Rhoda-level witticisms. He got the non sequiturs and the specifically confused moments of the sitcom dummies. I am not complaining. This was precisely what I moved to California to do—make a living as an actor, at something I loved, and be good at it. And I was apparently excelling at being a sitcom dummy.

Zucker came to every taping, effusively shaking my hand. People liked what I was doing. People said things like "You're going to be a star" and "John, you are the Kramer of this thing."* I was flattered but not sure; I'd watched too much TV to think that we actually had a guaranteed hit on our hands. The show was good and we had a very solid cast—Ana was a terrific addition, and Scott was everything you wanted in a straight man, flexing dry comedic muscles that *Felicity* never gave him a chance to show. But there were so many cooks at this point that the show's tone was erratic and some of the jokes handed down from on high were . . . not great. I don't blame Rich or his coterie of writers (there were a ton of *Simpsons* alums on staff, including George Meyer, Brent Forrester, and Greg Daniels, although Forrester got so

---

* This was before Michael Richards imploded his career by hurling the N-word around the Laugh Factory like so much confetti—it was still a good thing to be the Kramer of something.

frustrated with the process he quit).* No, most of the lame comedy came from Jeff Zucker.

Premiere day rolled around, February 4, 2003. The reviews were tepid—the *New York Times* review reads like a cry for help. A NEW SITCOM BLESSED FOR WHAT IT ISN'T was the headline, and it sort of damned us with faint praise for not being another reality show. There was one highlight though: the old Gray Lady, the paper of record, said that Wally was "played with considerable finesse by John Ross Bowie."

I had never been told I had "considerable finesse"—indeed, any finesse—by anyone. I had once injured myself in the testicles playing air guitar, for fuck's sake, and here I was being praised with a word often reserved for ballet dancers or pastry chefs. It would have been nice had the whole show garnered such praise, but it was awfully sweet to be singled out.

I told my dad in a phone call. He had a typically conservative take on the *Times*, which resulted in a bemused "So, Pravda West liked you?"

Eleven million people watched the premiere that Tuesday night when we aired after *Frasier*. At the time, these were mediocre numbers. Nowadays those numbers guarantee you five seasons and a lucrative syndication deal. But in a pre-streaming economy with only a handful of original shows on cable, 11 million was just . . . *OK*. Also, my dad thought the "laugh track" was too loud, which was frustrating, as there was no laugh track; I explained that that was an actual studio audience, and perhaps they were overenthused, sure. But he maintained that it was distracting.

"Well, regardless. I'll pass that on. We're gonna be on *Entertainment Tonight!*" I added.

"Who?"

---

* Worth mentioning that Forrester wrote *Homerpalooza*, the *Simpsons* episode that Egghead. watched on tour. I was so awed by this credit that I never even mentioned it to him.

"The cast! All of us. Tonight at seven."

"Ah," Dad replied. "We watch the French news at seven." Both my father and Carol spoke French (Carol fluently) and kept this skill up by watching *l'actualité la nuit.*

"Well, if you decide not to, your son will be interviewed on *Entertainment Tonight.*"

The *Entertainment Tonight* interview was maybe three minutes—a small camera crew wandered around the main office set, we all introduced ourselves, and Foley fielded a lot of questions, many about his then wife, *Alias* star Jennifer Garner. I gave my best—I like doing interviews, and I like bantering with a host, and I always think about sitting in a dismal North Carolina hotel room watching MTV with Mike Faloon when he sagaciously said, "Fame is wasted on the wrong people." The segment went well.

Dad watched it and said it was "fine." He had designed this fascinating cocktail of pride and condescension. It might have been the aforementioned jealousy. Or just not understanding how his son could be making that kind of money while still enjoying himself. And of course there's absolutely no way he could have known how much money I was making . . . had I not told him.

It came up organically, sort of. I had asked him for a loan before leaving New York, just so I wouldn't have to completely lean on Jamie, and he had come through, and I had promptly paid him back. Now—having just seen me on TV—he was telling me not to let things go too long before I asked for more money. This felt like something deeper than patronizing, this was some sort of Corleonesque power move that I was going to have to squash immediately, now and forever.

I told him what I was making.

"Per episode?" he asked, after a truly delicious pause.

"Yes."

"Well," he said. "Very well. Wow."

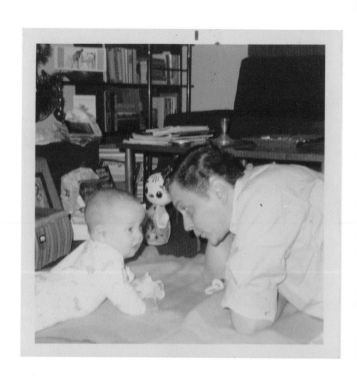

ABOVE: Dad and I. Trying to see eye to eye. BELOW: Christmas 1979 with the original Broadway cast recording of *Sweeney Todd: The Demon Barber of Fleet Street.*

ABOVE: Tenth or eleventh birthday—my parents splurged and got me one of those horse-drawn carriage rides around Central Park and the guy let me drive which was exhilarating but in hindsight maybe a terrible idea. BELOW: At the Lincoln Center, having just seen *The Mikado* with my parents in 1977. My parents were still married. People wore beige.

ABOVE: It's hard to pick the worst school photo of my childhood, but 1981's submission is a strong contender. OPPOSITE: High School for the Humanities, class of 1989. SC stands for Stage Crew (of which I was technically captain, I guess), *Humanitarian* was the school newspaper for which I reviewed new Ramones records, and *Lard* was the zine I had with several friends. "Oner" was a tag on a tag—graffiti writers would put that at the end of their own tags as an indication that they were one of a kind. Jim Nachlin wrote it in my yearbook.

John R. Bowie

SC 10-12 capt; Hum 11, 12;
Lard 11-12
This world is full of people who
think a lot about bowling balls.
                    -The Dead Milkmen

ABOVE: Egghead. at CBGB in 1996. BELOW: Naked Babies, 1999. Seth Morris, Rob Corddry, me, and Brian Huskey, who set a timer on his camera.

ABOVE: Jamie and I celebrating our first Halloween together, fall 2000. She had a Marilyn costume. She suggested I go as Joe DiMaggio. The Yankees had just beat my Mets in a Subway Series. "Fuck no," I said, setting clear boundaries. We compromised and I went as Arthur Miller. BELOW: Crowd-surfing during an Egghead. acoustic set. Baltimore, 2007. *Photo by James Kim.*

"The Killer Robot Instability," filmed in 2008, aired in 2009. Barry Kripke's first appearance in *The Big Bang Theory*. Back Row: Kunal Nayyar, Johnny Galecki, Jim Parsons, me. Front Row: Mobile Omnidirectional Neutralization and Termination Eradicator (M.O.N.T.E.).

There is a misconception that acting is an all-or-nothing game—you are either making a million dollars for a week's work, or you are waiting tables and hoping no one suggests you pool your tips. I had firmly ensconced myself in the less-discussed middle ground.

And that was the last time my father and I discussed money in any meaningful sense.

I met Corddry for a lot of drinks later that night, and he suggested I meet my father halfway and do something to get on the French news myself.

"Kill Gérard Depardieu?"

Corddry nodded. "Yeah, something in that area."

I mimed being led away in handcuffs, screaming at the camera, "Aime-moi!!" and we both laughed.

◆

My mom called every Wednesday to tell me how much she liked the previous night's episode. She even claimed that she heard people talking about it on the street ("We've gotta get home to watch *A.U.S.A.*!"), which was *very* unlikely but was the sort of lie one appreciates because it came from a well-intentioned place. I was still enjoying the work, the audiences were fun and warm, I was getting my laughs and putting a little backspin on jokes to surprise the writers with their own material, but the ratings were starting to slip. Castmates had taken to crying in their dressing rooms. Jacobson missed his wife, who was back home in New York. On top of everything else, two key marriages on the production were unravelling. Everyone was the pinnacle of professionalism, but there was a clenched-teeth bitterness filling the air wherever you went. People were concerned that the show just wasn't funny enough, and signs were posted in the writers' room that encouraged the staff to focus less on legal procedure and more on jokes. As such, the signs read:

LESS PERRY MASON, MORE JACKIE MASON

and

LESS LEGALESE, MORE GIGGLES PLEASE

We had a new director every two weeks—not unusual in TV, but what was striking was how often they, too, were replaced midweek. An East Coast law magazine summed us up as *"A.U.S.A.*—Another Useless Stereotyped Attorney."

The network had ordered twelve episodes. They then cut the order short based on our declining ratings, shot ten, and aired eight. Foley was served with divorce papers on the very same day we got canceled in May 2003. At the end of the TV season, *Variety* posted the results of two polls: one was a list of shows that their readers wanted to see renewed, one was a list of shows that their readers wanted to see canceled.

A.U.S.A. was on neither list. People did not care if we lived or died.

Rich Appel had been an assistant United States attorney. He'd written a spec script for HBO's groundbreaking comedy *The Larry Sanders Show* on the side and gotten his *Simpsons* gig that way, but writing a show about his time as a federal prosecutor had always been a dream of his. That dream came together and then fell apart, while *Good Morning, Miami* got a second season. Like most TV shows, every episode of *A.U.S.A.* cost around $1 million to make, give or take. The show employed some two hundred people, to say nothing of incredible guest stars (David Proval from *Mean Streets*! Kathryn Joosten from *The West Wing*! Robert Guillaume from *Benson*, although he, too, got suspiciously recast!) and all the people at the network who were dedicated to our promotion and accounting. And this goes for most shows—for every *Friends* or *Big Bang Theory*, there are dozens of shows that people pour their hearts and time into the work—or try to, anyway. And despite all this . . . it's gone, it doesn't stream anywhere, you can't find it on DVD. All that work sort of just . . . vanished.

(As did *Good Morning, Miami*, a season later.)

Don't read this as bitter—it's honestly not, although I don't wish Jeff Zucker (recently deposed head of CNN as I write this, giver of unlimited screen time to Donald Trump until an inappropriate relationship at work forced his resignation) well. There is work that vanishes into the ether in every field, even architecture, but this was the first time I'd been really invested in a job and watched it go away. And despite this, I had been good at something, it had paid well, and I wanted to keep doing it.

◆

Back at home, Jamie and I got a dog—a rescue pug that we got at an adoption fair also attended by small dog enthusiast Mickey Rourke—and we named him Yohei, after the sad-faced farmer in *Seven Samurai*. The dog was clearly, openly an experiment. Jamie and I were living together, we were talking about marriage—the logical next step was *let's see if we can keep a thing alive*. Ideally, a dog, before we took the plunge and decided to have kids. The dog thrived, curling up in bed with us like a barely sentient hot water bottle. I had had hamsters as a child, but those last two years and are easy to maintain. Dogs have emotions, needs, and energy. Jamie and I argued over the care and training of Yohei, but never in a meaningful way, and it was centering and peaceful to walk around our neighborhood with him on a leash, pre-smartphones, just stopping when he stopped and smelling the cool night air.

There was no disagreement that couldn't be instantly abated by her saying, "When I say Shabu, you say Shabu. Shabu!"

"Shabu!"

"*Shabu!*"

"*Shabu!*" And then we'd both walk down to the Shabu Shabu place at Hollywood and Highland, where you could cook your own meat in a pot of boiling water with your hot, funny girlfriend.

Jamie and I were married the following year, in June 2004. Rich Appel was unable to attend the wedding, but he sent an original *Simpsons* animation cel featuring Krusty the Clown, with a beautiful inscription telling me that, like Krusty, I was "a true original." It now hangs in our son's room.

The wedding was held in Boston and was a fun buffet of our backgrounds: We got married under a traditional Jewish chuppah, the canopy that hangs over the bride and groom and yet is open on all four sides as a sign of welcome—and our chuppah and the men's yarmulkes were made of the Bowie family tartan. "Mazel tov!" everyone said as I crushed the glass, and the piper-for-hire escorted us out with "Wild Mountain Thyme," because he swore that one simply could not play "Sunrise, Sunset" from *Fiddler* on the bagpipes. My father was unable to stand for most of the service. Thanks to a lifetime of smoking, his lungs were losing their elasticity with increasing speed, down to something like 25 percent of their capacity. Now wheelchair bound, he got out of his chair just for photos and a brief moment during the service. No one from my family spoke—Mom seemed to hide during the speeches, and my father quite literally just saved his breath—but Jamie's dad gave a sweet speech with a lot of Yiddish, and Corddry's best man toast was funny and warm. Ana Ortiz sang "Somewhere" from *West Side Story*. Dad stayed sober, as he had stopped drinking due to a calcified pancreas a couple of years before. I didn't drink much, but I made up for it on our Hawaiian honeymoon. We called in favors from old friends and got most of Conan O'Brien's band to play the reception, and as they bounced through "Love Train" by the

O'Jays, I danced with my new bride and was a very happy adult. Get on board.

◆

For a show that is largely forgotten, *A.U.S.A.* still opened doors—to have been a series regular, even just for ten episodes, is to be in a slightly exclusive club, and I immediately was thrust into the world of guest work, popping into shows to play co-workers, jilted lovers, or, as was often the case, murder suspects. This was actually what I expected and desired when I moved to L.A.—steady work as a "that guy" character actor, playing the geometry teacher on *Joan of Arcadia* (mouthfuls of dialogue about math and a lengthy tracking shot—very exciting!). Playing a beleaguered Bob Cratchit type opposite Tim Allen (complimentary of my comedic skills and perfectly pleasant on a day when he was out of his Santa Claus drag—apparently after four hours of makeup and wardrobe, most days he would emerge from his trailer a very irritable Kris Kringle which is, by any estimation, hilarious) in *The Santa Clause 3*. Another cut-proof scene—my dialogue might as well have been "Pay attention, sir, or the last ten minutes of this movie won't make any sense!" This felt like temping, but this time the ronin samurai was a bit better at his job and enjoyed it more.

There was a distinct period of time in my mid to late thirties when I was making a very solid living playing guys who were accused of murder but were very quickly judged to be far too incompetent to have actually committed the crime. My hand to God, almost every one of these audition sides contained the line "Wait—you guys think I killed her?" and this became such a frequently deployed trope that I started to have fun with it, switching the emphasis to shift the meaning and amuse only myself.

"Wait—you guys think *I* killed her?" was the fairly straightforward police procedural reading, suggesting that the speaker could not believe he was being accused of this. Probably the best way to deliver the line.

"Wait—you guys think I *killed* her?" A creepier interpretation, suggesting that yes, some shit went down, but I didn't kill anybody, how dare you suggest such a thing?

"Wait—you guys think I killed *her*?" Hands down the ickiest delivery, rife with a strong subtext that sure, I've taken a life or two, but not hers.

I booked a few of these—getting interrogated by Gary Sinise (consummate pro, and one of the handful of actors who introduced himself to me and welcomed me warmly to set) on *CSI: New York*, and playing a skeezy con artist on location in Florida on a short-lived show called *The Glades*. I even got to be the actual killer once on an episode of *Monk*. They spend the hour trying to pin the murder of a prostitute on a cult leader played by Howie Mandel, and at the end Tony Shalhoub (actor's actor, couldn't be kinder, told rich stories of working with the Coen brothers) figures out it was actually the guy who first reported the killing—me. After years of suspect work, I was finally led away in handcuffs at the end of an episode.

There were also a staggering number of roles in which I played the dork who shows the audience how rough it is out there for single women—imagine! Being stuck on a date with this sad sack! Watch the film *Because I Said So* carefully; I'm in one of those dating montages. Diane Keaton (incredible, literally sitting across from Annie Hall; she still has that halting cadence) interviews prospective suitors for her daughter and comes across a guy who can't stop spitting the peanuts he's shoveling into his mouth. That's me. And you know why Diane Keaton is incredible? Why she's an icon with an Oscar? Because she insisted I wasn't spitting enough, and she was right, and on the next take I fucking showered Kay Corleone with peanut shavings. It was beyond gross and much funnier.

My father watched most of my stuff—even, on occasion, complimenting my work on random shows like the UPN's *Kevin Hill*, where

I played such a loser that I was suing a dating service because they'd been unable to find anyone for me.

"That was really moving work, Tiger," my father said over lunch. It was early spring of 2005. Jamie and I were on one of our biannual trips—a tradition we'd established when we first moved to L.A.—back to New York. He had taken a cab to the restaurant, only a few blocks from his apartment, as walking was out of the question.

"Wow. Thank you, Dad."

"The main guy is kind of a dud, though."

"Taye Diggs? I dunno . . . I think he has a sort of . . . appealing naturalism."

"Eh. I just found him sort of wooden."

"OK, well, agree to disagree, I guess."

Jamie stepped in. "Your son is doing great, Bruce. Very solid steady work. He's certainly working more than I am."

"Really?"

"Yeah," I said. "The business, like a lot of businesses, can be rough for women."

And my father shrugged, and then he said, "That makes no sense. You've got great jugs."

Jamie was not nearly as offended as I was. I was mortified. Purple with embarrassment and rage, I seemed to leave my body, the shell remaining just staring at him dumbly. I didn't know what to say. I felt a little dizzy and lost my appetite for my half-finished lunch. My father apparently did not realize anything was wrong, and while I recognize that there is a certain generational misunderstanding about what constitutes flirting, this was his daughter-in-law.*

---

* A week later, my therapist would remark, "I'm sorry to use this word, but what your father did? That's just . . . that's just retarded. It speaks of an actual cognitive delay. Again, I'm sorry to use the word, but I can't think of another one."

And then, shifting gears with a whiplash carelessness, my dad asked, "You ever think about doing Shakespeare?"

"Um. Of course I do, Dad."

"Don't you want to do Shakespeare?"

The idea—exceedingly common among actors' parents—that we just get to go to some sort of actors hall and sign up for the jobs we want (Shakespeare! Marvel movie! Series regular on a show set in a hospital because those run forever!) is infuriating. It ignores gatekeepers and economic realities with a naïveté that would be scoffed at in any other profession. You never say to the junior counsel, "Wouldn't you rather be partner?"

"I'd love to do Shakespeare, but there are several things standing in my way. One, no degree in theater. Two, Shakespeare, especially in Los Angeles, is not being done that often. Three, Shakespeare on TV or in the movies? Strictly the purview of movie stars who are looking to stretch themselves."

"Still. Might be nice," he said.

"Yes," I replied, tight-lipped, quietly resentful in the manner of my mother. "It might. I'll keep trying."

A week later he called me. "You said something weird the other day, Tiger."

"I did?"

"At the end of lunch, when we hugged," and he lifted the word "hug" a little, clearly embarrassed by the vision of two men hugging, "you said, 'Watch your mouth.'"

"Well, yeah. That was probably in reference to you commenting on my wife's breasts."

"Oh," he said, lightly thoughtful, as if I'd not called him out on something egregiously inappropriate but had instead introduced him to an as-yet-undiscovered tie knot.

"Well," he said. "Sorry about that."

CHAPTER TEN

GENUINELY FAKE NEWS

s my father grew older and less ambulatory, emphysema
shortening his breath with a creeping persistence, each
"exacerbation" grimly benchmarked with a number ("I've
only got about 40 percent of my lung capacity working, Tiger"),
he took great refuge and solace in cable TV. His viewing habits were
eclectic—there was some Fox News in there, certainly, leading to
his firm belief that climate change was a myth, because "the climate
has been changing for centuries," but he also watched MTV (which
brought about clarifying follow-up questions like, "Morrissey is the
same guy from the Smiths, right?") and Comedy Central. And for all
his right-wing bona fides, he loved *The Daily Show with Jon Stewart*.
And he particularly loved my friend Rob Corddry's work as a correspondent on it.

"Rob had the funniest bit last night" went a typical phone call with
my dad. "Did you see it?"

I had. Rob had been interviewing some right-wing politician with
a history of misogynist comments and had hilariously sunk to the guy's
level. "Yeah, it was pretty—"

"That moment when he put the baseball cap on and started chugging beers, saying 'I don't trust anything that bleeds for five days and doesn't die' was *beautiful*."

"I mean, yeah. I mean. That's Rob sort of . . . doing a character, he's not really that boorish in real life."

"No, I know, I know, I remember him from the wedding. Just tell him I think he's doing a great job."

"I will."

"So. How are you?"

"Eh. I'm OK. I drove up to Van Nuys today for another audition for *The Office*."*

"Oh? Have you heard anything?"

"No. Probably won't."

"Well. Hang in there. Hope it works out." He coughed a little. Then he added, "I gotta hand it to you. It's a tough business. Spencer Tracy used to say it's 'no job for a man.'"

Conversations went on like this for a few years—my father reminding me of something Rob did on *The Daily Show*, asking that I pass on his compliments, clicking his tongue at my frustrations. It was inevitable that he would catch me on the wrong night. It was cold out, and I was walking the dog around Hollywood, and I was tired, and he was painstakingly recounting a bit I had *not* seen. "Anyway, tell Rob it was great."

"You know what?" I spat out. "Rob has his own dad who can tell him that."

There was a sharp intake of breath. It would appear I had caught my father on the wrong night as well. "I don't get enough shit from Carol?" he said and slammed his land line down, severing the call.

---

* God, I went out for *The Office* a lot. First for Dwight, and then I was handed new sides on the spot and asked to read for Jim. Obviously neither worked out, and both roles were filled by great actors, but it was an interesting microcosm of my career—I was neither weird enough nor wholesome enough to work.

My first reaction: *What the fuck is my dad's wife doing except taking kind and patient care of a guy who can't get groceries on his own and lives with an oxygen tank?* And then a deep sadness crept over me. There had to have been a nicer way for me to say what I said, but in that moment, a cold night, walking the fussy dog during a career lull, I wasn't even remotely interested in being nice. I was interested in standing up for myself a little and reminding my dad who his son was—and who his son wasn't. I was working steadily and had been since moving to L.A., lots of guest work on TV shows, some good and some terrible, all of which meant I didn't need to borrow any more money from him. No, none of it was Shakespeare (I was doing some scenes in acting classes—my Leontes in *The Winter's Tale* was a *breakthrough*, said the teacher, even though I was paying for the privilege), and my work was sporadic but it paid honest money, and I enjoyed it. I was not going to apologize.

I recognize there is a part of me that is apologizing right now.

I called him back the following day.

"Hey, I'm, uh, sorry I snapped at you about Rob and everything."

He took a labored breath. "Yes, I'm sorry, too."

"I'm making a living, Dad, and I love what I do."

"Yes. Good for you. I guess that's everything."

◆

It was not long after that that I got an audition for *The Daily Show*.

This was summer 2005, and my viewing of the show had tapered off somewhat, as I was incredibly depressed by the reelection of George W. Bush.* But the country's fascination with the show was not slowing

---

* *How could the American public have made such a terrible mistake?* I wondered with an amusing, almost adorable naïveté, some twelve years before Election Day 2016.

down, and my manager was quick to point out that "Steve Carell is going to be a movie star, and he has *The Daily Show* to thank for that."

This was a good point, but getting the job would mean moving back to New York, just as I was getting really comfortable in Los Angeles. It would mean Jamie either coming with me or staying in L.A., where she was working steadily and testing for pilots. And we were earnestly talking about having a child soon, having kept a dog alive for three years.

But also, how dazzling would it be to actually be on a show my dad watched regularly? To move the needle so that phone calls were less "I loved what Rob did on *The Daily Show*" and more "I loved what you did on *The Daily Show*?"

I went to the audition.

It was very casual, a conference room at the Comedy Central headquarters in Century City. Dressed in a suit, sides in my hand, I stood in front of a video camera and two casting directors like at any other audition. There had, apparently, been a time early in *The Daily Show*'s run when they had had people come in with their own material, but by this era they had a pretty clear idea of what worked and what didn't, and as such they provided you with a road-tested script, one of their fake remote pieces done in front of a green screen. I was supposed to be at the Neverland Ranch (2005!) reporting on new developments in Michael Jackson's legal woes, a bit that Ed Helms or Jason Jones had already done on the show. I was, let's say, 85 percent off book, but I understood the show's tone: dry, professional but not flat, mocking not just the news but the self-important way in which it's presented.

I was told they liked the tape back in New York, and they were going to fly me out to test for the show. Fly me back . . . to the city I had left just three short years earlier. Jamie was super supportive. It was fine either way, she said. *If you don't book it, our life in L.A. continues unabated. If you book it, boom, you're on the fucking* Daily Show, *and we'll make it work!*

We decided not to worry about what "making it work" would look like.

The plane landed on the soft August tarmac at LaGuardia, and I took a cab into Midtown Manhattan, laden with a suit bag that held my best suit (which was probably bought at the outlet malls way up in Camarillo). I hadn't told my parents I would be in town and certainly hadn't told them I was getting close to a job on *The Daily Show*, even though I was staying a few blocks away from my mom in Hell's Kitchen. I didn't want follow-up questions, I didn't want raised hopes, and I didn't want the prospect of their son moving back to New York to be introduced at all. This was, for the moment, just my business.

Checkout time the next morning was noon, and the test for *The Daily Show* was three P.M. I suited up in dark navy blue, a thick cotton shirt, and a nice, crisp tie with a perfect dimple in the center of the knot. It was a damp eighty-five degrees in New York City.

The Daily Show studios are over on Eleventh Avenue, the far west side of Manhattan, and my hotel was near Central Park, so I lugged my suit bag over to the Whole Foods underneath the Time Warner building—right off Columbus Circle—and waited. Too nervous to eat, I had a smoothie. Ran into an old friend from UCB. Told her what I was auditioning for. She smiled and said, "Perfect." There was a sense—and I felt it, too—that *The Daily Show* was a good fit for me, a chance to use my dry wit, my political engagement, and my one nice suit. There was just something vaguely preordained about me being on that show.

Having killed two and a half hours at an air-conditioned Whole Foods (pre-smartphone!), I emerged into the summer heat. The extremes of New York weather are well documented, but they still can't be overstated: August in New York feels like you're walking across someone's armpit. I elected to walk to the studio, in my suit, because I guess I just couldn't justify taking a cab for such a short distance. Or because I felt, somewhere deep down, below the parts that words can reach, that I should sabotage myself and throw a grenade under this opportunity. Did I *really* want to move back to New York City? Wasn't it just a well-populated ghost town to me, every corner the site of a wrong that had been done me or, exponentially worse, a wrong I had done? Here's where my dad took a swing at me because I was making us late for church. Here's where, in a fit of impotent rage, I dumped a half-full McDonalds milkshake into a mailbox. Here were broken hearts and harsh words and ignored opportunities.

By the time I got to the studio, my eyeballs were sweating.

They were seeing about six guys for the correspondent's job, and we were all shuffled into a small greenroom, harshly lit by fluorescent lighting. The cool air dried my sweat as we were told we would line up outside the studio. One at a time we'd go in, do the bit in front of the green screen, do another bit at the desk with Jon, and then come back to the greenroom to wait. I knew four of the five other guys. We chatted, did dumb bits, swallowed our anxiety, and then we shut up when Stephen Colbert walked by.

I went third or fourth. Like all TV studios, this one was smaller in person than it looked on TV, but it was still clean and magnificent, and it felt like stepping into famous person. Jon Stewart jogged down from the desk and extended his hand. "Hi, John. Thanks for coming in," followed by a spiel you could tell he had delivered several times before. "So the key here is the show has a certain presentational style, but we're not looking for Kent Brockman. It's a joke, but it works best if it's a little conversational. Have fun." I nodded a lot during this, making sort of vaguely nervous grunts of assent. I stood in front of a green screen. To my far left, Stewart sat at his desk in a T-shirt and jeans. Right in front of me was a camera equipped with a teleprompter.

Off to my right was a monitor where I could see myself, suited up, in front of the Neverland Ranch with a chyron that read JOHN ROSS BOWIE, CORRESPONDENT.

"For more information, we go to our correspondent live at the Neverland Ranch, John Ross Bowie," said Peabody and Emmy Award winner Jon Stewart. "John, what's the scene like there?" And I was off.

It's a bit of a blur, but I remember landing the jokes the way I wanted to land them, being fairly loose while trying to keep up with the teleprompter—and let it be said, reading off a teleprompter is nowhere as easy as it looks. There's something counterintuitive about reading moving text while staring into an all-seeing but unresponsive black eye, and its odd how you find yourself doing it even though you're off book by this time. But I did it, and when the segment was done, there was that quiet thrill that comes with a good audition. Maybe I didn't do *the* best, but I did *my* best.

"Okay," said Jon Stewart. "I wanna do it again, only faster."

Ever the eager-to-please actor, I said, "Sure."

And that's when I heard the laughter.

It was coming from the stands, the bleachers where the audience sits. Squinting, I could make out a group of what I correctly assumed were the writers, laughing at Jon's joke. And it *was* a joke. Like a lot of New Yorkers, I speak quickly—I have places to be, you have places to be, there's someone behind me in line at the deli, let's go—and I'd apparently done my audition so quickly that the mere idea that I could do it faster was *hilarious*. A slow burning shame crept up from the small of my back until it engulfed every part of me. There's an argument to be made that the truly brave thing to do at that point would have been to run screaming out of the studio.

A week later, my therapist would say, "Ridicule is hard."

That was just it: This fucker had *ridiculed* me. Me, a guy who was just auditioning for the smartest show on TV! Why would he—wait.

The smartest show on TV. Smart. I'm not smart. I can't be smart. Why would I think I could possibly be smart? I was a mediocre student at best!

"No, but let's do it again," Jon said. "Just slow down and relax into it."

I made a laugh sound with my mouth that I hoped would say, *Hey, fair enough, I'm a good sport. Let's have fun!*

"For more information, we go to our correspondent live at the Neverland Ranch, John Ross Bowie," said Peabody and Emmy award winner Jon Stewart. "John, what's the scene like there?"

Deep inhale and speak: "Well, Jon." Don't overthink it. Just slow down. Elongate the words. Like that. Yes. You are slowing down. *Drip*. "Child molestation joke, Jon, cutting gibe at the twenty-four-hour news cycle." You don't have to keep telling yourself to slow down because you are slowing down. *Drip*. "Another child molestation joke, perhaps a play on 'Man in the Mirror.'"* You are fine. Everyone had a good laugh at your expense, but don't dwell on that part. *Drip drip drop*. And this sudden sweating is absolutely no cause for alarm. Soldier through. *Drip*. Yes, it's getting in your eye, but tally ho. "Live from Neverland Ranch, I'm John Ross Bowie."

The problem with talking slower is that things take longer, and that's hard and difficult when you really want things to be over, especially when you are starting to sweat profusely. But the segment was eventually over, and Jon said, without making eye contact, "Nice adjustment."

I thanked him, waved to the writers (I will die wondering why), and headed for the doors that would take me out of the studio into anyplace that was not the studio. "Not yet," whispered a headphoned production assistant. "The desk segment." Fuuuuuck. The desk segment. Yes. Right. I was only half finished.

---

* I have long since blocked out the monologue. I know someone else had done it first, but I don't remember the words.

You know the desk segments on *The Daily Show*. They're staged like interviews, Jon sitting directly across from the correspondent. Jon would ask a series of questions of the correspondent, who would answer into the camera (the teleprompter again). I have zero recollection of what the desk segment was about, but it was 2005 so . . . rising gas prices? Rebuilding New Orleans? Jon teed me up again, but I was dealing with a sweat globule dangling off the end of my nose, so pronounced I could not just feel it, I could see it, and I missed my cue. "I'm sorry," I said. "Can we start again?"

"Sure," said Jon Stewart, with a small smile that did not say *Why not? You're crushing this anyway.* We started again. I slowed down. I sweated copiously. Projectile-ly. I thought about Albert Brooks in *Broadcast News* and that made me sweat more. It was a sweaty, out-of-focus mirage, those three or four minutes, and when it was over, Jon thanked me. He might have shaken my hand, which would have embarrassed me further, as my hand was drenched.

Back in the greenroom, I grabbed a bottle of water and gulped it down. "How'd it go?" asked another auditioner. "Terrible," I said. "Shit the tub. Sweat like Albert Brooks." A little taken aback at my candor, the other auditioner said, "Oh. Uh. That's okay."

And then Rob Corddry stuck his head in. "How'd that feel?" he asked.

"Not my best work," I said. "Very sweaty, and I was rushing."

"Albert Brooks?" he asked.

"Yeah. Very much so."

And then Rob said, "It wasn't that bad."

Jesus Fucking Christ. "You saw it?"

"Yeah."

"You were in the bleachers?"

"No, no," Rob said, which offered some temporary relief until he said, "They broadcast it on a live feed all over the building."

Another production assistant came by to tell us we could go. I left the studio—maybe nine blocks north of my mom's apartment—and got into a cab heading back for LaGuardia airport. I wanted to call my father, to reach out and say, "Dad, I really tried to impress you."

Instead, I called my manager and told him not to expect a call from *The Daily Show.*

Then, I called my wife, who had tested for *The Daily Show* a couple of years earlier and also not gotten it. There's an argument to be made for people marrying "outside the business" so that home is a refuge from auditions and tests and egos, but I'm not interested in that argument. I thank God that I was able to call Jamie and commiserate specifically with someone who knows *exactly* what it's like to whiff an audition for a show you actually occasionally watch.

Years later, mid-2017, we were driving into Manhattan without a place to stay, so I got on HotelTonight.com and we looked for places in Midtown. "I just want to make sure that we . . ." I started, and she finished, "Don't stay in the place where *The Daily Show* puts you up?" We both nodded fervently, and I wouldn't trade that shorthand for all the accountant or lawyer wives in the world.

At any rate, I took a cab back to LaGuardia and got on the plane back to Los Angeles and got so shithoused in coach that the flight attendants stopped serving me.

I never told my parents about the trip.

CHAPTER ELEVEN

HARDLY GETTING OVER IT

I t's a little early to announce, but Jamie is eight weeks pregnant!"

"A week pregnant?" said my dad. "That *is* early."

"No, dad. *Eight* weeks."

"Oh, ah, ha. Well. Congratulations."

I was pretty used to my dad's lukewarm enthusiasm, but this non-reaction was a lot to process. I was making the guy a grandfather, and he was reacting the way you'd expect someone to react when you finish Monday's crossword in a timely fashion.

This was February 2007, and winter was typically tough for my dad. The snow and cold made it difficult for him to do whatever meager outdoor exercise he was still capable of, and his untreated seasonal affective disorder was in full effect, so I wrote his tepid reaction off as a symptom of all that. Jamie painted the bedroom. We put together a crib and made a ridiculous *Funny or Die* video about it—it's still on the site; you're welcome to go look for it. Jamie's hilarious in it. Things were slow for me, but Jamie was working fairly steadily at the time, well into her pregnancy. Nothing crazy, no stunt work or anything, but doing a local comedy act where she played a character named Beverly Ginsberg, loosely based on her mom, her grandmother, and a bunch of their friends. To explain the sizable bump, it was established that Beverly was "carrying triplets for my niece Shira." This was hilarious and absurd, and it was invigorating to watch my baby mama annihilate an audience while being visibly my baby mama.

Then it was July. Jamie was in her third trimester with our first—a girl—who was, by now, quite the high-kicking tenant. I don't think Jamie would recommend doing your third trimester during a Los Angeles summer, but it was a summer of inopportune timing. Despite her delicate condition, I had booked a ticket back to New York for an Egghead. reunion show—and my dad went into hospice.

He'd had another exacerbation, a decline in his lung capacity, and now the drugs that were helping him breathe were chipping away at every other aspect of his health: The steroids had given him osteoporosis, and the blood thinners that assisted his sedentary lifestyle had thinned his blood so much it was showing up in his stool. One morning he woke up with dark red shit and an inability to breathe and was ambulanced to Beth Israel Hospital, across town from where he lived in Chelsea. These exacerbations were a twice-yearly occurrence at least, and I often flew back for them, terrified that *this was it*; once, he'd even landed in St. Vincent's psych ward when his suicidal ideation got to the point that he felt safer in a room where they took his shoelaces away and wouldn't let him hold sharp objects. He'd stayed for a week before calming down and feeling a deep need to get away from the "real crazies" with whom he was sharing quarters. I had flown home at the last minute a half dozen times, fearful that this was the end, only to watch him rally, be released, and go back home. But this was different—Carol called to let me know that the emergency room had examined him thoroughly and sent him upstairs to the hospice wing for "palliative care."

"Hospice usually means he only has six months," she explained.

"Jesus. OK. Are we . . . are we sure about this?"

"I don't think they make these decisions lightly," she said. She then added with a sigh, "This is one of those times where I really wish you lived here."

"All right. I'll be there Monday."

"You will?"

"Yes, I was coming anyway."

"Oh."

I landed in New York on a Sunday evening—Jamie, being by this point eight months pregnant and unable to fly, stayed home—and took a cab to my mom's place in Hell's Kitchen. It was the same apartment I'd grown up in, the same couch on which I'd crashed after leaving the Firm (and High School Sweetheart), the same apartment where my dad had come home drunk and thrown a samurai sword at my mom. She and I went for Italian food at a corny little place called Don Giovanni's, in the very space where the original improv nightclub was, where George Carlin and Jerry Seinfeld and other legends of stand-up practiced their craft, where today there's a plaque that commemorates the comedy legends that performed in front of the brick wall—a plaque that misspells Richard Pryor's name.

"This is really upsetting me," my mom said about my dad. She was even more tight-lipped than usual, but she didn't cry, and her voice sounded calm and smooth. "I guess I'm not the heartless bitch he said I was."

"We all say things when we're angry."

"He said it a lot." She never had a long-term (over a year) relationship after my dad moved out, which always saddened me. When I went to college she was a relatively spry and cute forty-seven, with no pesky teenager taking up space in the small apartment; it might have been a perfect time to get out there, but she could be incredibly shy, and she claimed to just really enjoy her alone time ("I can fart whenever I want.") We ate pizza and sat outside so she could smoke. It was a cool summer evening, and she went through three or four cigarettes while my dad was dying of emphysema a few miles downtown.

The next morning, I got up, showered in the tiny bathroom (after five years in Los Angeles, New York apartments feel comically small—you wander through a two-bedroom feeling like a less-wieldy Gulliver), and headed downtown, barely remembering how the subways work, all of that knowledge usurped by freeway exits. I stopped at a coffee cart near the old Stuyvesant High School, got a cup of drip and a cinnamon roll the size of my head (because I was thirty-six and could eat whatever I want), and signed in on the ground floor of the hospital.

The hospice wing was located literally down the hall from the maternity ward—a devastating proximity that fed into my somber circle-of-life mood at the time. About to become a father? About to lose a father? Welcome to the eighth floor: dramatic irony and a weird smell! Right this way! A nurse led me down a hallway of incredibly old people, hanging on to breath and little else, and way-too-young men, purple with Kaposi sarcoma sores. And then my father. Sitting up in bed. A catheter sneaking out from below the blanket and an oxygen tube wrapped around his head, blowing air directly into his nose. He spoke haltingly but seemed sharp and alert.

"Hey, Tiger."

I went in to hug him and kiss him on his head. He had been five foot ten, but even in bed I could tell he was shorter than me now.

"How are you?" I asked.

He gestured around the room by way of answering.

"OK. So what do they think is going on?"

"They thought I was dying. Now, they're not so sure."

He went on to explain that despite the consignment to hospice, the doctors were now hemming and hawing that a "six months or less" prognosis might be a little premature. We talked details—medications, who was in charge—and then he addressed the elephant in the room.

"Why do you have your bass?"

"I have rehearsal this afternoon."

"Ah. How are the Mikes?" he asked, using his shorthand for Mikes Galvin and Faloon, who were fine and would meet me at a rehearsal studio in the Garment District in a few hours. I hadn't canceled the reunion—I told myself it was because the fans (such as they were) wanted us to reunite, but the truth was I needed it. I was about to become a father. My childhood would be officially, irreversibly over, and my band playing a pop-punk festival in Baltimore would be a last gasp of independence before the responsibilities of fatherhood. And I didn't want to cancel.

"They're good. Faloon has two kids!"

"Hey, good for him. Sit, sit."

I sat next to the bed and watched him interact with the hospital staff. You'll recall my father spoke a couple languages fluently and could at least say hello in a dozen more. "Kamusta," he flirtatiously greeted the Filipino orderly who fluffed his pillow. "Namaste," he said, replete with the hand gesture, to the Indian cardiologist who checked his heart rate. It was a reminder that my father had spent twenty years in customer service and, though he claimed to hate it, was probably pretty good at it.

Around lunchtime my dad said, "Go get us some dirty waters," referring to the hot dogs they sell in mobile stands around the city.

"Oh, uh . . . is that a good idea? Should you be eating something that you just called dir—"

Again, my father gestured around the room, a gesture that clearly meant *I'm in hospice care. Let me have my gross street meat.*

I went downstairs to First Avenue and found a stand on the corner of 14th, near the Blimpie where Stuyvesant stoners used to cut school. I bought four dogs and smuggled them back into the hospital, eating lunch with my dad while we watched old films on Turner Classic

Movies. People came in and out all day, checking on him, seeing how quickly he could get up, stethoscope to the lungs, everything. He was wearing an adult diaper but was still able to make it to the bathroom with some assistance. The doctors asked a lot of questions but didn't give a lot of answers. That was how I spent the day: next to my dad in his hospital room while Carol was at her publishing job. It was understood that she would replace me for the evening shift with my dad.

Around five P.M., I got on the N at Union Square, took it up to 34th, then walked over to the weird little rehearsal studio tucked in one of those old green buildings around 32nd, around the corner from interchangeable bodegas and Irish pubs. The studio smelled like sweat and weed, and there were the Mikes, still youthful in their late thirties. They were all smiles, but also filled with genuine, concerned questions about my dad. I tuned my bass and talked and talked and talked—I was pretty caffeinated and pretty shaken up from spending the whole day watching my dad be charming and sharp and yet very incapacitated. But there was music to play and nostalgia to be indulged. We dug in, played an older song, a simple little Jackie Chan ode called "Hong Kong." Faloon teared up. So did I, for a million reasons, but it was nice to play music—loud, dumb music. And at the same time it felt almost disrespectful, as if I wasn't actually coping with my issues. We rehearsed for three hours and then went out for Japanese food and beer served in tall cans. A couple of them, as I recall.

The next morning, I walked into my dad's hospital room to find a woman with a small puppy in her arms, talking to my father. "Would you like a puppy visit?"

"No, thank you."

"You're sure? He's hypoallergenic!"

Smiling thinly, my father said, "I'm sure."

I followed the woman out into the hallway, and she let me take the dog—a Wheaten terrier—from her for a moment. The Wheaten went trustingly into my arms and lavished me with kisses. Who wouldn't want this? "You're missing out, Dad!" I called into his room.

"I'll be okay." He wheezed back. It was family lore that my father had had but one pet, a tiny Lab mix named Laddie, who was a faithful companion in my father's Long Island childhood. Laddie lived to be about nine or ten before picking a fight with a German shepherd down the street, who quickly bested Laddie and left him perfectly, hor- ribly still on the sidewalks of New Hyde Park. My father was around twelve and had seen the whole gruesome thing happen. Laddie had never—would never—be replaced.

I gave the terrier back to the puppy visit volunteer and headed into my dad's room. Kissed him on the head. He looked a little more tired today, a little less animated. The novelty of his son's visit had under- standably worn off, but I sat next to him and read a magazine, sharing funny items with him while he dozed through the morning. Before lunch, a stern-looking woman with short hair and a black shirt walked in and introduced herself as a chaplain.

"Hello, Mr. Bowie," mispronouncing it as everyone does on their first dozen or so tries. "I'm just here if you need to talk."

"Thank you," he said. "I'm talking to people—my reverend has visited. And it's *Bao-ee*."

"I'm so sorry, sir."

"That reminds me," Dad continued. "Tiger, remember to let Bishop Roskam know when I go, she'd want to be notified. I'd love to have her at the funeral."

"Yes, I can do that."

"And reach out to Tony, Carol will have his number."

"Sure, of course."

The chaplain teared up. "That's . . . wonderful, that you can say that to your son. What a great relationship." Maybe she had a point, it *was* a credit to our relationship that we could openly discuss such matters, but what she didn't realize was that my father and I had been talking about death—his, mine, other peoples'—for years. My father talked about death so much that Carol gave him a weird little celebrity death day calendar one year for Christmas—every day you pulled off a leaf, and there was the anniversary of the death of one person of note.

"Do you know Bradley Nowell?" my father had asked during a phone call years ago.

"Yeah, wait, yeah—that name sounds super familiar."

"Sublime?"

"*Right*. Bradley Nowell sang for Sublime. Heroin over—"

"Heroin overdose, yeah, that's what the calendar says."

So the chaplain said she was here to offer prayers or counsel, and maybe my father would have taken her up on it if I hadn't been there—maybe my agnosticism made him self-conscious. I hardly ever went to church anymore, and that bothered him, just like it bothered him that we weren't going to have my incoming daughter baptized.

"You're not?"

"Well . . . no. I mean, Jamie's Jewish, and I don't really . . . It's just not important to me. Anyway, Jamie's Jewish and, you know, that means . . ."

"Right. Your kids will be Jewish. It's matrilineal," said my dad, making absolutely sure he used the word *matrilineal*.

It's hard to say what went wrong between me and religion. Punk rock? My dad being hungover at church? My dad taking a swing at me for making him late to church? My dad calling me an asshole for making him late to church? Or just some sort of vague, collegiate dismissal of all religion—that according to most Christian doctrine, children who are born in Sudan and never encounter a minister of Christ and, as such, never accept him as their savior are doomed to torment? Was my father—a sinner, though repentant—doomed to eternal torment?

Whatever it was, the chaplain left, and my dad and I turned on TCM.

After lunch, two doctors came in to check on him. He was tired but lumbered slowly to the edge of his bed, perching there on the side, his legs dangling. This effort cost him, and he pursed his lips, sucking in air, trying to inflate his sagging lungs the best he could. He looked frail. He had been getting frailer every time I saw him. The doctors were new and didn't notice his progressive illness. He was just another sick old man. They checked his blood pressure. Made him blow into a tube. Checked his heart rate. Then they asked me to come outside.

In the hallway, the taller of the two doctors—a zaftig woman resting her hands in the pockets of her lab coat—looked at me with great concern as she said, "Your father is not dying."

"He's not?" This was an awful feeling. It's not that I was rooting for my dad to die, but he was sad, and tired, and wearing a diaper, and even more bitter than his baseline, and I found myself wishing for him to be out of pain and have some sort of dignity restored.

The doctor continued: "I can't say for sure that he's only got six months. It could be a couple of years. His lung capacity is down around 12 percent, but it can go lower, and your father can still live for quite some time."

"So . . . where do we go?"

She sighed. "Well, there are a couple of options. Assisted living facilities. He can go home, of course, but he would need round-the-clock care."

"OK."

"There are ways to pay for this . . . there are a lot of financial routes you can take."

"OK. Well. When would he check out?"

"Well, we can keep him a couple of days to make sure we're right."

I nodded. This was all a great deal to process. My father had seemingly been at death's door for years—there was a moment when we weren't sure he'd live to see our wedding—and here we were three years after the ceremony. I was used to him getting a reprieve from a doctor. But this was a serious downturn, and it had to have serious ramifications. Didn't it?

I went back into the hospital room—my dad knew what was going on, and his old gray-blue eyes were wet. "I came here to die, and they won't even let me do that."

"Maybe it's not time, Dad."

He groaned and looked out the window, not quite able to make eye contact with me. I sat on the side of his bed and held his hand. His wrist was horrifically bruised from all the needles and IVs that had been pushed in and pulled out of his arm for years, but especially in the past few weeks. He squeezed.

I had no idea what to say. I was a vacuum. I couldn't ask him what he wanted, because he had just told me. I couldn't ask him if he was scared, because I was too scared to ask him. So I just sat there quietly, uselessly holding his hand. Two guys. One a father, one about to be a father, just sitting there, holding hands.

A little while later an enormous woman in a floral summer dress walked in, followed by a much smaller woman toting an acoustic guitar. "Hello," announced the larger woman. "Would you like me to sing for you?"

She had an incredibly rich voice—trained, eloquent, every consonant heralding the arrival of a new syllable. My father, unable to contain a chuckle, said, "Oh, no, thank you."

"I see you have a guitar?" the woman said to me. "We could collaborate on something?"

"Uh, it's a bass?" I said. I was suddenly more uncomfortable than I had been moments before when my father talked about his own death. "It's electric . . . I'd have to plug it in . . . I think we're OK."

"That's fine," said the woman, in a tone that suggested maybe it wasn't at all. "Have a good day."

She and her accompanist left. When she was out of earshot, my father said, "That woman loves the sound of her own voice."

We sat quietly in each other's presence, both of us breathing lightly. After five or six minutes, we heard something from down the hallway.

It must have been cold there in my shadow,

To never have sunlight on your face.

You were content to let me shine, that's your way.

You always walked a step behind.

DAD: Jesus Christ.

We laughed, my father and I, silently acknowledging that there were very good reasons a person might want to not postpone death. I got up to close the door just as she hit the chorus . . .

Did you ever know that you're my hero?

And everything I would like to—

SLAM.

◆

The next day was Wednesday, July 4, and TCM was full of war movies and jingoistic actors that led with their chests. We watched together, even politely talking about politics—my father was a Republican, but a New York one, and he was pro-choice, and though he called homosexuality "aberrant," he had tons of gay friends because, duh, we're Episcopalians. And he was way too smart, way too articulate, to go all in for a president like Bush, who was astonishingly unable to get through an extemporaneous sentence without butchering it. The night after Barack Obama put himself on the radar with his rousing speech at the 2006 Democratic Convention, my dad called me and said, "Wow. I'll trade you ten of my guys for one of him." This was the safest way to discuss politics with him: treat it like a game, a free-agent fracas with low stakes. One of us would eventually go too far—I'd call Bush a fascist as the Patriot Act kicked in; he'd dismiss global warming as an "alarmist myth"—and we'd have to change the subject. But this July Fourth, there was an understanding that there might not be any more July Fourths, so everything was quite civil.

It got quiet. We talked softly about the future. Our incoming daughter not being baptized came up again. "We talked a little, Jamie and I, about how to raise our children. Frankly, I wanted to raise them . . . sort of with nothing. Just a sort of polite . . ."

"Nothing? Nothing at all?" said my father at the precipice.

"And then Jamie said if you raise them with nothing they tend to go way off in the other direction, start looking for meaning later in life and end up in cults."

This made sense to my dad, and he even managed a smile. "Huh. Alright."

"So I said, 'Why Judaism? Why not Episcopalianism?' And here's where she got me, Dad. She said, 'Jews don't believe in hell.'"

"Well, it's more complicated than that," said my dad. "Right now, the Church of England has shifted its official view of hell. It's not . . ." He waved his tired hands like a menacing monster for a moment. "It's not a lake of torment, pitchforks and fire and all that. It's just sort of being absent from the light of Christ. Closer to the Old Testament idea of Sheol, a shadowy land of the dead."

"So not being chewed on by demons for infinity, just sort of . . . bad seating."

He laughed weakly. "Yes. Sort of like that." He caught his breath. "That's good, Tiger. Very good."

We talked about it very abstractly; not in a literal *Where do you think you're headed, Dad?* Way but more of a vague, *John, there are those who believe . . .* It got quiet again and my dad told me, "I don't want to leave this world without telling you how special I think you are."

Something shifted. The room seemed to let in more air and get brighter, while at the same time chilling with this candid discussion of leaving the world. He'd told me he was proud of me before; I'd book an episode of, say, *Las Vegas* and he'd say, "Proud of you, Tiger," and it felt cursory, obliged. It had never really distracted me from the harshness of my father also telling me he was jealous of me. Or hitting me. Or getting drunk and playing with swords in front of me. As vulnerable and sad as that was, it made my eyes cross with anger. But this was different—this was a declaration, a last-minute attempt at fatherly affection, a toss from the free-throw line, said with fear, sadness, and truth.

I wish I'd said, "I know." I think I said, "Thank you," and then added, "You were the first funny person I ever met. And now . . . look at what I do for a living." It was a quiet lull in my career at the moment—maybe not the most impressive time to cite my accomplishments, but it was true. My father was funny, and he knew what was funny, and it was he who introduced me to George Carlin, and Richard Pryor, and *Laugh-In*. It was he who stayed up late with me to watch *Rhoda* and *WKRP* and *Taxi*. It was he who made sure I watched early TV like *Your Show of Shows* and *That Was the Week That Was* at the Museum of Broadcasting. It was he who came home with jokes from work (a distressingly large number of them ethnic, but one thing at a time). I was often too young to get the jokes, so it was all about delivery and timing. Sometimes he could just make me laugh parroting one of the crude things his frat brothers would say. After all, why claim to be "famished" when you could claim to be "so hungry you could eat the asshole out of a skunk"? Why claim to be aroused when you could claim to "have a hard-on a cat couldn't climb"? I loved the way laughing with my father felt, and I loved the way I was eventually able to make other people do it. I loved the way it broke tension and quilted strangers together. My father, who didn't trust the lifestyle of an actor, particularly a comic one, had no one but himself to blame for his son becoming one. And maybe he made peace with that.

I wish I'd said more. But I told him how funny he was, and I told him I loved him. The band didn't rehearse that night, so after he drifted off to sleep, I just walked from Beth Israel back up to my mom's place in Hell's Kitchen, fireworks reddening the sky over my head.

◆

Thursday night came. Egghead. played a warm-up gig at the Lost & Found in Brooklyn, a bar so remote you had to take the G train to get there. I'd spent thirty years in New York, and this was my first time on that line, the only subway that doesn't go into Manhattan. The bar was a striking harbinger of gentrification in the deeply Polish part of Williamsburg. We had a dinner of pierogis and soda at a nearby diner—no beer; we never played drunk or even buzzed—and took the stage around nine, after local faves Lost Locker Combo. Egghead.'s ridiculous mythos lived on, and we had our buddy Steve read a pro-foundly dumb speech about our hiatus (our corporate overlords Gentech had dispatched us to Upper Slobovia, where we had installed ourselves as rulers, à la *The Man Who Would Be King*) while we changed into fake NASA flight suits in the cramped bathroom of the bar, engaging in a clumsy group hug before walking out to applause from the small gathering. I had just turned thirty-six a couple months prior.

We took the stage and tore through twelve sweaty songs, playing to a crowd of close friends, my mom, and my cousin from Jersey. It was exhilarating, yelling to the choir, but we knew it was but a soft prelude to Friday night: a four-hundred-capacity venue in Baltimore, larger than we'd ever played in our actual career, and we would be featured late on the bill, playing for pop-punk fans from all over the country—nay, the world! I couldn't wait to get in front of a huge, rapt audience, who would bathe in our hooky shtick. I can't speak for the Mikes, but did I entertain some ideas about another, bigger band on the bill liking us so much that they would maybe invite us on tour? Stranger things have happened in punk rock. We could open for them—this amorphous bigger band—on the road, share a merch guy. Oh, the times we would have, Egghead. And this hypothetical more popular pop-punk band—maybe we'd finally get the record deal that eluded us during our initial run. Maybe we'd finally get the validation that we sought. This could be the break that never came! We closed with "Jetpack"—we always closed with "Jetpack," because it was so fast and hard that we almost always broke a string and/or a kickdrum pedal in the playing of it. The set didn't end so much as it crashed gloriously into a wall, and we staggered off the stage, ready for the real gig the following night.

Friday was a shorter day. I wasn't too tired; I'd slept pretty deeply. My dad politely asked how the show went. The questions were on the order of how many people were there rather than how the actual performance went (really well, actually) or how I thought we sounded (better than ever). He was in increasing discomfort and was struggling to understand his ever-weakening body. The doctors were still not sure if he was going to have to stay. At one point in the late morning, my dad grimaced, his face tightening and then reddening. "I have to . . ." he murmured. "I need some help."

Oh God. I had figured out all too quickly what had gone wrong. "Oh. OK. Do you want me to try and walk you over to the bathr—"

"No. Too late. I need some help."

Oh. The poor guy. "I'll go get a nurse—"

"Just use the intercom."

I leaned over him, pushed the button on the small speaker. A nurse said, "Yes, Mr. Bowie?"

"Yes," I said, and then, loud enough so she could hear me: "My father needs to be changed."

"*Jesus Christ, John,*" said my dad.

"What? I didn't know what to . . . I mean . . ." I started to equivocate, but he was right, there had to have been at least ten more graceful ways to call a nurse. "I'm so sorry, Dad."

"It's *fine,*" he hissed. "I do. I need to be changed." He was sixty-nine years old.

I sat with him until the nurse came, and then I turned my back to look out the window as she checked his diaper. It was a false alarm; it might have been the small dose of morphine making him feel . . . unstable. Either way, my father did not need to be changed. The nurse left, and I apologized again. He gestured with a wave of his hand, which I took to mean, *It doesn't matter. Very little does.*

I left after lunch that day, loaded my bass into Faloon's car, and the three of us drove down to Baltimore. I'd had a few too many coffees, using caffeine to keep my energy up and also to supplement my Paxil. We listened to music—some of the bands we were going to see, some bands like the Kinks that we would never see—and made each other laugh. I barely talked about my dad. I'm not usually that stoic; I tend to wear my heart on my sleeve in my dealings with the world, but this was all too much. If I started, if I unlocked, I didn't know when I'd stop. I stuffed my emotional turmoil way down deep and made jokes of varying quality as we sped down I-95.

The sun was going down when we pulled into the parking lot at the club in a very desolate, very *The Wire* area of Baltimore (GALVIN: "The Big Easy!"). There were a lot of old friends there to greet us—people from the scene in New York, people we'd met on our brief tours back in the day, people we'd never met but whose bands we listened to. Everyone milled around; this subset of punk rock did not thrive on the ohawks and spiked leather jackets one associates with the genre, just a lot of jeans and T-shirts that seemed to be engaged in a sort of mortal combat to out-obscure each other. The biggest name on the bill was the Bay Area's Mr. T Experience, authors of brilliant lonely hearts anthems like "I'm All Yeah, and She's All No" and "Even Hitler Had a Girlfriend." But despite not having an enormous head-liner, the club was big and sweaty, and the crowd was warmed up for a show. People seemed excited to see us—one kid even stopped me to make a request! Why, yes, young man, we would be playing "Hong Kong" tonight, in fact we're opening with it. I chatted with the kid a bit more about the other bands playing the fest, and at one point he looked down at his Converse, shook his head and said, "Wow. I can't believe I'm talking to John from Egghead." Stunned, flattered, I said something like, "And I can't believe I'm talking to Sean from New Jersey." Seemingly levitating, I went into the club and caught a little of the Unlovables' set, tight as a fist, as quickly accessible as a gourmet Pop-Tart.

After a couple of songs, I went back out to Faloon's car to grab my bass. We were on next, a fairly plum seven thirty–ish slot. My mind started to race. *Should we change into our outfits? Nah, we'll do that in the bathroom, we can't go into the greenroom until the Unlovables clear out, and they only just finished, and wow people seem really excited to see us and wait—*

What's. That. Weird. Silence?

The neighborhood had plunged into darkness; the city's hum flicked off like a switch. The club went dark, and all the streetlights went out. A blackout like the one in my childhood, alarming in its silence. The main drag about a block and a half away seemed to have power, but it was clear that this was a significant outage that covered everywhere else. Failure has many fathers, but a large nightclub pumping its AC and several amps could not have helped what I'll bet was a pretty old grid. There was a low-key panic as everyone realized a rock club in a shitty neighborhood is a fire hazard under the best of circumstances, but a rock club in a shitty neighborhood in which no one can fucking see could get really dangerous. Punk rock kids spurted out of the club by the dozens.

"Who knows what's going on? Does Mark know anything?" Mark being Mark Enoch, one of the organizers of the festival and an Egghead. fan so zealous he had a tattoo of us on his calf.* Mark knew very little and was all apologies. It was no biggie, he said, they called the power company, and they should know more soon.

The power company showed up, and a guy shimmied up a pole to survey the situation and said, yeah, there was no way the power was coming back on tonight. Show's canceled. "Sorry kids," he said, adding a knife twist: "Punk rock? Do people still do that?"

The club emptied out into the parking lot, and a lot of people decided to cut their losses and head home. But there were still a couple dozen people hanging out, and it wasn't long before one of the bands produced an acoustic guitar. (It was a punk festival; we were lucky to have even one.) It got passed around, and someone—Mark?—decided that Egghead. (as ever too pop for punk, too punk for pop) would sound all right unplugged.

You can still find chunks of our parking lot set on YouTube. Galvin plays guitar, for a little, while Faloon claps along, and I'm just standing there, nervously giggling, singing my heart out. "Hong Kong." "Neighborhood Palm Reader." "Donna's Always Mad at Me." "Data Entry." We got to "Jetpack," and I had nothing to lose. Accompanied only by an acoustic guitar, I hopped up on a precarious folding chair and leapt into the sea of hands, crowd surfing to what sounded like fast folk music. It was exactly the insouciant dipshittery I had been looking for during our big Egghead. revival, although it wasn't entirely carefree—on

---

* Seriously. It's a tiny little cartoon from the cover of one of our seven-inches. We're in good company; he has a Madness tattoo as well as a little red Devo energy dome.

NO JOB FOR A MAN

the video you can hear me cautioning my carriers to "watch the back, watch the knees."

We stayed at a friend's house that night—our buddy Skyzz, who had been in Berserk and the Jennifers and was a mainstay of the Baltimore punk scene. Skyzz didn't play music much anymore; he'd been making documentaries about Baltimore and curating a series of film screenings called MicroCineFest. Not a get-rich-quick scheme by any stretch, not even a straight day job, but his job was doing something he loved.

◆

The next morning—Saturday—the Mikes and I drove back up to New York, the reunion partially out of our system, the itch *sort of* scratched. We were a little let down by what was not quite the heroes' welcome we had hoped for. I can't speak for anyone else in the band, but I've always been pretty sure that the power outage was some sort of karmic punishment for me not canceling the gig entirely to stay by my father's side. Still, this time around, there was something less weird about returning to my regularly scheduled life from a couple of concerts—a mini tour, after all. This is still what I do for a living. Perform. Galvin would fly back to L.A. ahead of me by a couple of days, a draft due on a screenplay he was writing for MGM. Faloon would drive back up to the Hudson Valley, where he was teaching elementary school. He had gone to grad school for that and had the gentle-but-not-condescending demeanor of a great educator of young people.

Faloon dropped me off at the hospital. I lugged my bag and my bass back upstairs, past the maternity unit, my inner voice yelling, *How's Jamie? What if the baby's early? Are you ready to be a dad finally, now that you got your little punk rock reunion out of the way?* It had only been twenty-four hours, but my father had taken another sharp downturn. They'd upped his morphine to make him more comfortable, but all downers are respiratory suppressants, so in exchange for less pain he became very short of breath. We sat together watching TV, Dad and Carol and me. The Live Earth concert of 2007 was on, and we all enjoyed Alicia Keys helping Keith Urban through "Gimme Shelter"—the three of us digging one of those quiet, culturally agreed upon moments, like laughter. I felt a cold coming on. I was emotionally and physically exhausted, and there was a telltale tickle in my throat, an inability to quench my thirst. It was getting late—a lot of the other rooms on the floor were dark, and I could tell my father was fading fast into a dopey sleep. I kissed my hand and placed it on his thin, hairless shin; this seemed like the easiest way to show him I loved him but not to infect him with my cold. He opened his eye and smiled softly at me, then he looked at the TV. Kanye West was performing. My father looked at the outspoken rapper (this was already a couple years after "George Bush doesn't care about Black people") and whispered, "Bigmouth."

Carol and I talked in the hallway. She looked tired, but not exhausted; she never once looked exhausted. Her hair was neatly styled, her skirt pressed. "We don't know what's going on."

"I'm getting nervous about staying, Carol," I said. "Jamie is eight months pregnant. She could pop at any time. I hate leaving her like this. A friend had a baby at eight months, and if he's not even going to stay here . . ."

"I know," said Carol. "Well. You should probably go home. If he checks out of here, we'll have to figure something out."

"OK. We will," I said, hugging her. I told her I loved her and left the hospital, my pace quickening after I turned the hallway corner and headed to the elevator bank. I called Jamie.

"Hey, how is he?"

"He's not great," I said, throat tight. "He's in and out. They're just trying to make him comfortable. I don't know if I should . . . I don't know."

"John. Come home."

"OK," I said after a moment. "Probably going to get pretty drunk first."

Galvin and I went out that night to a tiki bar right down 14th Street, where I got polluted, submerging myself in absurd Technicolor cocktails while a surf band in the back of the bar made any meaningful conversation irrelevant. I ended up closing the night in a cab and then with my head in my mom's toilet, my drunk lasting about a quarter the length of my hangover, which was so bad as to seem vindictive. This was life. Joy and excretion and grief hand in hand.

I flew back to Los Angeles on Sunday. When we landed, I turned my iPod to shuffle, and, hand to God, the first song up was Randy Newman's "I Love L.A." I took a cab back to the house and found Jamie nestled on the couch, beautiful and full of life.

My dad and I didn't speak much that week. He was sleeping a lot, and I would miss him when I called.

On the following Monday, I spoke to Carol. She was crying. The doctors told her that with my father's rapidly shrinking lung capacity, he would probably never walk again.

On Tuesday, it became clear that things were not going to get better. The decline was swift and had momentum. He was in and out of consciousness: Some of it was the morphine; some of it was just the kind of deep exhaustion that I think you only know once in your life, toward the end.

On Wednesday night, Carol put the phone up to his ear so I could say what I needed to say, which wasn't much: "I love you, Dad. Thank you for everything you taught me. I'm sorry I'm not there."

Maybe I should have rushed back to New York. Maybe I should have stayed the whole time. The tough call I had to make was whether I wanted to miss my dad's death or my daughter's birth.

Later that evening, I was out walking the dog when my phone rang. Carol had sat watch next to him as he was in and out of a quiet consciousness—she had interrupted her vigil not even to leave, but just to turn her back, just for a couple of seconds to adjust her chair, and he slipped away.

His last words to me were when he called Kanye West "Bigmouth."

I flew back to New York on Friday.

My father had arranged for everything—the funeral at the Church of the Transfiguration, his cremation, the internment of his ashes in the columbarium (a sort of large wall of lockers filled with niches where urns can be placed, this one on the southeast corner of the church, where his mother's cremains were installed alongside John Morris's, the old choirmaster who had gotten us choirboys into *The Piano above Heaven* and had succumbed to AIDS a few years later). My father's obsession with mortality—a dire state that often made him less than fun to be around—paid off in that he knew exactly how he wanted to be sent off. There was to be a piper. There was a wee Scottish dagger (look it up, it's called a *sgian dubh*) locked up next to him. He'd picked the music—somber, tear-jerking, also Scottish.

I wandered around his apartment while Carol tidied the morning of the funeral, poking through all the film books: *Bogey, War Movies, The Films of Tyrone Power*, a collection of character actor volumes simply entitled *Who Is That?* The framed photo of an ad for Spam that he kept on his desk, commemorating the fact that both he and that weird meat stuff were born in 1937. I found an old collection of Robert Burns poetry and tore through it to punch up the eulogy I'd written on the plane. I had had trouble finding stories to honor him—they were all filthy, or at least inappropriate, and while the Episcopalians are cool, they're probably not cool enough to excuse saying "motherfuckly" from the pulpit.

The bishop spoke fondly of my dad. The piper played. I got up and stood on the altar right near where I used to sing alto in the choir.

Friends from high school came. Jamie's parents came down from their town just north of Boston. My mom was there, polite, stiff-upper-lipped, and respectful. I condensed all of his ridiculous college stories (a fraternity brother shouting, "Let Bruce drive, he's too drunk to sing," and similar stories that led to him calling *Animal House* a "documentary"). I closed with a paraphrased Robert Burns quote:

> *If thou, at friendships sacred call*
> *would life itself resign, man,*
> *thy sympathetic tear must fall*
> *for Bruce was a kind man.*

Of course, everybody at the service told me how proud he was of me, how he was constantly touting my accomplishments. This was how he made peace with my career—by taking a little bit of ownership of it, but rarely letting me know about it. Fine. Some of the parishioners even shared some inappropriate Dad stories that I hadn't heard yet. And they all talked about how funny the guy was.

He was installed in the columbarium, and a plaque was placed over his urn with his dates. He had been born on December 26, 1937.

"I forgot his birthday more than once," I said to Carol by way of apology. "Right after Christmas, it was always a blur."

Carol smiled and told me, "He'd forget your birthday sometimes. Couldn't remember if it was May 30th or 31st."

"Really?"

"Oh, yes." And then she added, "Recently he would just check IMDb to make sure."

I rushed back to L.A. later that night, terrified of missing my daughter's birth.

◆

A month later, Nola was born, and God, it was striking how much she looked like baby pictures of my father—the circular head, the tight smile, the slate gray-blue eyes. I showed side-by-side pictures to friends just to make sure I wasn't completely fucking crazy, and they gasped. Standing in our room at Cedars-Sinai, I held this little ball of perfect as tightly as you can hold a newborn: like a football (or so I'm told), with her head in my palm and her body stretched down my forearm, and Jamie knew what I was thinking: "He would have loved her, John. And he knows how much you love her. This is probably why he was so nonchalant about the pregnancy. He knew he wasn't going to be around to see her. But he gave you room to be a father, he left so you'd have less to worry about." I took it all in with a deep breath—my wife, my daughter, the maternity ward with its weird smells. This was everything. Intense beauty and weird smells. As if to really drive this point home, my gorgeous daughter—a day old, pink and glowing with the light of the future—stretched, yawned, and then farted so hard she nearly dislocated my elbow.

She smiled wistfully and fell asleep in my arms.

CHAPTER TWELVE

THAT'S WHY WE FIGHT ROBOTS

I had recently been let go by my agent. Not "fired," per se, and this is an important distinction: Your agent works for you as a sort of independent contractor, and you pay them from the work you've gotten through auditioning, and it is necessary that you grasp the chain of command before embarking on a career. But either way, my first agent was no longer my agent. I had a newborn, my father had just died within the past year, we were gearing up for our second child, and my agent thought that she should just rip off the Band-Aid and make the whole year pretty intense. I still had my manager, Joel—well-dressed and unflappable—and it had fallen to him to let me know that my agent was no longer going to work with me.

I was a decent client, and I was booking steadily, but I hadn't booked a pilot in a couple of years and had even been fired in early 2005 from a pilot by a director who did not think I was funny—and I probably wasn't. I had been in New York visiting my dad in the hospital right before I started work on said pilot, and this time we thought he had tuberculosis, so no, I was not at my most cheerful or comedically adept. So my agent had looked at me as dead weight and decided to throw me off the boat. I had a new agent, but it was the early days of that relationship, and there was no telling how we would get along going forward.

My improv team at the newly opened UCB Los Angeles had been dismantled and a bunch of my friends had found new shows to do that didn't involve me, and I was left a little bit adrift. Jamie and I had recently bought a house, endured the writers strike that shut down production for months, and watched the country slip into a recession all while welcoming our firstborn. Our house was now worth less than its asking price, and while our accountant neglected to use the term "subprime mortgage," he did say, "It's likely you wouldn't be able to get a mortgage like that anymore." The circle was complete: As I had feared back in New York, as early as seven years old, I was an unemployed actor not entirely certain how I would feed my child.

I needed something steady. A series regular gig would be great, but I had tested for something like eight pilots in a row and not gotten the job, so that was looking like an impossibility. I'd settle for a steady recurring, some sort of home base, a north star that would use me a couple times a year. But man, that kind of lottery win looked increasingly unlikely.

On one particular night a couple of weeks shy of Christmas 2008, it was raining, that kind of thick, sideways, making-up-for-lost-time rain that only Los Angeles in December can do, when, out of the blue, I got a same-day audition in the valley for *The Big Bang Theory*.

"Hm," I said to Joel. "I've been out for that show a bunch. I auditioned for Leonard twice. Are they just dicking me around?"

"Well, they wanna see you. Not too many guys going in. I guess they offered this role to Kevin Sussman, and he can't do it, he's doing a movie"—*Jesus*, I thought. *Kevin's doing a movie? I cannot catch a break*—"so they need to book this tonight to work tomorrow. There's a chance it could recur. You should go."

I looked over the sides. The character was named Stuart Kripke, and I was intrigued. He was a nerd bully, and while I've met a few in real life (I remember one particularly nasty LARPer at Ithaca)* and had maybe occupied the role myself at some points, I'd never seen that type represented in media. It was a meaty role. Also, a long shot. A plum guest role like this on a show that was doing well in the ratings? They could straight offer it to a name. But what if they didn't? And it might recur! *But, John, they always say it might recur. You've played roles where you were led away in handcuffs at the end of an episode that "might recur."* And it was at this moment in my increasingly high-pitched internal dialogue that I remembered the thing that my acting teacher Caryn West had told me: The casting directors need you to solve their problem. And if the role starts work tomorrow and they still don't have anyone to fill it, they have a sizable problem.

I slipped into my car at five P.M. and crawled through Hollywood at rush hour, finally getting to the audition in Burbank around six. (Look at the distance on a map to see how bad L.A. traffic can be; it was maybe four miles from my house in Silverlake to the studio, and I was averaging around four mph.) I signed in, and yeah, they weren't kidding—the casting directors had called in a mere four actors for this role. One in four is *very* good odds in this business—one in four is decent odds in Vegas—so I committed the cardinal sin of starting to hope: *What if this turns into an actual recurring gig? What if this gives me a steadier footing on the slippery deck of this business? What if this actually works out?*

They saw the other three actors first, and because this role worked the following day and there wouldn't be time for callbacks, they asked everybody to stay put after their read. They called my name,

---

* Live action role player: a young man given to epic battles staged on the blood-soaked fields . . . behind campus, up near the radio transmitter.

mispronounced it as ever, and I entered a room with the casting directors and producers Chuck Lorre and Bill Prady, both of whom I'd
met the previous year while auditioning (twice) for Leonard. Lorre
is a legend in the business—created *Dharma & Greg* and *Two and a
Half Men*, worked on *Roseanne* and *Cybil*. Sitcom royalty. Prady was
a former computer programmer who had turned a lucrative career into a
different, even more lucrative career by bottling his experience as
a professional nerd into the show for which I was now auditioning.
Pleasantries were exchanged. I was told I'd be reading with the casting
director, and I could start whenever I was ready.

Again, the key to sitcom work is filling in the blank in the following
sentence: "This character is the most _____ person in the world." I
played Stuart aggressively, shifting my posture so I was leading with
my crotch, getting as full-on alpha as a full-on beta like me can get.
"Kripke is the most confident person in the world." I got some snickers
and a warm giggle from Chuck Lorre, and then a pronounced, head-
back laugh at the exchange that ends with Kripke saying, "We're all
pathetic and creepy and can't get girls. That's why we fight robots." At
the end of the first scene, Chuck suggested something: "He should have
a vulnerability. Maybe a . . . a speech thing?" Prady nodded. "Yes. Can
you do a sort of Tom Brokaw liquid *L*?"

Ever the compliant actor, I said something like "Sure, absolutely!"
having no idea what was about to come out of my mouth. What did come
out was a sort of weird, Elmer Fudd thing—"If you have any iwusions
about beating the Kwipke Kwippwah . . ."—and Chuck leaned back his
head again and erupted with a cackle that would become very familiar
over the following decade. It was a big move, but it gave the character a
weakness, a vulnerability, the kind that all supervillains have. Lex Luthor
has alopecia. Kripke has this ridiculous speech impediment.

Remember that scene in *La La Land* when Emma Stone is in the
middle of a pretty good audition, there's a knock on the door, and

someone walks in, interrupting her flow? That actually happened at that very moment. An assistant poked her head in and said, "Chuck, I'm so sorry to bother you, but there's a phone call. It's Leonard Nimoy."

What the fuck is going on? My inner monologue asked. I am *killing* it over here, and Mr. Spock is fucking up my read!

Chuck leapt up from the couch the way anyone would when Leonard Nimoy calls. "John, I'm sorry, I gotta take this."

I did the next scene and Bill, the less effusive of the two, gave a polite smile. I thanked them for their time and headed back out to the waiting room to grab my bag and do the same hour drive back home, figuring out what I would say to Joel if he called. I mean—I guess it went well? Chuck vanished in the middle, but I felt pretty good about it? The casting director, Nikki Valko, announced, "Everybody stay put for a moment" and headed back into the room. There was some muffled conversation, and the other three actors and I just sat, dumbly trying not to stare at each other. After roughly thirty-six hours (actually, two minutes) Nikki came back out.

"Thank you guys so much. You can go; your agents will call you." I reached for my bag and umbrella when she added, "John, can you hang out for one second?"

◆

Production started the next morning, a clear, blue-skied, post-downpour Wednesday with a ten A.M. table read. The Warner Bros. lot is special because you can actually see it in the Warner Bros. logo that runs before Warner Bros. films—those sun-warmed soundstages reflected in the enormous WB icon before, say, a Harry Potter or Batman film. It looks like a casting director's idea of a movie studio.

My character's name had been changed to *Barry* Kripke, as it is funnier to say with the speech impediment. I said hello to everyone and shook hands. The only one of the cast I knew before that day was Simon Helberg, who played the part of Howard Wolowitz and until recently had been on the same "auditioning for the nerd in the commercial" track that I was on. The show was in its second season and growing in popularity (I googled it when I got the firm offer the previous night and was alarmed to see that *Big Bang Theory* the TV show was the first result, before any mention of the *actual theory about the creation of the universe*). There is a fun, fizzy mood that you'll find on the set of any show doing well in its second season, and *Big Bang* was no exception. I got a hug from every member of the cast at the end of the day, except for Johnny Galecki, who stubbornly did not hug me until the second day I was there. The director, Mark Cendrowski, was a tall, amiable TV nerd, and the assistant director was a guy named Anthony Rich whose father, John Rich, directed the pilot of *All in the Family*. They were both founts of fun TV history. Cendrowski had cut his teeth on *Family Ties*, and Anthony remembered being scared of Carroll O'Connor until the day O'Connor let him sit in Archie Bunker's chair. Also on the episode—or at least heard on the episode—was a brash yet sweet older woman named Carol Ann Susi, who played the offstage voice of Howard's mother. "I do the show a few times a year," she told me at the opulent craft services table. "You're gonna love it here. They're *so nice*."

This would be a perfect time to share a lot of dirt about the show and the people who work on it. Alas, there isn't any. Kaley Cuoco and Johnny Galecki had been dating for a couple of years, and I could tell that was a secret, so I kept my mouth shut. Jim Parsons never talked about his personal life in interviews—*got it*—I won't talk about his personal life either. Nobody yelled; I never saw any tantrums or diva behavior. The actors on that show either came into it without a lot of TV experience (Kunal Nayyar, Jim Parsons) and were very grateful to be there, or they'd been at this wildly erratic line of work since they were kids (Johnny Galecki, Kaley Cuoco, Mayim Bialik) and were very grateful to be there. I was treated like family, and when my second child, a fierce little guy named Walter (not Wally), was born in late 2009, we brought the newborn to visit the set, and he was cooed over and passed around with great affection. Fully aware that the older child can feel left out in the presence of a baby, Kaley gave Nola a tour of the set, and Nola was enraptured and has since been in every one of her school plays. The worst thing I can say about the *Big Bang* cast is that they dress almost self-consciously well when they're not in *Big Bang* wardrobe, as if to say *Hey, look, I may play a nerd on TV* . . . Nonetheless, they were terrific co-workers. If you ever spend a decade recurring on a show, my wish for you is that it be a lot like *The Big Bang Theory*.

And look—I know that there is nothing particularly punk rock about recurring on a CBS sitcom. It's as establishment as it gets. But there is something very punk rock about doing something that fills you with adrenaline and serotonin, and not caring what anybody thinks because you're feeding your children by playing like a child. I've heard acting likened to the priesthood—not in the sense that it's a deeply spiritual calling, but in the sense that if you can do anything else for a living, you probably should.

I cannot do anything else.

There would be plenty of time for punk rock around the house. Like a lot of people my age, I introduced my kids to the Ramones early on, and welled up with tears when Walter, at age three, asked, "Can we listen to 'Hey Ho, Let's Go'?" without being prompted. There will come a time when my kids introduce music to me that I just don't get, that screams at me and questions my choices, but so far, so good. There will come a time when my kids make choices to do things—maybe even be actors, God help them—and I hope I just throw every pound of myself behind them, pushing them up to their goals. Nola has the acting bug. Walter is getting very good at guitar and announced recently that he wants to be a musician—the one field with even less stability than acting. He's feisty, Walter, he has some of the Bowie anger, but in hindsight, he's not nearly as volatile as I was. He's funny, too, and I'll bet punk rock finds him before long. Everyone thinks their kids are beautiful, and they should, but Jesus, my kids are good-looking. They don't take after me—they have blue eyes, yes, but small noses and good strong chins, and I look like God's clumsy first draft of both. And if it turns out either kid has inherited my mental health issues, we're here, and we'll handle it, and I'll try to do a slightly better job than my parents did. When my kids are upset now, I skip the cursory "What's wrong?" and jump ahead to the more inquisitive "What are you afraid of?" This narrows the focus a bit, and there's almost always an answer. When I ask them how school is going and they say "fine," we're not done. I ask what they're reading—*"Animal Farm?* It's wild, right? Did you know Boxer the horse represents *all* workers?" I ask them to explain whatever math they're working on—and they're going to have to, because after basic geometry I am going to be no help at all. There's a visceral, dopamine-flooding thrill when they introduce me to a band or a movie I haven't encountered yet (I can thank my kids for introducing me to *Coraline* and the British songwriter Beabadoobee). I try to dig deeper with them than my parents did with me, in the hope that they'll feel heard as children. It helps to be sober now. Bless them both. I can't wait to see what happens.

◆

Tape night was exciting. The audience giggled nervously at my first entrance (you can hear them when you watch the episode "The Killer Robot Instability"—they're not *quite* sure what to make of me). The weird speech impediment went over OK. My first scene ended initially with Kunal looking to the guys after my exit and asking, "What part of America is that accent from?" Laugh. Fadeout. On tape night, they added a new line—an alt, as they say in the trade—which was Galecki looking up from his lunch tray to say "Whode Iswand." The joke was a hit, drawing huge laughter and applause, an enthusiasm that really could only be called . . . cruel. The audience didn't just dig the joke, they liked stepping down on its target. I was relieved when it was cut for air. Kripke's strength is that he is *never* a victim. It could also be argued that this exchange—

> RAJ: He's depressed because he's pathetic and creepy and
>   can't get girls.
> KRIPKE: We're all pathetic and creepy and can't get girls.
>   That's why we fight robots.

—is the whole show in a nutshell. For a guy who was on tech crew in high school, getting called "nerd" when he had to run out on stage to adjust AV equipment, a guy so presentationally nerdy that I was mugged and harassed with alarming frequency as a child, there is a profound satisfaction in taking the "nerd" label and going pro with it.

I was immediately called back to do a second episode called "The Friendship Algorithm," and that back-to-back exposure concerned me. Too much of this character at once seemed excessive to me. I was not alone. The *A.V. Club* set off my Google alert by wondering if I was helping the show "jump the shark" this early in its run. But the audience got used to me, and I to them. There's a terrific episode around season 5-ish where I'm greeted with a dangerous *groan* upon my entrance, like I'm a malevolent Chachi (it's a pretty famous scene, and it's my only one in the episode: voice recognition can't understand Kripke). Years later, the show would syndicate and I would still be appearing on it, and suddenly people would stop me on the street—in Los Angeles, in London, in Johannesburg—and tell me they loved my work, and people would insist on selfies with me, and I would get actual fan mail (some of it from China!), and I would get to talk with great authority to Wayne Knight (Newman on *Seinfeld*) about the curious paradox of being a sitcom villain, and there would be a racehorse in England named Barry Kripke that was doing very well, cheers, and I would become friends with fellow recurring cast member Wil Wheaton and go see—yes, again—the Dickies with him, and I would meet Adam West (complimented my hair) and LeVar Burton (sent me one of the children's books he's written for my kids to enjoy) and Mark Hamill (got to tell him that my confirmation name was Luke and it was *not* for the saint) and Christine Baranski (we talked about Sondheim) and Stephen Root (got a pep talk from him about how it actually gets *easier* to be a character actor after forty because a lot of other people quit) and Bob Newhart (not much of an interaction, just shook his hand, but wow, what a fucking legend). The imprimatur of recurring on a monstrously huge hit sitcom would give me a leg up on future auditions and slowly pull me out of both debt and the sense that my career was just treading water. No, it wasn't Shakespeare, Dad, but it was funny and smart and popular, and there was time to do Shakespeare in acting classes, and I would do a professional run of a play by the second most popular playwright in the English language (Neil Simon's *Laughter on the 23rd Floor,* my professional theater debut just a couple months before turning forty-seven), and recurring on a show of this size cleared a path that got me a lead role on *Speechless,* number two on the cast list, second only to an Oscar nominee.

My mom even came to a taping one time—sat up front, met the cast, was shy but impressed with everyone. She had a cackle you could hear from the stage, loud and viral, and she'd get embarrassed by it. But it was great. My mom might not have been that funny herself, but she knew what was funny, and it was a great joy to make her laugh. She loved being part of that incredibly pumped audience on tape night, and it was heartening to hear her while I was on set with Parsons. She was in her seventies by then, moving a little slower. Still sneaking cigarettes. Getting forgetful. But she loved visiting L.A. and was dazzled by production. Her life at home was quiet, maybe a little lonely, but content. She never asked for financial help, but I gave it anyway. And I got to tell her, after I'd had two children, how much I underestimated how hard parenting was, and how sorry I was that I'd ever made it difficult for her. "Kids are kids," she said, and gave me a hug.

One June morning in 2018, shortly before the last seasons of both *Big Bang* and *Speechless*, my mom finished the *New York Times* crossword puzzle (in *ink* on a *Friday*, thank you very much) and apparently just fell down in the living room of her apartment in Hell's Kitchen. A few days later, the NYPD was called to investigate, and they called me to get permission to enter her apartment, permission that I gave with my heart in my throat. It had been a massive coronary.

I flew back to New York on a red-eye, suddenly overwhelmed. Mom and I hadn't spoken in about a week, which was not unusual, but just days before she passed away, she had sent me an incredible birthday card with a long, uncharacteristically heartfelt message about what a father I had become. What a son. What a man.

It was going to take some paperwork to get her out of the medical examiner's office. I called my cousin Katie, the sole lawyer in the family, and asked her to meet me at Penn Station, which she did, on an otherwise shiny Thursday morning.

"Oh, John," she said, mid-hug. "I'm so sorry. What do we need to do?"

"Well. It's pretty awful," I started, underslept and in a sort of numb grief. "She died a few days ago, and it's been hot, and you know she never had air-conditioning—"

"She hated air-conditioning."

"Hated it, so . . ." Deep breath. "So the coroner says she's in such an advanced state of decomposition that I can't photo ID her and we need to locate some medical records so that we can get some X-rays, get a positive ID, and then get a death certificate, and then I need to take that to the local precinct and—"

Just as I said this, a short, clearly excited woman wearing a big hat and earbuds pointed at me from across the waiting area at Penn Station and said, "What's going on, Kripke?"

I smiled at the woman. Waved. Then turned back to my cousin and said, "Should I . . . Should I tell her what's going on?" I've never heard my cousin laugh harder in her life. It's OK. Eileen would have found this hilarious, too.

Jamie flew to NYC a day after me, leaving the kids with a close family friend, and helped me through the worst scavenger hunt in history: tracking down my mom's dentist to get her most recent X-rays. Jamie called this particular treasure hunt "bummer *Goonies*," thus affirming the sanctity of our marriage. I had actually paid for my mom's dental work, so tracking down the dentist (an odd duck in the West Village with massive sleeve tattoos) only took the weekend, and in a few days, everything was sorted, and I splurged on an obit that ran in the *New York Times* and mentioned her fondness for the paper's crosswords. We held a memorial service on her favorite pier on the Hudson, and Jamie held me as it drizzled on the small gathering. Eileen Bowie had asked to have her body donated to science, but the circumstances of her death made that impossible. She was cremated—some of her ashes sent into the Atlantic Ocean, some into the Pacific.

Everyone in the cast of both of the shows I was working on reached out to me, lovely texts, moving emails from Parsons and Minnie Driver, and a truly amazng basket of food from Scott Silveri, the showrunner of *Speechless*. The boy who played my son on the show had grown to be over six feet over the past season, towering over me. Scott's note read: "With deepest condolences on being shorter than your TV son." This got a huge, tearful laugh from me—there was always time for dumb jokes. I still have the note, as it validated every choice that had come before it.

◆

The *Big Bang* gig felt like being on dry land for a while after years of treading water. Now—once you are on dry land, the work isn't over. You still have to forage for food, you still have to build shelter. But you're no longer at any risk of drowning. Show business is mercurial and unfair and filled with hideous abuses of power, much like teaching, or management consulting, or publishing or any of the fields into which I had strolled. Try to do something that makes you happy and doesn't hurt anyone. It won't make depression go away, and the crazy old uncle will still drop by from time to time. But now it is always temporary.

But there was no way to see the career uptick coming on that first week. On tape night, I did my first scene and then had some time to myself. Jamie got a sitter and came to the taping, cheering me on, grabbing a couple of snacks from the craft services table, and then heading back home to tuck our daughter in. Multi-cam sitcoms are shot in order in front of the audience, so you can end up with a couple hours off in the middle of the shoot. The buoyant mood on the set was lovely but also overwhelming, so I caught my breath by going outside into the cool Burbank night.

Big Bang shot on stage 25 on the Warner Bros. lot. Most studio lots put plaques on the stages, commemorating the productions that have shot there, and 25's is impressive. I found myself weirdly itching for a cigarette (I've never smoked, and I had just watched it kill my dad the previous year, but it just seemed like a thing to do between scenes outside on the Warner Brothers lot) as I read over the titles.

Who's Afraid of Virginia Woolf?
My Fair Lady
Ocean's 11 (not the George Clooney one, the OG Frank
Sinatra one)
Rebel Without a Cause
And . . . *Casablanca.*

I stopped breathing for just a second. Look at that. *Casablanca*, starring Humphrey Bogart, Paul Henreid, Claude Rains, Dooley Wilson,
and my dad's and my old friend from the playground: Ingrid Bergman.
Casablanca had been the film where my father first fell in love with
her—it was one of his favorites—and here I was, working in the same
building where her delicate Swedish feet had walked some seventy
years earlier. Here I was, thirty or so years after I knocked over her
grandson in Central Park and apologized, and she noticed and spoke
to my dad about it. The plaque was brass, and, as corny as it sounds, I
let myself touch the raised letters.

*Look, Dad. Look at that. This is something. This puts me on a continuum,
however thin, with the greats. With a thing you love. God, you were so scared
I wouldn't make a living, and maybe a little scared that I would, but it's
fine, Dad. It's working out.*

At the end of *Casablanca*, Rick lets Ilsa go—gives her money and
safe passage to get out of Morocco and go help Victor with the French
Resistance. Rick's stuck in the titular city, and it's not entirely clear if
he'll live to see the end of the war. But just because he's stuck there, he
realizes, doesn't mean the person he loves has to be.

It was the last *Big Bang* episode of 2008, and after the taping there
was a holiday party on the set. Kunal spoke movingly of missing his
family back in India around the holidays. Simon followed him and got
massive laughs when he spoke of missing his family back in Malibu
("It can be thirty, forty minutes, depending on traffic"). Carol Ann

Susi left us a few years later, and Stephen Hawking was on the show for the last time a year before he died, and they were mourned like beloved cousins. That night at the end of 2008 there was fun loud pop music and dancing on the cafeteria set, and Kunal stopped dancing and pretended to throw a fishing line at me—and I let myself be hooked, and I let him pull me into the dance.

AND ONE LAST THING

"Acting is no job for a man" is not actually a Spencer Tracy quote—it's a quote attributed to Clark Gable's father. Who apparently said it—quite often—to Clark Gable.

ACKNOWLEDGMENTS

We overuse the term "patience of a saint," but there should be some level of canonization for Todd Shuster and his team over at Aevitas, and I am very grateful.

Thanks to Jessica Case and everyone at Pegasus Books for their commitment and enthusiasm.

Lori Paximadis had to accommodate several quirks (the period after Egghead., the capitalization of the first 'The' in 'The The') that are above and beyond the call of any copy editor and she handled them grace and patience.

Thank you to Joel Zadak for two decades of trust and support.

Emily Flake was exactly the person for the job of cover artist, and she exceeded expectations.

The teams at Paul Kohner, Pakula-King, Talentworks, and Innovative Artists have shepherded calls and been strong advocates at various times over the years.

Everyone who is mentioned in this book, certainly, but also Portia Sabin and Heather Scott and Chris Gethard and others who have answered calls at dire times.

Huge chunks of this book were developed as either personal essays or monologues or components of a one-man show—with that in mind, I must thank various editors, producers, and directors: Andrey Slivka and John Strausbaugh of the *NY Press*; Bo Blackburn, late of Power Entertainment; Natasha Vargas-Cooper and Stephen Falk of Public School; Matt Price; Liz Warner; and lastly Michael Delaney, intrepid director of *Paid to Stand Around*.

I must thank my parents for teaching me how to read, only to be repaid with this slim volume. Every creative position I've been in can be traced back to you two, and I love you both very much.

For the Naked Babies and Egghead., without whom there is little to write about.

For Nola and Walter, without whom there is little to write for.

For Jamie, who is often right.